THE TELEPHONE
INTERVIEWER'S HANDBOOK

THE TELEPHONE INTERVIEWER'S HANDBOOK

How to Conduct Standardized Conversations

Patricia A. Gwartney

JOSSEY-BASS
A Wiley Imprint
www.josseybass.com

BICENTENNIAL
1807
WILEY
2007
BICENTENNIAL

Published by Jossey-Bass.
A Wiley Imprint
989 Market Street, San Francisco, CA 94103-1741   www.josseybass.com

Library of Congress Cataloging-in-Publication Data

Gwartney, Patricia A.
The telephone interviewer's handbook : how to conduct standardized conversations/
by Patricia A. Gwartney.
    p. cm.
Includes bibliographical references and index.
ISBN: 978-0-7879-8638-4 (pbk.)
1. Telephone surveys. 2. Market surveys. 3. Interviewing. I. Title.
HF5415.3.G88 2007
658.3′1124–dc22

                                                          2006035832

Printed in the United States of America
FIRST EDITION
PB Printing   10 9 8 7 6 5 4 3 2

CONTENTS

FIGURES, TABLES, AND EXHIBITS

Figures

Tables

Exhibits

I dedicate this volume to the memory of Karen A. Garrett. We began our survey research careers together in 1973, and they ran parallel for twenty-six years.

PREFACE

T*he Telephone Interviewer's Handbook* brings together the best practices for telephone interviewing, with the goal of minimizing interviewer-related error. It is also rooted in the empirical and experimental literature on survey interviewing.

It is intended for use in call centers for all types of survey organizations, from market research to public opinion polling to academic settings. It is not intended for organizations that handle incoming calls from customers or clients. It is also written specifically for use in the United States, and Canada to a lesser extent, due to the widely varying laws and regulations governing telephone survey research in other nations.

This book is written to interviewers, in the voice of an interviewer trainer. Ideally, all telephone interviewers will have their own copy to read and mark up during training and then to consult as needed on the job. Although this book is rooted in academic survey research, citing each relevant book or journal article in the text would distract interviewers from the training process. Those interested in research on interviewers and the interviewing process may consult the comprehensive bibliography at the end of the book.

The following chapters offer a substantial amount of detail. Where they offer more detail than your survey research organization needs—for example, the section on probing industry and occupation questions—you can easily bypass the sections that do not apply. In addition, the workplace routines and policies of employers using this book may vary from those presented here. Interviewers are responsible for learning the extent to which their employer's customs and rules differ from the examples presented here, as this volume frequently reminds the reader. In addition, this *Handbook* is just one part of interviewers' training.

February 2007   Patricia A. Gwartney
Eugene, Oregon

ACKNOWLEDGMENTS

In 1996, the National Network of State Polls (NNSP) asked academic survey research organizations to share and review each other's interviewer training materials. The participating organizations—the University of Nebraska's Bureau of Sociological Research, University of Georgia's Institute for Behavioral Research, University of South Carolina's Institute of Public Affairs, Ohio State University's Laboratory for Political and Social Research, and Survey Research Laboratories at the University of South Carolina, University of Oregon, Virginia Commonwealth University, University of North Carolina at Chapel Hill, and University of Wisconsin-Extension—generously shared their interviewer training materials and learned a lot from each other. Several NNSP newsletters later summarized the best practices derived from those manuals (see http://survey.rgs.uky.edu/nnsp/newsletters/newsltr.htm).

The idea for this *Handbook* originated from participating in that exercise. In addition, it benefited from materials shared by Karen A. Garrett at the University of California, Berkeley, Survey Research Center and by Joe Spaeth and Mary Spaeth on their retirement from the University of Illinois Survey Research Laboratory, and materials gleaned by me when working with the University of Michigan's Survey Research Center in the late 1970s—before telephone interviewing existed much at all. Special thanks go to John Tarnai for helpful suggestions, to Diane Davis for remarkably detailed comments and valuable ideas, and to Barnie Jones for permission to use the survey that serves as a continuing example through-out the volume. I would also like to thank the thirteen anonymous persons who reviewed the proposal for this book and offered detailed comments and sug-gestions. Most important, thirteen years of suggestions from interviewers, lead interviewers, interviewer supervisors, and research assistants at the now-defunct University of Oregon Survey Research Laboratory are contained herein. I, of course, remain solely responsible for any errors.

P. A. G.

ABOUT THE AUTHOR

Patricia A. Gwartney is professor and associate head in the Department of Sociology at the University of Oregon. This *Handbook* has its foundations in her more than thirty years of survey research experience. She started as a face-to-face interviewer in 1973, and she still remembers vividly numerous respondents and experiences—and mistakes—from her first project. In the ensuing years she worked on surveys as a coder, sampler, research assistant, research analyst, project director, and principal investigator. In 1992, she founded the Oregon Survey Research Laboratory, directing it until 2003 and overseeing the conduct of approximately 290 studies. She has trained at least one thousand interviewers. Occasionally, she has also been a telephone survey respondent. Those interviewers who called her, she is convinced, would have done their jobs much better if they had been trained using this *Handbook*.

CHAPTER ONE

INTRODUCTION

This *Handbook* speaks directly to you, new telephone interviewers just starting your training. It aims to teach you the basic principles and procedures for conducting telephone interviews, from the moment you dial the telephone to the moment you say good-bye. It emphasizes best practices for collecting the highest-quality telephone survey data possible, minimizing interviewer-related error, and avoiding bias. This *Handbook* is based on standardized interviewing techniques. It incorporates psychologists' and sociologists' findings from studying interviewers, interviewing, and the interview process. The bibliography at the end of this volume presents the books, articles, and Web sites that underlie the guidelines presented here.

This *Handbook* will also help you understand how your job fits into the wider world of survey research. You will find explanations of what surveys are all about and why they are important. You will learn about the types of organizations that conduct telephone survey research, as well as what you can expect from your employer in terms of training, work culture, workplace policies, and the physical environments that you may encounter in the organization in which you work. You will also find out about your ethical responsibilities and your respondents' legal protections. If your employer's training materials and policies differ from those presented here, however, do not think something is wrong. Many reasonable variations occur across different types of survey organizations.

All organizations that conduct scientific telephone surveys to advance the understanding of society and human behavior should find this volume practical. Asking questions by telephone of a representative sample of people has been an accurate and efficient way to obtain survey data for decades and will continue to be so for many years into the future. This *Handbook* will enhance interviewers' ability to collect high-quality data about people's opinions, attitudes, beliefs, behavior, needs, knowledge, and characteristics. Interviewers can apply this training to surveys on all kinds of topics, for all types of survey sponsors, for studies representing large populations, such as a county, a state, or the nation, and for studies of special populations, such as elderly patients, welfare recipients, customers, or members of an organization.

I speak from experience, starting as an in-person interviewer in 1973 and ultimately founding and directing a survey research organization from 1992 to 2003. Even as a director, I always tried to find the time to conduct some telephone interviews side by side with the interviewers I trained. Why? The one essential lesson of my experience is that interviewers are critical to the success of any telephone survey project or organization.

Without highly trained and well-motivated interviewers, a telephone survey organization cannot persist. Consider this scenario. The finest thinkers develop a clever new theory that may help answer a pressing human problem. They find the most talented survey researchers to design an ideal instrument that will test the theory. A statistician selects a perfectly representative sample of people to take the survey. A computer programmer programs the survey software flawlessly. Everything up to this point is precise and complete. But none of it matters without highly trained interviewers to gather the data.

You are the one who dials the telephone and determines whether each telephone number belongs in the sample. You introduce the survey and orient respondents to it. You select the appropriate adults to interview in households and organizations. You ease reluctant respondents' concerns and convince them to participate. You ask the survey questions. You record respondents' answers. Without your knowledge, skills, and integrity, none of the rest matters. Poorly trained interviewers can sink the best-designed survey project.

> Interviewers are critical to the success of telephone survey projects and organizations.

You are the heart and soul of all data derived from telephone interviews. A great deal of data crucial to public policymaking, human service delivery, and business come from the telephone surveys you conduct. For many surveys, telephone interviewing is the best way or the only way to collect the data needed for planning and decisions. Your responsibility as a telephone interviewer is enormous. Fortunately, this job is also varied, flexible, and can be a lot of fun.

Finally, this *Handbook* is just one part of your training. Your employer is likely to have its own training materials to complement this volume. For example, the software for computer-assisted telephone interviewing (CATI) systems varies from one organization to the next. Therefore, this volume provides you with only general information about them. It is up to you to learn your employer's CATI system on the job. You are also responsible for learning your employer's workplace policies and procedures to the extent that they differ from those you find here.

To be an excellent telephone interviewer, you should refer back to this *Handbook* frequently to refresh your skills. If you encounter words or terms that you do not understand, refer to the glossary in Appendix A for definitions.

The rest of this chapter presents the big picture of survey research and your essential role in the survey process. You will learn why surveys exist, as well as the kinds of practical problems and theoretical issues that surveys help to solve. The last section introduces the concept of survey error and interviewers' role in minimizing it.

Why Have Surveys at All?

Why do surveys exist? A survey involves collecting data from a sample of people who have been specially selected to represent an entire population. Everyone in the sample is asked the same questions in the same way by interviewers, or they fill out a questionnaire themselves. Respondents' answers are then organized in a way that allows researchers to analyze the information and draw conclusions.

If all people were identical to each other, surveys would not be needed. Surveys help researchers, public policymakers, and businesses understand why and how people vary across groups. For example, how do Democrats' political beliefs systems differ from those of Republicans? Which people are most likely to buy gas-guzzling SUVs, and how do they differ from those who buy more fuel-efficient vehicles? Why do some people enjoy visiting shopping malls but others avoid them? Do the elderly encounter different barriers in obtaining adequate health care than younger adults? If people were all the same, politics, transportation, and health care could be delivered in the same way to everyone, because no individual would need anything different from another. Of course this is not the case. Each human differs deliciously from every other. Surveys enable researchers to examine broad-scale patterns of similarity and difference across human populations.

Surveys can be used for an infinite number of purposes, all of which help people to understand themselves.

The persons you interview are most likely to be adults speaking on behalf of themselves, but they may also speak on behalf of their family, their household, or an organization. Each person with whom you speak will have been selected randomly from a defined population of persons, families, households, or organizations. Random selection is a scientific procedure based on statistical probabilities, ensuring that each unit in the population has a known chance of being chosen for the survey. The persons selected are called a *random sample*, or a *probability sample*. A random sample of 400 persons can accurately represent tens of thousands of people in a population.

Handing out questionnaires in a shopping mall or on a street corner is not random, because the population is not defined and every person in the population does not have a known chance of being selected. These are called *intercept samples*, or *samples of convenience*. The results of such pseudosurveys cannot be generalized to any known population. They are not scientifically valid or accurate. They might, however, prove useful for initially exploring a topic.

Surveys are conducted on behalf of private companies, nonprofit organizations, school districts, counties, hospitals, and various agencies in federal, state, and local governments. The governmental agencies that might need a survey include crime prevention commissions, air pollution monitoring groups, local libraries, economic development organizations, state boards that accredit teachers, health insurers, and wastewater management districts. This variety keeps your work interesting.

All of these organizations have one thing in common: They need survey data to solve a problem, answer an important question, evaluate a program, or track social or economic indicators over time. Table 1.1 describes several studies in which a telephone survey helped to meet such needs. (The study details have been changed to protect the confidentiality of the persons and organizations involved.) The questions in the surveys were carefully designed and tested to address the issue at hand while also minimizing inconvenience to respondents.

These few examples only partially represent the wide array of telephone surveys conducted all the time, every day, in every state and almost every nation. The federal government requires survey data in order to calculate unemployment rates and poverty rates, to predict enrollment in educational institutions, and to track crime victimization, consumer purchases, energy consumption, and health care. State and local governments use surveys to gather information for planning and programs. Government agencies use survey results to examine trends, to help decide public policies, and to find out what citizens think about those policies. Governments also use survey results to determine whether certain places need

TABLE 1.1. EXAMPLES OF TELEPHONE SURVEY RESEARCH PROJECTS.

The Problem	How a Telephone Survey Helped Solve the Problem
A dangerous highway ran through a medium-sized town. The state legislature found funds for the Department of Transportation (DOT) to reroute it. DOT estimated the project would take a year. DOT knew it would disrupt citizens' daily lives with dust, delays, noise, rubble, and potential danger from big machines rumbling through town. DOT needed data to help minimize these disruptions.	DOT hired a survey research organization to conduct three representative telephone surveys. (1) The first took place before the highway reconstruction project began, to obtain citizens' input on the best times of day and days of week to delay traffic, the maximum number of minutes citizens could bear delays, how they preferred to contact DOT when problems arose, and related matters. (2) DOT deployed a second survey partway through the project to find out how citizens thought the project was going, learn about particular problems, and solicit ideas for improvements. Respondents praised the project to date but said they could not see driveways for certain local businesses, causing near accidents and endangering pedestrians. DOT immediately made signs and placed them pointing at the driveways. (3) When the project ended, DOT conducted a third survey, asking respondents to evaluate the project overall and suggest what DOT could have done better. These surveys helped DOT plan future highway projects in other communities.
A regional newspaper publisher needed to convince advertisers that their limited budgets were better spent on his newspaper than on competing news outlets.	The publisher engaged a survey research organization to conduct a random sample survey of households in the newspaper's region. The interviews asked how often adults read the newspaper and for what purposes; how often they got their news from television, radio, and elsewhere; and which source they considered most accurate and fair. The results did not portray the newspaper as favorably as the publisher had expected, but he got enough data to persuade his advertisers.
An economically distressed county needed to determine the best ways to allocate scant resources to child and family services.	A county child and family services commission worked with a survey research organization to develop parallel surveys for both families and the agencies that provided services. The interviews asked about the

(continued)

TABLE 1.1. *(CONTINUED)*

The Problem	How a Telephone Survey Helped Solve the Problem
	adequacy of recreation, library, child care, medical, substance abuse, crisis intervention, crime prevention, arts, religious, and other family services, as well as why children and families did not get the services they need. The survey results showed that families and agencies voiced similar opinions about service adequacy. However, agencies said families themselves were the main barriers to service, believing they did not need help when they actually did and thinking it was too much hassle to get help. But families said the agencies created barriers, with bad locations, restricted operating hours, rude staff, fees for service, confusing rules, waiting lists, and overly personal questions.
President Clinton's welfare reform policy in the 1990s drastically changed how states deliver services to needy families. State welfare employees had to change how they did their work, and needy families had to find ways to adapt.	A state human services department (HSD) hired a survey research organization to conduct parallel studies of affected families and HSD staff over time. Interviewers called a random sample of needy families in the months that HSD denied them food stamps or Temporary Aid to Needy Families, then again six months later and ten months after that. Questions asked how the families adapted in jobs, housing, child care, food, health, and so forth. The interviews were difficult. They lasted over one hour. Many families had moved and could not be located. Families' situations upset interviewers. The telephone company had often disconnected and reconnected service. The paperwork to pay families $25 per interview was complex. Interviewers also conducted semistructured in-depth conversations with HSD staff when the new policies started and a year later. These interviews proved difficult too. The policy changes conflicted with HSD employees' beliefs about how to serve the poor best. Some distrusted the confidentiality of the interviews. Some quit before the second interview. The survey findings resulted in a book.

TABLE 1.1. *(CONTINUED)*

The Problem	How a Telephone Survey Helped Solve the Problem
A foundation planned to build a museum to celebrate a famous athlete's life. This man inspired many people, but enraged others. The planners needed ideas on how to present his life in a balanced way.	The planners estimated that most visitors would travel four hours to visit the museum in its planned location. That four-hour radius included ten states and over 130 counties, from which a random sample of households was selected. Respondents familiar with the athlete were interviewed about their impressions of him, why they held those impressions, and whether they thought certain qualities or themes in this man's life would inspire teenagers.

certain programs (for example, Meals on Wheels) and to identify the geographical areas needing those services most (for example, counties with large populations of impoverished persons aged sixty-five and over). Once a program is in place, surveys can help evaluate how well the program does what it intended to do. Each year in the United States, surveys help the federal government distribute over $200 billion in funds and services to states, local governments, and tribal jurisdictions.

A census is an ancient type of survey. Censuses count all persons in a specific geographical area (usually a nation) within a specified time period. The first-known censuses were conducted in Egypt, Rome, and China as early as 95 B.C. for purposes of taxation and military conscription. Think about the biblical story that Christians tell at Christmas, about Mary and Joseph traveling to Bethlehem and Mary delivering baby Jesus in a barn. Why would Mary and Joseph go to Bethlehem when she was nine months pregnant? Because their government was conducting a census that required people to return to their home villages to be counted.

The U.S. Constitution requires a census of population every ten years. Since 1790, the U.S. Census Bureau has counted every person in the nation in each year ending with a zero. The last U.S. census took place in 2000. The nation needs this count to reallocate the 435 seats in the House of Representatives across the fifty states, based on the number of persons in each state. Researchers, businesses, students, and others also use census data to describe the U.S. population and track how it changes over time.

A census differs from a survey in that everyone participates in it. In contrast just a small, representative group is asked to participate in scientific random sample surveys. Surveys also differ from a census in that they are cheaper and less intrusive. Interviewing a few people who represent an entire population burdens that population much less than asking everyone.

Although we tend to think of surveys and censuses as uniquely about people, many surveys and censuses concern animals and inanimate objects. For example, in between conducting the population census every ten years, the U.S. Census Bureau conducts the Census of Agriculture, Economic Census, Census of Commercial Fisheries, Census of Construction Industries, Census of Manufacturers, Census of Mineral Industries, Census of Transportation, and numerous other censuses and surveys. The Census Bureau conducts these studies because the U.S. Congress requires it to do so. Private, for-profit companies and businesses widely use and benefit from regular data published by the federal government on such things as crop values, milk production, land use, communications, consumer prices, employment, earnings, inflation, salary trends, insurance, auto accidents, personal injuries, banking, and much much more. Almost all of these data come from surveys.

Political polls are another type of survey. Polls differ from surveys in that they tend to ask just a few questions (usually fewer than ten), they are often conducted in just a day or two, and the private companies that conduct them vary widely in their scientific rigor. Polls are typically used to determine what voters think about candidates for public office and about how well elected representatives perform their jobs.

Market research is one more type of survey research, differing from others mainly in subject matter. The market research industry uses surveys to assess consumer responses to products of all types, from toothpaste to Toyotas, and in all kinds of dimensions, such as color, name, taste, smell, associations, and feelings. This type of research helps both companies and nonprofit organizations develop advertising and public relations campaigns, identify their market niche, and test ideas for new products. (Would you buy grape-flavored toothpaste? Why or why not? What is the most you would pay for four ounces of this toothpaste? Would you prefer to use it from a plastic tube, a metal tube, or an upright container? Which do you like better, a screw-off end or a flip-top end? You get the idea.)

Respondents' cooperation with marketing surveys has steadily declined. Many say they do not trust the promise of confidentiality (especially when an interviewer asks for their name and address at the end of the interview). Respondents complain that market researchers' telephone interviews are too long and that interviewers do not display professionalism and courtesy on the telephone. They may also wonder about the extent to which such surveys contribute to their communities and advance understanding of human behavior.

Telemarketing is not survey research. Just because telemarketers call people at home on the telephone does not mean that they conduct a legitimate form of survey research. Rather, they engage in practices that professional survey researchers call *sugging*—selling under the guise of survey research—or *frugging*—fundraising under the guise of survey research. Similarly, *push polls* are not a legitimate form of election polling. These illicit forms of surveying presented serious challenges to the scientific survey community in the 1990s. Chapter Three discusses these issues in more detail.

> Telemarketing is not survey research.

Thus, people conduct surveys for many reasons. Asking questions of a random sample of persons remains the most accurate and efficient way to obtain information about a population's opinions, knowledge, needs, attitudes, beliefs, behavior, and characteristics. Surveys are more valid and reliable than educated guesses. Indeed, sometimes surveys find the opposite of what researchers expect to find. Surveys are not new in human history, but they have become pervasive as societies have grown in numbers and become more complex and differentiated.

Why Have Interviewers?

Why not just give survey respondents a questionnaire on paper or on the Internet? Why bother with interviewers at all? Don't most people prefer completing surveys on their own? Sure, some people would rather complete a questionnaire on their own, but a certain number "forget" their promise to do so, or their partner "helps" by filling it out for them. Others are too embarrassed to admit they cannot read very well. When people completing self-administered questionnaires do not understand a survey question, no one is immediately available to help them. They might skip the problematic question or throw away the entire questionnaire in frustration. Many other reasons also underscore interviewers' importance.

The most recent National Adult Literacy Survey estimated that over one-fifth of adult Americans have limited reading and writing skills. This means that over forty million people might not be able to write a check, locate a meeting time on a handout, identify a piece of specific information in a short newspaper article, or accomplish other brief, routine, and uncomplicated reading tasks. Semiliterate people experience great difficulty completing questionnaires. They have problems understanding a survey's purpose, accurately reading questions, correctly recording their answers, and following *skip logic* (that is, instructions to skip over questions that do not apply to them).

People with literacy problems are diverse. Some are well educated but have vision problems. Many can converse with ease but barely completed high school and did not fully develop their reading skills. Some were educated in another language and perform less well in English. Others might have temporary physical or mental conditions that limit their literacy. If no interviewer is present, these citizens' opinions, attitudes, beliefs, and knowledge could easily go unrecorded, making a survey unrepresentative. Thus interviewers are essential for accurate and representative data collection from this portion of the population.

> Never underestimate your importance as an interviewer.

Interviewers can also answer respondents' questions about a survey's purpose or about a specific question. Interviewers make sure that the randomly chosen person takes the survey, not a well-meaning but nonrepresentative volunteer. Trained interviewers can guide respondents through complex parts of a survey, screen out a fourteen-year-old trying to have some fun, and keep impatient respondents on the telephone (who might have quit partway through a self-administered questionnaire). Good interviewers know when to probe an open-ended question, which cannot be done in a self-administered questionnaire.

An interviewer's presence can enhance the survey experience for respondents who might otherwise not understand, care about, or participate in a research project. In these ways, interviewers improve the quality of data that respondents provide, ease the respondents' burden, reduce potential respondent error, and—overall—optimize the value of survey data.

The Basic Survey Process

Before going further, you need to gain some understanding of the overall survey process. Every survey involves six basic, predictable steps. As an interviewer, you will participate mainly in the fourth step.

1. Study design and planning
2. Survey instrument design
3. Sampling
4. Data collection and entry
5. Data analysis
6. Reporting

Stages in the Survey Process

The first step in a survey is study design and planning. Survey research organizations work with clients to define the scope and content of the study's objectives, assess their feasibility, and consider alternatives. What does the client need to know? What information is necessary to describe and analyze it? Could the information be obtained somewhere else? Will the results of the survey be used in such a way that it is worth the time and cost for respondents and survey sponsors? At this stage, researchers identify the survey's target population; define key concepts; select methods of sampling, data collection, and analysis appropriate to the survey's objectives; and develop budgets and time schedules.

The second step is survey instrument (questionnaire) design. This step involves determining the content, structure, and sequence of survey questions. It includes writing each question in a way that makes sense to respondents and maintains their interest, while simultaneously avoiding bias and minimizing inconvenience. In addition, instrument designers must ensure that respondents' answers are clearly recorded in an efficient form for later data processing. Then the instrument is pretested, revised, and pretested again as needed until it is as perfect as possible. Experienced interviewers often participate in survey pretesting and offer suggestions on question wording, answer categories, and question ordering.

The third step is sampling. This includes choosing an appropriate sample size to meet study objectives, deciding the best sample design for the project, and identifying potential sample sources, such as lists, directories, organizational records, or vendors that sell sample lists. The sample size is based on the number of persons in the target population and the sample design. Some sample designs are simple, involving just a certain number of completed interviews from the target population. Other sample designs are complex. For example, in quota, cluster, and stratified samples, interviewers must obtain a specified number of completed interviews with population units having certain characteristics or residing in certain geographical areas.

Sampling itself is the process of selecting a certain number of units from the target population. For simple random samples, it involves randomly selecting a small fraction of a target population in such a way that that fraction represents the whole population. When a simple random sample is properly executed, each person in the target population has a known and equal chance of selection; that is the definition of a probability sample.

Telephone interviewers typically work from *listed* samples or *random-digit-dial* (RDD) samples. A list sample is drawn from a record of all members of an entire population, such as all the patients treated at a certain clinic in a given month or all the automobile owners who paid Jiffy Lube to service their cars in a certain period. Certain businesses specialize in compiling and selling sample lists to survey research organizations. Purchasing lists from vendors can be very useful for rare and difficult-to-locate populations, such as households with known tobacco users. Once a list is obtained, a staff person in the survey research organization selects a random sample from that list. List samples can be very efficient for rare populations, but for general populations RDD samples tend to be more up-to-date, comprehensive, and representative. For this reason, RDD samples are very common in telephone surveys.

The RDD sampling process goes something like this. Statisticians use a computer to generate all the telephone numbers that could possibly occur in a particular geographical area (that is, all the telephone numbers that could follow each area code and its assigned prefixes). Then they randomly select telephone numbers from this list.[1] Often interviewers are responsible for further sampling, for example, by randomly selecting an adult in each household. Legitimate survey research organizations never sell lists of working telephone numbers or cooperative respondents to others, such as list vendors.

After sampling, some send precontact letters to randomly selected respondents. Precontact letters explain that an interviewer will call, from where, and why. They present the survey's purpose and tell respondents how they were selected and why they are important. These letters explain confidentiality and other elements of informed consent. They also offer contact information (such as a Web site or telephone number) for respondents who have questions. Some survey research organizations involve interviewers in the process of signing these letters, stamping envelopes, and folding and stuffing the letters into envelopes. Interviewers often welcome these tasks as a break from interviewing.

> Legitimate survey research organizations never sell lists of working telephone numbers or cooperative respondents.

The fourth step, data collection and data entry, is your job. Telephone interviewing is not always fun and easy. People contacted in an interview situation may be unlike anyone you have ever met, and most do not know how to be a "good" respondent. Some are anxious to tell their opinions and flattered to be chosen. Others will talk because they are lonely. Some will hang up before you have a chance to explain why you called. You will find respondents who are sincerely interested in the survey topic, answer questions frankly, and are a delight to interview. Other people honestly know little and care nothing about the survey subjects and tell you so from beginning to end; but you still must interview them.

Respondents represent the opinions and attitudes of many others in their community. Each respondent's participation is intrinsic to the survey's integrity. The great diversity of people makes interviewing a demanding and challenging, yet interesting, job. The best interviewers genuinely enjoy the variety. A good interviewer is committed to obtaining the best possible data in every interview and will rise to the challenge of a difficult interview by using the techniques described in this *Handbook*. As a practicing interviewer, you will learn to relax and guide each interview with more and more success.

As a telephone interviewer you are very important because you are the link between the researchers who need data and the respondents whose answers provide it. The statistical validity of the survey results depends on many interviewer qualities, such as your ability to persuade reluctant respondents to participate, your skill in reading questions exactly as worded yet conversationally, and your proficiency in accurately recording answers. More qualitative aspects of interviewing also affect the quality of survey results, such as your tone of voice, pace, timing, awareness, sense of impartiality, and professionalism.

Your presence as an interviewer should not affect respondents' perceptions of questions or the kinds of answers they give. Each interview demands and exercises skills in different combinations. Your importance in the survey process is why survey research organizations conduct intensive interviewer training, carefully supervise and monitor data collection, and randomly verify completed interviews by calling respondents back. The bulk of this training manual is about this step in the survey process.

But this fourth step is not just about interviewers. In modern telephone interviewing you will work interactively and seamlessly with a CATI system, which integrates sampling, calling, interviewing, and data entry. You will sit under a telephone headset in a sound-reduced carrel at a computer workstation connected to a computer network. In CATI the survey instruments and telephone numbers are preprogrammed to appear automatically on the computer monitor at each workstation. You enter the data into a computer as you speak with each respondent. The CATI system helps you gather high-quality data by eliminating out-of-range responses and by accurately guiding you through complex skip logic. The CATI system also helps maintain standardized calling and callback procedures, and it automatically stores your call records. Thus, high-quality telephone survey data collection in this fourth crucial step involves two components: (1) a specially trained staff of interviewers to collect data one on one from carefully selected and motivated respondents and (2) a CATI system that facilitates interviewers' work and helps prevent errors.

> Interviewers must not affect respondents' perceptions of questions or their answers.

Data reduction and data analysis is the fifth step of the survey process. Once the survey data have been gathered by the interviewers and entered into the computer, programmers clean the data of any wild codes (out-of-range numbers), prepare variable labels, construct statistical weights, create scales and indexes, and combine the data with any necessary linked or nested files. At this stage, open-ended coding also may occur. For example, specially trained coders may translate respondents' narrative answers to occupation questions into the U.S. Census Bureau's detailed occupational code categories.

In the final step of the survey process, researchers produce reports explaining all the survey steps up to this point. They also prepare descriptive statistics on each question asked in the survey and present full documentation on the survey data set's structure and content. Sometimes clients also need detailed data analysis reports describing the survey's findings, with graphs and statistical analyses. All this is delivered to the client, sometimes with a formal, in-person presentation. This step may also involve a press release describing certain survey findings for the media. After a number of months or years, many survey organizations publicly archive their data for future researchers' use.

Note that not all research organizations perform all these research operations. Your employer might specialize in just one or two, subcontracting one or more steps to another organization. Some clients prefer to conduct some of these steps themselves. At some point, however, each of these steps will be performed by someone, somewhere in the survey process.

How Telephone Surveys Compare to Other Survey Modes

You are being trained to conduct telephone interviews using your employer's CATI system. Telephone interviewing is a significant tool of survey data collection but not the only one. In order to understand how telephone interviewing fits into survey data collection more generally, this section briefly reviews different survey modes, why researchers choose them, and some of their advantages and disadvantages.

Researchers have used face-to-face interviewing and self-administered questionnaires for generations. But telephone interviewing became feasible only in the 1970s, when the percentage of U.S. households with telephones exceeded 90 percent.[2] Early on, telephone interviewers recorded respondents' answers on paper questionnaires. CATI systems became widely available in the 1980s and 1990s. Currently, the U.S. Census Bureau estimates that over 96 percent of U.S. households have at least one telephone line. Telephone surveys are cost effective, reaching the maximum number of people in the shortest period of time while maintaining representative samples. Interviewers can speak with respondents living all over the nation from a single location. Calling from one location allows interviewers to obtain on-the-spot directions from supervisors as needed, and supervisors can easily monitor interviews for accuracy, completeness, and comparability.[3] Also, many respondents are more comfortable discussing sensitive topics on the telephone with an interviewer than doing so face-to-face with a stranger in their home (see Exhibit 1.1).

But telephone interviewing also has important disadvantages compared to in-person interviews and self-administered questionnaires. For example, telephone surveys need to be short, with simpler questions, fewer questions, and fewer answer categories than other types of surveys. Most telephone interviews last ten to twelve minutes or less, while face-to-face interviews often last thirty minutes or more. Telephone interviewers also cannot use visual aids to help respondents understand a complex concept or calculate something. Although

EXHIBIT 1.1. WHY ARE SENSITIVE TOPICS EASIER TO DISCUSS ON THE TELEPHONE?

The social psychologists Argyle and Ingham[4] discovered that people have *personal space,* something like little social bubbles. People invite others into their spaces with nonverbal cues, such as eye contact and body language. In experiments on social distance, eye contact, and surveys, Argyle and Ingham found that people need more social distance when discussing sensitive topics. Thus respondents who speak with interviewers on the telephone about sensitive topics should feel more comfortable and give more accurate answers than they would with in-person interviewers.

In additional experiments, Argyle and Ingham found that when the physical distance between two people remains the same (say, when sitting at a dining table in a face-to-face interview), they start avoiding eye contact when a conversation's topic becomes sensitive, to increase their social distance. For this reason, face-to-face interviewers are trained to look down when asking sensitive questions, giving respondents more personal space.

telephone interviewers may be able to "read" a respondent's tone of voice for impatience or misunderstanding, they cannot see that respondent's body language for the additional nonverbal clues that an in-person interviewer can.

Telephone surveys also do not reach all households. The growth of cell phone–only households, especially among young adults, is problematic for telephone surveys, because RDD samples typically exclude cell phone numbers. To date, however, most cell phone users maintain land lines at home. Telephone surveys also tend to exclude households whose residents are rarely home (for example, unmarried young men living alone). By definition telephone surveys exclude the homeless and households lacking telephones (typically those who are very poor or living in very remote places). These issues contribute to low response rates and low coverage rates, which can cause random sample telephone survey results to not represent their underlying populations.

Face-to-face or in-person interviews put the respondent and the interviewer together in the respondent's home or a neutral location to complete paper-and-pencil or laptop computer questionnaires. They include persons without telephones, but hard-to-reach and homeless persons remain as difficult to reach as for telephone surveys. In-person interviewers have a high degree of control over the interview situation. For example, by observing body language, they can judge respondents' understanding, attention, and the appropriateness of responses. Interviewers also can employ visual aids—for example, handing respondents a card that lists complex answer categories. To obtain sensitive information, interviewers can turn a laptop computer toward respondents to let them type in their own answers or hand them a short self-administered section that respondents can seal in an envelope when they finish.

The process of conducting face-to-face interviews builds rapport and trust between the interviewer and respondent, which allows for longer interviews and may enhance data quality. Rapport can backfire, however, when interviewers inadvertently influence respondents' answers. For example, respondents sometimes answer questions in ways they think will please or impress the interviewer. This is called social desirability bias. Sensitive questions—about religion, money, social status, sexuality, drugs, alcohol, culturally deviant behavior and opinions, and political and moral issues—are particularly vulnerable to social desirability bias. Face-to-face interviews are more susceptible to social desirability bias than telephone interviews because respondents can see and react to interviewers' social characteristics, such as age, sex, race, and ethnicity, as well as perceived social class and educational attainment.

Telephone interviewing minimizes the potential effects of interviewers' social characteristics on respondents' answers, because all respondents experience is a voice. Voice is not a reliable predictor of age, race, ethnicity, social class, or education. Voice is not even a consistent indicator of sex.[5] Only interviewers with strong regional or foreign accents might affect respondents' answers, but few survey research organizations hire interviewers with strong accents. Instead of seeing you, telephone respondents can create a visual image of the type of person they want you to be, consistent with their decision to cooperate.

Additional disadvantages for face-to-face data collection are trust and cost. Survey research organizations must completely trust their interviewers to carry out the interviews in exactly the way they were trained—and trust them not to fabricate the data altogether. Supervisors cannot tag along, monitoring interviewers' skills. Instead they verify each interviewer's work by recontacting a certain percentage of respondents who completed interviews and checking the accuracy of the answers interviewers recorded. But the biggest issue in face-to-face interviewing is its extreme cost in time, training, tracking, and travel. Many face-to-face interviews cost over $500 each, compared to $30 to $100 for each completed telephone interview.

Respondents complete self-administered questionnaires without an interviewer's assistance. Researchers distribute such questionnaires via the postal service, Internet, e-mail, or in group settings. Mailed questionnaires are typically sent to a random sample of homes or businesses, with an explanatory cover letter, a token incentive (for example, a crisp dollar bill), and a stamped envelope for return to the survey research organization. Interviewers are sometimes employed to drop off questionnaires that respondents will mail back, to pick up questionnaires that were mailed out, or to call respondents to remind them to complete their questionnaire.

Internet and e-mail questionnaires are most appropriate for closed populations, such as employees of a firm or members of a voluntary organization. Even these populations, however, often lack universal Internet access. No list of e-mail addresses is available for the general U.S. population. Moreover, household Internet access varies significantly by geography in the United States, with higher penetration in the West than the South. Although very cheap to administer, these self-administered questionnaires typically suffer very low response rates. Nonetheless, self-administered Internet-based surveys will continue growing in importance as Internet access grows.

Self-administered questionnaires in group settings include customer service evaluations and teaching assessments. They generally seek short-term appraisals rather than represent basic research that can be generalized to the social world. Similarly, questionnaires distributed at special locations, such as a ski lift or county fair, and questionnaires strategically placed in a motel, restaurant, or doctor's office, are not scientific surveys because they lack random samples.

The advantages of self-administered questionnaires over interviewer-administered surveys include the ability to employ visual aids, such as photos or charts. Respondents also can take their time to think about questions before answering and answer sensitive questions outside the presence of a stranger (the interviewer). Hard-to-reach respondents may be more reachable by mail or e-mail.

However, self-administered questionnaires are not necessarily cheap, and data collection can take many months to complete. When mail questionnaires are properly administered, with multiple mailings, incentives, and telephone reminders, the cost-per-complete is about the same as for a telephone interview, with similar response rates. Data collection for mailed surveys often takes several months, because multiple mailings must be staggered over many weeks. In contrast, many telephone surveys can be completed in two or three weeks.

Additional disadvantages of self-administered questionnaires include potential biases associated with illiteracy, non-native language speakers, and lack of control over who actually completes the questionnaire. Respondents may skip questions or entire groups of questions, or answer questions out of order. If they become confused by skip logic, do not understand a question, or have unanswered concerns, they may set aside the task indefinitely or toss it into the recycling bin. For such reasons, a persistent problem of self-administered questionnaires is a low response rate.

This overview of the advantages and disadvantages of different survey data collection methods has illustrated how telephone interviewing compares to other types of survey data collection. It should now be clear why telephone interviewing is the most appropriate method for collecting data for certain types of surveys. This summary has also given some clues about potential sources of error and bias in survey research, which is the next section's topic.

Interviewers and Survey Error

The goal of a random sample survey is to accurately represent the target population under study. Any difference between a sample estimate and a population parameter is considered an error. For example, Census 2000 found that 25 percent of persons aged twenty-five and older in Oregon had completed a bachelor's degree or more. This is the best available population parameter defining Oregonians' educational attainment. If I had conducted an RDD survey of 400 adults in Oregon in the same year and found that 28 percent of my sample had completed a bachelor's degree, the 3 percent difference between the population and the sample would be considered error.

> This *Handbook* aims to minimize survey errors attributable to interviewers.

The problem is to determine the source of that error and, for the purposes of this *Handbook*, whether interviewers contributed to that error, and if so, how interviewers can avoid it. Standardized interviewing aims to minimize errors attributable to interviewers.

Random Error Versus Bias

The process of designing and administering a telephone survey is complex, involving many separate but interrelated tasks, often conducted by different people. Errors can emerge at any step in this complex process, from instrument design to programming to interviewer training and so on down to what respondents say. Some errors are accidental or random—for example, a respondent says she is age forty-five, forgetting that she just celebrated her forty-sixth birthday last month. Or an interviewer's finger slips and hits the wrong key—for example, accidentally typing in "45" instead of "46." Random error is difficult to locate and correct because it has no pattern. Careful interviewer training and supervision helps to minimize random error. Researchers hope that random error is infrequent and balances out in the end, thereby minimizing its effect on survey findings.

Bias is a type of error much worse than random error because it is systematic. Often bias is not discovered until the last step of a survey project, during data analysis, when something seems wrong, or "off," in the survey findings. Here is one example of a situation in which a systematic error had the potential to cause bias:

> A research assistant noticed several *outliers* (out-of-range numbers) during data analysis. In tracing the source of those outliers, she discovered that a certain interviewer accidentally hit the "6" key about half of the time when he intended to hit the "5" key. He finished 55 out of the 403 completed interviews in that survey. Fifteen of the seventy-five possible questions in the survey allowed interviewers to record a "5." To determine whether the interviewer's systematic

error actually caused bias, the research assistant had to examine all of his 4,000 or more possible keystrokes across his 55 completed interviews.

Errors such as this can be very costly to identify and correct, especially when they remain invisible until the late stages of a survey project. By then, bias is often impossible to correct. Respondents may need to be recontacted but can be difficult to locate—and they may give different answers many months later than they did the first time. Rarely can researchers just throw away the contaminated data. If a potential source of bias is noticed and corrected early in the survey process, its damage is less. Because both systematic and random error can occur at any step in the survey process, research teams build in checks and balances to try to avoid sources of error altogether.

Total Error

To understand the sources of error, survey methodologists divide it into two logical groups: error due to sample selection, called *sampling error,* and error due to everything else, called *nonsampling error.* Together, they comprise *total error.* Both sampling and nonsampling error can have random and systematic components. The next sections describe sampling and nonsampling error and the telephone interviewer's role in avoiding and catching both. Chapters Five, Six, and Seven provide specific techniques for minimizing interviewer error.

Sampling Error   Sampling error occurs naturally when researchers interview a random sample of the population instead of the entire population. If I had asked the entire population of Oregon adults their educational attainment in 2000, I should have found the same results as Census 2000, that is, that 25 percent had completed a bachelor's degree. But few researchers have the means to interview millions in an entire population. If I had conducted numerous RDD surveys of 400 adults in Oregon in 2000, some of my estimates of educational attainment would likely have been high and some low, but the average across all surveys should, theoretically, have equaled the true population parameter. Again, few researchers have the means to conduct numerous RDD surveys to prove such correspondences. If my original sample size had been 4,400 respondents instead of 400, the results would more likely have matched the population parameter, but my clients could not have afforded me to conduct so many interviews.

Instead, researchers rely on a single, well-chosen, and well-implemented random sample to provide the best sample estimates of a population. A random sample of a population is like a slice of bread representing the whole loaf or like a spoonful of soup representing the entire pot of soup. Sampling theory, combined with strategic decision making about how to best use a survey's budget, allows researchers to predict the amount of sampling error a survey can tolerate.

> A random sample of a population is like a slice of bread representing the whole loaf or spoonful of soup representing the entire pot of soup.

The keys here are the terms *well-chosen* and *well-implemented*. If something goes wrong with the way in which a random sample is chosen or implemented, sampling error can result. For example, once (and only once) one of my research assistants programmed a computer to generate an RDD sample, but he forgot to *randomize* the list after it was selected. The computer generated a *sequential* list of random telephone numbers, which was then distributed sequentially to the interviewers. This meant that the telephone numbers at the bottom of the list did not have as much chance of being called as did those at the top of the list. If telephone companies assigned telephone numbers randomly, this would not pose a problem. However, telephone companies assign area codes and prefixes to geopolitical areas, such as towns, cities, and counties. (For example, where I live, these combinations of area codes and prefixes are common: 541-343-xxxx, 541-344-xxxx, 541-345-xxxx, and 541-484-xxxx.) This error resulted in the systematic underrepresentation of several counties whose telephone numbers fell at the bottom of the list. We saved the survey from bias only by quickly going back into the field with additional RDD telephone numbers for the underrepresented areas, proportional to their representation in the target population.

Alert interviewers can help prevent difficulties such as the one described in the preceding paragraph. For example, you might notice that you have not called telephone numbers or conducted interviews in a county or city that should have been in the sample. If you notice a potential sample problem, tell a supervisor right away. In this way your awareness can help to ensure that the sample is adequately put into practice and help to avoid sample bias.

Properly trained telephone interviewers should never be a source of sampling error. However, interviewers can directly contribute to sampling error if they fail to follow sampling-related instructions. For example, random sample telephone interviews with individual adults typically require two steps: (1) obtaining the cooperation of the household attached to a telephone number, and (2) obtaining the cooperation of the randomly selected adult in that household. The second step can be difficult if the person who agreed in the first step is not the same as the person randomly selected. The second step is especially tricky if the person who agreed in the first step adopts a gatekeeper role or if the randomly selected adult is rarely home. Lazy or easily intimidated interviewers may be tempted to substitute another person for the randomly selected but difficult-to-reach respondent, but substitutions are not allowed. Interviewers who do not consistently follow random selection instructions contribute to sampling error and restrict a survey's generalizability. When such deceit is discovered, the interviewer will be promptly fired.

> Interviewers should never allow substitutions for the randomly selected respondent.

Sampling theory allows researchers to predict the amount of sampling error in their surveys. Sample implementation problems are avoidable and should never contribute to sampling error. Interviewers, in particular, should never contribute to sampling error. Moreover, by attending to your work closely, you may help to prevent sample problems.

Nonsampling Error   Every step of the basic survey process outlined earlier is a potential source of nonsampling error. For example, in the design and planning step the principle investigators may overlook a key concept. In designing the survey instrument, pretesters might not understand a concept well enough to realize that a question is misworded, or in a rush to get into the field, they might neglect to notice an error in complex skip logic. Even when a researcher has created a perfect RDD sample, a certain number of persons will always refuse to participate, and even willing respondents can err in reporting. (Not all people can accurately recall, for example, how many hours they exercise or commute to work each week.) While conducting an interview, you might not notice that your finger slipped on the keypad, recording a "1" instead of a "4." During data analysis, researchers can easily make mistakes in sorting their data sets or in creating scales and indexes of respondents' answers. Survey researchers invoke many techniques to check and recheck their work to avoid common errors.

Minimizing Errors Attributable to Interviewers   Telephone interviewers are a potential source of four broad types of nonsampling error and must exercise vigilance to avoid contributing to it.

First, avoid unit-level refusals. (A unit is the household, person, organization, or other entity that the survey seeks to ask questions of.) You will learn to use all techniques and personal powers of persuasion effectively in order to avoid such refusals (Chapter Six provides specific methods). Each person, household, or organization that refuses to participate represents hundreds of others like them. If certain types consistently refuse to participate in a survey, the results will be biased and misleading.

> While individuals are an absolute puzzle, in the aggregate they become a mathematical certainty. You can never foretell what any one person will do, but you can say with precision what an average number will be up to. Individuals vary, but averages remain constant.[6]

Second, avoid item nonresponse, that is, answers such as "don't know," "refuse," "other," "no opinion," "no answer," and "if volunteered"—unless specifically instructed otherwise. Respondents most often refuse to answer sensitive questions, such as those related to sexuality, religion, illegal behavior, and drug and alcohol use. Nonresponses are nonanswers; they give the researchers no data to analyze for those cases. Use the techniques in Chapter Seven to encourage respondents to select from the answer categories provided.

Third, make sure that the numbers you record and words you type are accurate. Although most survey research organizations require only minimal typing speed of their interviewers, accuracy is essential. Expect to be tested and retested on this. If your finger often slips down when you intend to record a "4" to the adjoining "1" key, you may be accidentally recording, for example, "strongly agree" instead of "strongly disagree." Consistent errors such as this will bias the data. Failure to correct a tendency to such errors may result in dismissal. No one wants this. Your employer invests a lot in your skills, so keep them accurate.

Although you will most often use the number pad on the right-hand side of your computer keyboard, for recording answers to open-ended questions and *thumbnail sketches* (or *interviewer observations*) you will use the letters on the regular keypad. Naturally, interviewers find it difficult to type as fast as respondents speak when answering open-ended questions. To make this task easier, use the shorthand, acronyms, and abbreviations in Table 1.2, or use other shortcuts approved by your employer. After you have completed an interview, review your narrative answers to open-ended questions to ensure their legibility.

Fourth, use standardized interviewing techniques combined with your knowledge of how respondents answer questions (see Chapter Seven). In brief, read all questions in their entirety, in the order presented, and exactly as they are written, using a neutral tone of voice. Use only scripted definitions and standard probes. Probe to clarify respondents' answers and offer neutral feedback only as scripted and as trained. Never utter a word or make a sound that could influence

TABLE 1.2. COMMONLY USED ACRONYMS AND ABBREVIATIONS IN SURVEY RESEARCH.

Term	Acronym or Abbreviation
Adult	A
Because	bc
Business	bus
Call forwarding	CF
Callback	CB
Cell phone	CP
Cell phone only household	CPO HH
Could you tell me what you mean by that?	WM
Don't know	DK
Elderly	E
Elderly female respondent	EFR
Elderly male respondent	EMR
Female	F
Female respondent	FR
Gatekeeper	GK
Household	HH
Identification number	ID#
Information	info
Interviewer identification number	Ir ID#
Inappropriate question; does not apply	inap
Interview	Iw
Interviewed	Iwed
Interviewer	Ir
Interviewing	Iwing
Institutional Review Board	IRB
Knowledgeable adult	KA
Male	M
Male respondent	MR
Message	msg
Not ascertained or not asked	NA
Number	#
Proxy respondent	PR
Question	Q
Question by question survey objectives	Q by Q
Random digit dial	RDD
Randomly chosen adult in household	RA
Refusal	ref
Repeat question	RQ
Respondent	R
Respondent unavailable	RUN
Standard neutral probe, such as "whatever it means to you," "uh-huh," or "thank you"	(P)
Survey research organization	SRO
Telephone	TP
Telephone number	TP#
Telephone answering machine	TAM
With	w/

or change a respondent's answers. Do not suggest answers, ask unscripted questions, make comments on a respondent's answers, or try to make a respondent's answers consistent across questions. Finally, use a congenial, methodical tone of voice that conveys self-assurance, attentiveness, and professionalism. These are the key elements of standardized interviewing.

Summing Up

This chapter has explained why researchers conduct surveys and the crucial role of professional telephone interviewers in survey research. You have learned the basic, overall survey process and where you, as an interviewer, fit into it. In examining the different types of survey data collection, you learned the advantages and disadvantages of interviewer-administered compared to self-administered surveys. You should understand now that the goal of a survey is to accurately represent the population under study, but the road to accuracy is fraught with potential error. By the end of your interviewer training, you will know the best practices for avoiding any contribution you might make to survey error.

Now you have some understanding of survey research in general and where you fit into it. The next chapter narrows our focus, discussing the types of organizations that conduct surveys, what you should know about your employer, and what your employer needs from you.

CHAPTER TWO

WHO CONDUCTS SURVEYS?

This chapter briefly introduces you to the types of organizations that conduct survey research and explains how they differ. Survey employers who assign this *Handbook* are likely to be professional and legitimate. Unfortunately, some pseudoscientific, fly-by-night survey organizations also flourish, and this chapter discusses how to identify and avoid them. This chapter concludes by describing what survey employers seek in their new interviewers.

Types of Survey Organizations

Three basic types of organizations conduct scientific surveys: governmental agencies, academic survey research organizations, and private research firms. These three types, however, crisscross in function and purpose. Some focus on market research, political polling, or public policy research. Some are for-profit businesses, some are nonprofit, and a few are employee owned. Many cooperate with each other. They vary greatly in size and structure. This variety means that your survey employer may not exactly fit the descriptions that follow. But in reading these discussions you will learn more about the major characteristics of survey organizations.

A few federal governmental agencies, such as the U.S. Census Bureau and Department of Defense, conduct their own surveys with their own interviewers, whom they hire and train. For Census 2000, for example, the Census Bureau recruited 2.6 million qualified applicants and hired sufficient staff to collect over 120 million questionnaires, containing data on over 280 million persons in the United States. During some follow-up operations, the Census Bureau issued an average of nearly half a million paychecks each week. Most of these employees worked part-time and for less than a year. The U.S. census is the largest survey operation in the nation, but it occurs only in one out of every ten years.

Congressional legislation requires other federal agencies to gather a large amount of survey data; among these agencies are the Bureau of Labor Statistics, Agency for Healthcare Research and Quality, Environmental Protection Agency, National Agricultural Statistics Service, National Center for Education Statistics, Social Security Administration, National Science Foundation, and Department of Justice. Many state and local governments also require their agencies to collect representative survey data on certain topics. But few governmental units have the specialized expertise to collect survey data themselves. Instead, they give grants and contracts to private and academic research firms, who in turn hire and train interviewers.

Academic survey research organizations tend to differ from private firms in several ways. They usually focus on research projects that benefit their communities, especially surveys for nonprofit associations and state, regional, and local governments. They also serve as resources and intellectual homes for university professors, staff, and students involved in survey-related research, including training and instruction in survey methods.

The communities surrounding state capitols, Washington, DC, and large research universities are fertile ground for private survey firms to develop. These firms often develop close relationships with certain public agencies, elected officials, or businesses that serve government and that need surveys. They also sometimes specialize in particular survey topics, such as health care, transportation, natural resources, or election polling.

Private political and election polling organizations represent a subgroup of private survey firms. They differ from other types of survey organizations in that their surveys tend to ask very few questions and their data collection periods are often very short—sometimes overnight. Sometimes they collaborate with large news organizations, such as ABC, CBS, NBC, NPR, the *Los Angeles Times*, the *New York Times*, and *USA Today*, to conduct specialized polls. Most state and regional newspapers, such as the *Minneapolis Star Tribune, Columbus Dispatch*, and *Oregonian*, regularly conduct special polls, especially around elections. On occasion, the large polling and news organizations subcontract their telephone polling to smaller, local survey research organizations with whom they have developed trustworthy relationships. During election seasons, small political polling organizations often emerge for a few months and then go dormant until the next election cycle.

Market research firms represent another subgroup of private firms. They vary widely, from large, highly professional, national and international organizations serving multinational corporations to small, local organizations. Almost every medium-to-large city contains several small market research organizations serving local and regional interests. Some local market research firms also do political polling during election seasons.

Small market research and election polling firms that serve local and regional interests tend to differ in several ways from the federal agencies, large research firms, and universities that conduct surveys. They less often belong to professional associations, which are important for the codes of ethics they promote, as discussed in Chapter Three. Small, local firms also rarely conduct basic research on the survey process. Some small firms do not even invest in computer-assisted telephone interviewing (CATI) systems for their telephone surveys. In contrast, the larger and more professional organizations often experiment with new and better ways to ask questions, record answers, and convince respondents to participate. The larger firms also tend to have the most up-to-date computer software and hardware for survey data collection, analysis, and reporting.

Exhibit 2.1 provides examples of over one hundred major private survey, polling, and market research firms and over one hundred major academic survey research organizations in the United States. The lists are not complete, for no single, comprehensive list exists of either type of organization. However, each organization listed has a Web site that you can visit if you are interested in seeing how these firms differ.

What You Should Know About Your Survey Employer

The survey employers who assign this *Handbook* are likely to be professional and legitimate. However, you should be aware that in this industry, as in any other, some unscrupulous, pseudoscientific, fly-by-night organizations exist. Thus telephone interviewers need tools to assist them in judging the character of a potential survey employer. Table 2.1 and Exhibit 2.2 are two such tools, listing the features of legitimate survey research organizations that tend to result in a positive work environment and incentives to perform well as an interviewer.

Before starting to work at a survey organization (or any employer), do a little homework on your own. Read over the questions in Table 2.1 and note the answers you should hear from a genuine, established, and scientific survey research organization.

EXHIBIT 2.1. MAJOR U.S. SURVEY FIRMS AND ORGANIZATIONS.

Major Private Survey, Polling, and Marketing Firms

A. C. Nielsen

Abt Associates

American Institutes for Research

American Research Group

Anderson, Niebuhr & Associates

Aspen Systems Corporation

Battelle Centers for Public Health Research & Evaluation

Bauman Research & Consulting

Behavior Research Center

Belden, Russonello & Stewart

Bisconti Research

Blum & Weprin Associates

Business Research Lab

California Survey Research Services

CALLC

Candace Bennett & Associates

CBS News, Election & Survey Unit

Center for the Study of Services

Central Research and Consulting

Charlton Research

Ciruli Associates

Clearwater Research

D3 Systems

Data Recognition Corporation

David Binder Research

Development Associates

Discovery Research Group

Eastern Research Services

Economist Intelligence Unit

Edison Media Research

Elway Research

EPIC-MRA

Fairbank, Maslin, Maullin & Associates

Field Research Corporation

(continued)

EXHIBIT 2.1. *(CONTINUED)*

Major Private Survey, Polling, and Marketing Firms

FSC Group
Gallup Organization
Garin-Hart-Yang Research Group
Gary Siegel Organization
GfK NOP World
Gilmore Research Group
Glenn Roberts Research
GlobeScan
Greenberg Quinlan Rosner
Group Health Cooperative, Center for Health Studies
Hamilton, Beattie & Staff
Harris Interactive, Harris Poll
Hollander, Cohen & McBride
Intermedia Survey Institute
Ipsos North America
Ivan Moore Research
J. D. Franz Research
Juarez & Associates
Kaiser Family Foundation
Kerr-Downs Research
Knowledge Networks
Kochevar Research Associates
L. C. Williams & Associates
Lake-Snell-Perry-Mermin & Associates
Leger Marketing
LHK Partners
Macro International, ORC Macro
Market Resource Group
Market Shares Corporation
Market Solutions Group
Market Wise
Marketing Systems Group
Mason-Dixon Polling and Research
Mathematica Policy Research
McLaughlin & Associates
Mitchell Research
Mitofsky International

EXHIBIT 2.1. *(CONTINUED)*

Monroe Mendelsohn Research
National Opinion Research Services
Neuwirth Research
Nielsen Media Research
O'Neil Associates
Opinion Access Corporation
Opinion Dynamics Corporation
Opinion Research Corporation
Organizational Research & Consulting
Peter D. Hart Research Associates
The Pew Research Center for the People & the Press
PricewaterhouseCoopers
Princeton Survey Research Associates International
Public Opinion Strategies
Pulse Research
QFACT Marketing Research
QSA Research and Strategy
Rand Survey Research Group
Reda International
Renaissance Research & Consulting
Research 2000
Research and Polling
Research Spectrum
Research Support Services
Riley Research Associates
Roper Starch Worldwide
RTI International
Schulman, Ronca & Bucuvalas
Scripps Research Center
Selzer and Company
Strategic Vision
Survey Sciences Group
Survey USA
TNS
Urban Institute
Westat
Wirthlin Worldwide

(continued)

EXHIBIT 2.1. *(CONTINUED)*

Major Private Survey, Polling, and Marketing Firms

Yankelovich Partners

Zogby International

Major Academic Survey Research Organizations

Arizona State University, Survey Research Laboratory

Auburn University, Survey Research Laboratory

Brown University, John Hazen White Public Opinion Laboratory

California State University, Chico, Survey Research Center

California State University, Northridge, Center for Survey Research

California State University, San Marcos, Social & Behavioral Research Institute

City University of New York, York College, Survey Research Laboratory

Columbia University, Lazarsfeld Center for the Social Sciences

Columbia University, Social Indicators Survey Center

Cornell University, Survey Research Institute

Farleigh-Dickinson University, PublicMind Poll

Florida International University, Institute for Public Opinion Research

Florida State University, Survey Research Laboratory

Fort Hays State University, Docking Institute of Public Affairs, University Center for Survey Research

Franklin and Marshall College, Center for Opinion Research

Franklin Pierce College, Center for Applied Public Opinion Research

Indiana University, Center for Survey Research

Indiana University, Public Opinion Laboratory

Iowa State University, Center for Survey Statistics & Methodology

Iowa State University, Statistical Laboratory, Survey Section

Kennesaw State University, Burruss Institute of Public Service

Kent State University, Survey Research Laboratory

Keuka College, Division of Basic and Applied Social Sciences

Louisiana State University, Reilly Center for Media and Public Affairs, Public Policy Research Lab

Mansfield University, Mansfield University State Poll

Marist College, Institute for Public Opinion

Michigan State University, Institute for Public Policy and Social Research

Mississippi State University, Survey Research Laboratory

EXHIBIT 2.1. *(CONTINUED)*

Muhlenberg College, Institute of Public Opinion
Northern Arizona University, Social Research Laboratory
Northern Illinois University, Public Opinion Laboratory
Ohio State University, Center for Survey Research
Oklahoma State University, Bureau for Social Research
Oregon State University, Survey Research Center
Pennsylvania State University, Survey Research Center
Pennsylvania State University Harrisburg, Center for Survey Research
Portland State University, Survey Research Laboratory
Princeton University, Survey Research Center
Quinnipiac University, Polling Institute
Rutgers University, Eagleton Center for Public Interest Polling
Saint Cloud State University Survey
Saint Norbert College, Survey Center
Sam Houston State University, Survey Research Program
San Diego State University, Social Science Research Laboratory
San Francisco State University, Public Research Institute
Savannah (Georgia) State University, Survey Research Center
State University of New York, Albany, Center for Social and Demographic Analysis
State University of New York, Stony Brook, Center for Survey Research
Temple University, Institute for Survey Research
Texas A&M University, Public Policy Research Institute
Texas Tech University, Earl Survey Research Laboratory
University of Akron, Center for Policy Studies
University of Alabama, Institute for Social Science Research
University of Alaska, Institute of Social and Economic Research
University of Arkansas, Survey Research Center
University of California, Berkeley, Survey Research Center
University of California, Los Angeles, Institute for Social Science Research
University of California, San Francisco, Health Survey Research Unit
University of California, Santa Barbara, Social Science Survey Center
University of Chicago, National Opinion Research Center
University of Cincinnati, Institute for Public Policy Research
University of Connecticut, Center for Survey Research & Analysis

(continued)

EXHIBIT 2.1. *(CONTINUED)*

Major Private Survey, Polling, and Marketing Firms

University of Connecticut, Roper Center for Public Opinion

University of Delaware, Center for Applied Demography and Survey Research

University of Georgia, Survey Research Center

University of Illinois, Chicago, Survey Research Laboratory

University of Illinois, Urbana, Survey Research Laboratory

University of Kansas, Survey Research Center

University of Kentucky, Survey Research Center

University of Louisville, Survey Research Center

University of Massachusetts, Boston, Center for Survey Research

University of Michigan, Survey Research Center

University of Minnesota, Center for Survey Research in Public Health

University of Minnesota, Cities' Institute for Public Health Research

University of Minnesota, Minnesota Center for Survey Research

University of Missouri–St. Louis, Public Policy Research Center

University of Nebraska, Lincoln, Bureau of Sociological Research

University of Nebraska, Lincoln, Gallup Research Center

University of Nevada, Cannon Center for Survey Research

University of New Hampshire, Survey Center

University of New Mexico, Survey Research Center

University of New Orleans, Survey Research Center

University of North Carolina, Odum Institute

University of North Carolina, Survey Research Unit, Biostatistics Department

University of North Florida, Public Opinion Research Laboratory

University of North Texas, Survey Research Center

University of Northern Iowa, Center for Social and Behavioral Research

University of Oklahoma, Public Opinion Learning Laboratory

University of Pittsburgh, Center for Social and Urban Research

University of South Carolina, Survey Research Laboratory

University of Southern Maine, Survey Research Center

University of Tennessee, Social Science Research Institute

University of Texas, Office of Survey Research

EXHIBIT 2.1. *(CONTINUED)*

University of Utah, Social Research Institute

University of Virginia, Center for Survey Research

University of Wisconsin, Institute for Survey and Policy Research

University of Wisconsin, Survey Center

University of Wisconsin–Milwaukee, Social Science Research Facility

University of Wyoming, Survey and Analysis Center

Virginia Commonwealth University, Survey & Evaluation Research Laboratory

Virginia Polytechnic Institute & State University, Center for Survey Research

Wake Forest University, Survey Research Center

Washington State University, Social & Economic Sciences Research Center

Wayne State University, Urban Studies Center, Survey Research

Wright State University, Center for Urban and Public Affairs, Survey Research Lab

---

Of course, survey research organizations vary in the volume and type of research they conduct, their workplace policies, and related activities. However, you should avoid those organizations that answer the fifteen questions in Table 2.1 with answers you do not want to hear.

In brief, steer clear of survey organizations that lack a regular office setting, that are difficult to locate in a telephone book or on the Internet, that operate under multiple "doing business as" names, or that cannot put together a few simple sentences explaining why they do what they do. Very small organizations run by one to three people, especially those that have existed for a year or less, are not likely to have well-developed workplace policies or much work for you—although they may suggest huge possibilities for business growth and the importance of getting in on the ground floor.

Be wary of potential employers who require you to complete minimal paperwork, who do not ask for references, or who do not speak with the references you supply. Survey organizations that hire employees with poor references are not likely to care about the quality of their survey data or to invest much in interviewer training. This in turn allows them to distrust their employees' honesty and treat their work products with suspicion. When any organization treats its employees poorly, work morale and motivation decline.

Keep away from organizations that pay per completed interview. When telephone interviewers are paid on a per-interview basis, their main work

TABLE 2.1. QUESTIONS AND ANSWERS ABOUT YOUR SURVEY EMPLOYER.

Questions to Ask Your Survey Employer	Answers You Should Expect to Hear	Answers You Do Not Want to Hear
Where is the survey organization physically located? What is its telephone number and Web site URL?	The organization has an address and telephone number listed in a telephone book. Web sites are now standard. Good ones should answer most of the questions in this table.	The organization operates out of someone's home or a location that changes from project to project. You can find neither its name in a telephone book nor its Web site on the Internet.
What is the organization's statement of purpose?	The organization has a written mission and goals statement and gladly shares it with you.	The organization has no formally stated reason for existing. Someone volunteers to tell you what it does.
What does the organization chart look like?	The organization has multiple employees filling clearly named positions. It is clear to whom employees should go with different types of questions. Interviewers' direct supervisor(s) are named.	There is no organization chart, or one or two people run the entire organization.
Who will be my direct supervisor?	One or more clearly identified persons with experience and authority supervise interviewers.	The owner or a senior interviewer supervises interviewers.
How many years has the organization operated?	More than one year.	Less than one year, or episodically over several years.

TABLE 2.1. *(CONTINUED)*

Questions to Ask Your Survey Employer	Answers You Should Expect to Hear	Answers You Do Not Want to Hear
Who are the organization's main clients? May I see a list of recent projects? May I see summaries of some recent projects?	Lists of survey sponsors and project titles are available on request or online. Project summaries are available for interviewers to examine.	Interviewers are not allowed to know survey sponsors' names; that information is proprietary. No project list is available. Only clients get to see survey reports. You should not trust a verbal (unwritten) client or project list.
Are prospective employees required to supply references?	Yes. Job applicants must provide contact information for a prior employer, teacher, or other person in a position of trust who can attest to their character.	No references are required, or no one actually contacts the references applicants provide.
What are the workplace policies that apply to interviewers?	The organization gives new interviewers a copy of workplace policies to review. These policies are discussed in interviewer training.	The organization is said to be too small, new, or collegial to need official policies. "We handle issues informally."
What are the hours of operation and work shifts?	Most survey organizations stay open long hours, sometimes twelve to sixteen hours per day, seven days per week, depending on the geographical areas that their surveys cover. Interviewers are assigned clearly defined work shifts. No one is allowed to conduct interviews forty hours per week.	Hours of operation vary week to week, or the organization is open only evenings and weekends. Drop-in work is available. Interviewers are encouraged to work as many hours as they can when many surveys are in the field.

(continued)

TABLE 2.1. *(CONTINUED)*

Questions to Ask Your Survey Employer	Answers You Should Expect to Hear	Answers You Do Not Want to Hear
How will I learn about upcoming surveys and training sessions? How do I know what work shifts I am assigned?	Survey organizations need multiple reliable ways to communicate regularly with interviewers about in-progress and upcoming surveys. Most have a secure Web site or dedicated telephone hotline for interviewers to obtain regularly updated information. Most also send interviewers e-mails or leave them telephone messages at home.	"You call us."
What is the method and frequency of payment?	Paychecks are issued at fixed intervals (weekly, biweekly, or monthly). Hourly rates exceed the minimum wage. Raises or bonuses are possible. Paychecks are itemized, allowing you to see how much is deducted for taxes, Social Security, and so forth. Direct deposit to your bank account is available.	Interviewers are paid a certain amount per completed interview or paid the minimum hourly wage with no raises or bonuses possible. Paychecks are issued irregularly or when projects end. Paychecks are not itemized, or interviewers are paid in cash.
How are interviewers trained?	Interviewer training is formal, and includes some combination of general, project-specific, and refresher training. General training lasts six hours or longer. Interviewers receive pay for training hours.	Interviewers receive five or fewer hours of formal training. Reading the interview script to yourself a few times does not count as formal training.

TABLE 2.1. *(CONTINUED)*

Questions to Ask Your Survey Employer	Answers You Should Expect to Hear	Answers You Do Not Want to Hear
How are completed interviews verified for accuracy and completeness?	The survey organization verifies a certain number of completed interviews. Good employers explain the verification process, such as the types of questions they verify and the penalty if data do not check out.	Interview verification is not transparent. Interviewers suspect it is used to avoid paying them for the full value of their completed interviews.
May I see the interviewing stations and work area?	Potential interviewers should be allowed to view the work area. It should contain sound-reduced carrels, ergonomic chairs, and individual (not shared) headsets.	Be wary if you are not allowed to see the interviewing area in advance. Avoid places in which interviewers sit at long tables without dividers to minimize conversation sounds. Do not agree to conduct interviews from your home.
Does the organization belong to a professional association whose members subscribe to a code of ethics?	The employer identifies the professional association(s) to which it belongs. Interviewers must review a code of ethics and sign a statement indicating that they will abide by those rules.	"Our work is always very ethical. Do you doubt our professionalism?" Interviewers see no document saying the organization will keep respondents' answers confidential or anonymous.

motivation is speed, not quality. The rate per complete can range from roughly $10 to $50, depending on whether the average interview length is five or twenty-five minutes. However, you cannot predict how difficult the calling list will be, how many refusals you will get, or the number of completes you will make. Moreover, you cannot predict the number of completes your employer will accept. They may find excuses to not pay you for each one.

> Be wary of organizations that pay per completed interview or expect you to conduct interviews from your home.

Be very careful about working for survey organizations that ask you to conduct interviews from your home. The reasons are several. (1) If you do not own your own telephone headset, either you will have to type respondents' answers one-handed while holding the telephone in the other hand, which is slow and can cause data entry errors, or you will have to tuck the telephone between your head and shoulder, freeing both hands to type but often causing head and neck problems. (2) Your employer will usually supply you with a single-person CATI system to use on the A: drive of your personal computer. But many A: drives are slow, especially on old computers, causing long gaps between questions, which both rankles respondents and embarrasses you. (3) Do not be surprised if your employer deducts $50 or more from your first paycheck as a deposit to ensure that you return the CATI diskette. Good luck getting that deposit back. (4) Because no one supervises your interviewing work at home, your employer can easily raise suspicions about various aspects of your work, such as whether you actually called all the numbers you were supposed to (or called friends and relatives instead), dialed the numbers correctly (since this CATI system cannot do it for you), did the interviewing yourself (or subcontracted it to a roommate), or read all the questions or all the words in each question. Suspicions like these can result in employers' having excuses not to pay you for the work you truly completed. (5) Find out in advance if and how you will be paid for long-distance calls. (6) Be aware that you will not be paid for wear and tear on your own computer and telephone equipment and that breakdowns will cause you to lose your job. (7) Realize that you may be required to record respondents' telephone numbers with their interview data, supposedly to allow your employer to later verify your interviews. But your employer might also be in the lucrative but unethical business of selling cooperative respondents' telephone numbers to other firms. The bottom line: interviewing from home often seems like a better idea than it actually turns out to be.

Also be careful about survey organizations that do not explain their interview verification process, because the less legitimate firms sometimes use verifications as a reason not to pay interviewers their due. The things you want to know about this process are the number of interviews checked, how many days after an interview the verification occurs, the types of items checked, and what happens with problematic results. Verifications should take place within a day or two after an interview is completed, otherwise respondents often forget the interview and forget what they said. Verifying factual answers, like age, makes sense. But people's answers to opinion questions often change naturally over a few days. Also, if the employer does not pay interviewers for a completed survey when an answer does not check out, the employer should delete the entire interview record. Some, however, record the new answers and use the repaired data. A survey employer that lies about a few verifications with each interviewer could save itself hundreds of dollars in interviewer pay for each survey. When interviewers feel that their employer is cheating them on verifications due to ill-founded suspicions because they work unsupervised, they may lose their incentive to do high-quality, ethical work.

One of the most distinguishing features of legitimate professional survey organizations is their interviewer training, so beware of organizations that do not offer formal, paid interviewer training that includes rigorous attention to the codes of ethics of the professional associations to which the organization belongs. Organizations that conduct surveys for scientific purposes generally take interviewer training very seriously, putting a great deal of effort and thoughtfulness into its planning and execution. They generally attend to their interviewers' experiences in order to achieve high-quality survey results.

However, in some survey and polling businesses, interviewers do not know what surveys they will work on until they sit down at an interviewing station. Their survey-specific training consists of the option of scrolling through the CATI script once or twice before commencing calling. They cannot clarify respondents' questions because they know little or nothing about the survey's purpose or sponsor or the confidentiality of people's answers. Their nonstandardized replies to respondents' legitimate questions could be wrong and might bias the answers. They do not know if they are participating in marginally ethical survey activities because they have never heard of sugging, frugging, or push polling (see Chapter One). Supervision consists of urging interviewers to make more dial attempts and completions per hour, without regard to whether they stick to the interview script, offer ad hoc explanations, or interact with respondents in nonstandardized ways. Interviewers who receive no hands-on CATI training can easily make data entry errors and may not be able to figure out how to correct errors that they know they made. This in turn can result in interviews that cannot be verified and excuses to not pay interviewers for their work. Organizations that do not take interviewer training seriously tend to conduct surveys of questionable quality. They also tend to not treat their employees very well.

> Interviewer training is one of the most distinguishing features of legitimate, professional survey organizations.

Unscrupulous and fly-by-night survey organizations exist because many businesses want to get their survey data as cheaply as possible. Avoid getting caught in their web by using the questions in Table 2.1 to help you judge the character of a potential survey employer.

What Your Survey Employer Needs from You

Successful telephone interviewers need a unique combination of personal traits, skills, attitude, and understanding of the survey process to perform well. However, certain employee characteristics that other employers consider desirable for their types of jobs are not at all important for telephone interviewing. The next two sections discuss what your survey employer needs, and does not need, from you. Exhibit 2.2 summarizes the main points.

Not everyone has the personality or potential to be an excellent telephone interviewer. This job requires a genuine interest in talking with all kinds of people. Excellent telephone interviewers are able to adapt quickly to different kinds of people, yet they forget quickly the specifics of any given respondent. They

EXHIBIT 2.2. SUMMARY OF WHAT SURVEY EMPLOYERS NEED AND DO NOT NEED FROM TELEPHONE INTERVIEWERS.

What Survey Employers Need of You

> An interviewer's temperament and personality
>
> Above-average reading, listening, and enunciation skills
>
> The ability to read an interview script exactly, yet make it sound like a conversation
>
> Basic typing and computer skills to record respondents' answers accurately
>
> A willingness to adapt your voice and speaking skills if needed
>
> Adaptability to irregular work hours
>
> A professional attitude and sense of dignity about your work

What Survey Employers Don't Need of You

> A certain personal appearance or dress
>
> The ability to walk or move around a lot
>
> A cigarette smoker's chronic cough and phlegmy voice
>
> Prior interviewing experience
>
> Doubling up on interviewing jobs

must be utterly indifferent about knowing any respondent's identity. Telephone interviewers also have thick skins, because they know they will experience a certain number of refusals, no matter how good they are or how hard they try. They do not take rebuffs personally. The best telephone interviewers go in and out of other people's lives so smoothly that their respondents do not even remember the conversation a few days later.

Beyond an appropriate temperament, perhaps the most important skill telephone interviewers need is literacy. Specifically, you need an above-average level of reading comprehension and the ability to read aloud. You will be reading training manuals, like this, project-specific instructions, densely scripted interviews, and various types of forms. You must easily and willingly follow interview scripts exactly, word for word, even if you do not like a particular question's phrasing. The best telephone interviewers learn to read an interview script exactly—only partially memorized—and make it sound to respondents like a structured, yet flowing, conversation. This takes practice and training, because interviewer scripts differ widely.

Hearing and listening skills are also very important for this job. As a telephone interviewer, you must hear and record respondents' answers accurately, even though many people do not answer questions in full sentences or with correct grammar. Sometimes loud noises—such as construction, (un)happy children, or a television—invade respondents' backgrounds. Careful listening enables you to understand respondents despite such distractions. Careful listening is also necessary to determine whether a respondent's answer matches the question asked or whether the respondent misheard or misunderstood the question. You must also listen closely for tone of voice and any emotion behind each respondent's words that could interfere with data quality.

Telephone interviewers need only basic computer skills as a platform for CATI training. Typing speed matters much less than typing accuracy. Generally, you will type one or two numbers into a computer for each answer to a question. Sometimes, you will also type in narrative answers to open-ended questions—in respondents' exact words. But these answers tend to be short, that is, five to twenty words.

Vocal characteristics are an important element of telephone interviewing, but perhaps not in the way you think. The clipped, breezy, slick, and rapid speech of television reporters and radio advertisers tends not to go over well with survey respondents. Such speakers seem to remind them of shysters and salespeople. In my experience, interviewers who have something unique about their voices, such as the hint of a foreign accent or a slight lisp, get fewer refusals than others, as long as they enunciate well.

I once had an interviewer, Clyde, who had no teeth on one side of his mouth, due to jaw cancer. In our first conversation his mumble-mouth delivery made me seriously doubt his ability to work as a telephone interviewer, but his high motivation made me give him a chance. Another interviewer, Scott, had an unusually mechanical way of speaking. Both Scott and Clyde became successful interviewers, by enunciating carefully and following interview protocols. Hannah's voice was naturally high pitched, bubbly, and sometimes childish sounding. Although she could lower the pitch of her voice only slightly, she became a successful interviewer by learning to use a firm, cool, businesslike tone.

An accent is not necessarily a problem, as long as the interviewer speaks clearly. But in some parts of the United States certain heavy accents carry negative connotations, especially Asian and southern U.S. accents. Motivated, attentive interviewers can find ways to compensate by finding and using the particular interviewing skills that work well for them.

Fluency in multiple languages can be helpful, especially for certain types of surveys in certain geographical areas. Even the ability to understand a few basic conversational sentences in order to direct a non-English speaking respondent to a bilingual interviewer can be helpful. Almost 11 percent of the U.S. population speak Spanish in the home, about 4 percent speak another Indo-European language, and about 3 percent speak an Asian or Pacific Island language.[1]

Some survey research organizations conduct interviews only in English. But in many geographical areas, such as Texas and California, Spanish language interviews are needed in order to accurately represent the population. Survey organizations either translate interviews into Spanish or allow bilingual interviewers to free translate questions for respondents who prefer it. Many survey employers pay a premium for interviews completed in a different language and to interviewers skilled in *back translation* (that is, translating instruments from, for example, English to Spanish, then from Spanish back to English, and then comparing the two English versions to determine translation accuracy).

> If you need a full-time, year-round job, telephone interviewing is probably not the right job for you.

Unlike the workdays for many other jobs, telephone interviewing hours tend to be nonstandard and irregular. Telephone interviewers must be willing to work part-time, episodically, and on evenings and weekends. Many small telephone survey research organizations conduct fewer than twenty surveys per year. Some conduct twenty-five to forty surveys yearly. But very few have enough surveys for all their telephone interviewers to rely on the job for a regular paycheck. In addition, many survey organizations do not allow telephone interviewers to work more than four or five hours per day, or more than twenty hours per week, because voices tire, the ability to stick to the script slackens, even thick skins get frayed, and burnout is just around the corner. This job can be perfect for retirees, homemakers, and students. If you need a full-time, year-round paycheck, you should probably find a different line of work.

Your new survey employer needs your flexibility and adaptability to irregular work hours. In thinking about the hours you will work, many interviewers find it useful to understand how a typical telephone survey progresses. At the beginning of a typical random-digit-dial survey, interviewers dial the telephone a lot (or your CATI system does), working through banks of telephone numbers, many of which are nonworking or nonresidential. Interviews at this stage usually occur with the most cooperative respondents. By a survey's end, few numbers are left to dial, and those represent the grouchiest, hardest-to-reach, and hardest-to-convince respondents. In the middle of a survey, work is somewhere between these two poles. Most telephone numbers have already been called several times. The remaining numbers are mostly residential with potential respondents. The interviewer's job is to reach them and convince them to participate.

Many telephone interviewers find that they like working one stage of the survey data collection process more than others. This knowledge helps interviewers plan their work over the survey's duration. Typically, the first week or two of a telephone survey offers the most interviewing work, and day shifts will be available. In the middle stage most work shifts will be available only on evening and weekend shifts. By the survey's end, only one or two interviewers might be assigned to work on it for a couple of hours each day.

Some interviewers prefer to work at the beginning of a survey because they like the sense of rapid progress as they work through the first telephone numbers. Some prefer the more challenging interviews at the end; they enjoy exercising their refusal conversion techniques. Many interviewers like the different challenges of working all three stages.

If your employer conducts only one survey at a time, be prepared for more work hours at its start and fewer at its end. As a survey winds down, interviewers might be sent home before a shift ends, or they might receive a call saying their interviewing shift is cancelled because the survey is complete. Understanding a typical telephone survey's progress can help interviewers avoid frustration and maintain an adaptable attitude.

Survey research organizations that conduct two or three surveys each month try to stagger them, so that one starts just as another is winding down. When arriving for a work shift, an interviewer might be asked to work through the numbers on the survey that is winding down and then switch to another survey. This requires a certain amount of mental flexibility.

> Telephone survey interviewers need to maintain a professional attitude and a sense of dignity about their work.

Finally, telephone survey interviewers need to maintain a professional attitude and a sense of dignity about their work. Interviewers collect valuable data that may be required by congressional legislation, helps to evaluate a social program, helps a town plan for its future, or benefits people in general. Interviewers understand that the integrity of the survey data—as well as the reputation of their employer—rests on their shoulders. This knowledge, combined with their training, motivates them and gives them the confidence and skills to do the best job possible. Their voices convey their professionalism and help lessen respondents' concerns.

What Your Survey Employer Does Not Need from You

Several things that matter for employees in other industries do not matter for telephone interviewers. A telephone interviewer's appearance makes no difference in his or her ability to be an asset to the organization. Style of dress, tattoos and piercings, or disfiguration from an accident might cause Wal-Mart customers to faint, but none of these detract from a telephone interviewer's work.

Because this job requires little movement, other than typing, it can be an excellent career for persons with certain physical disabilities or those who get around in wheelchairs. Telephone interviewers must be able to easily read, clearly speak, acutely hear, and use their hands to write and type. No other physical disability should affect their ability to work in this job. However, persons with a chronic cough or phlegmy voice (often resulting from cigarette smoking) tend not to make good interviewers because the involuntary noises they utter while speaking tend to sound gross to respondents and distract them from the task at hand. Most employers require no minimum educational attainment for telephone interviewers. But the degree of literacy required suggests that most interviewers will have at least a high school diploma. Needless to say, age, sex, race, ethnicity, and religion should make no difference in employability. Nationality will only make a difference for those who have a heavy, nonnative accent while speaking English.

Prior experience as a telephone interviewer may prove to be a liability on a new job, depending on the type of survey research organization for which the interviewer worked previously. Another potential liability is doubling up, or working for two survey organizations at the same time. I am increasingly aware of telephone interviewers who do this. For example, I know several interviewers who proudly hold a relatively well-paid telephone interviewing position at a well-respected scientific survey research firm. But, because that organization's telephone surveys are irregular, they fill in by working at a local market research organization, which offers more continuous work, at minimum wage, and allows drop-in work hours in addition to regularly scheduled work shifts.

The problem with this type of prior experience or doubling up is that interviewers can develop telephone interviewing habits at one place that clash with the interviewing methods at another place. The issue becomes acute when it clashes with the standardized, scientific model presented here. The market research jobs of the persons I know are easier than their jobs at the scientific survey research firm, because instrument delivery is casual, and no one supervises them closely making sure they do the job right. Interviewers who try to juggle two such widely differing types of telephone interviewing jobs often lapse when trying to use the model presented in this *Handbook*.

Doubling up may prove trouble-free if each employer uses the same standards for interviewer work. I know one interviewer who triples up, conducting both face-to-face and telephone interviews for three highly respected national survey research organizations. Because all three use the standardized interviewing techniques presented here, he does not experience difficulties going back and forth.

Summing Up

This chapter has described different types of survey research organizations, paying particular attention to how new interviewers can identify those that are professional and legitimate. It discussed the skills and personal characteristics survey organizations seek in new interviewers. In the process, it explained the life cycle of a typical telephone survey and how that can affect interviewers' work hours. Next, we turn to ethical issues in survey research and the professional organizations that protect telephone interviewers' work.

CHAPTER THREE

SURVEY PROFESSIONALISM

You might feel like a small player in the survey research profession as a whole, but your interactions with respondents are the profession's lifeblood. Thus it is essential for you to understand the ethical aspects of your work and to uphold them in your daily activities as a telephone interviewer. Ethics refer to moral principles, norms, and values. Researchers must collect telephone survey data in a manner that treats all respondents ethically. Ethical data collection relies on the integrity of interviewers in their interactions with respondents.

This chapter is designed to give you an overview of the voluntary codes and the federal rules that oversee ethics in the conduct of survey research. It will show you how these codes and rules affect your everyday encounters with survey respondents.

Ethics in Survey Research

The ethical treatment of humans involves a few basic principles. First, do no harm. Nothing in a telephone survey should cause respondents psychological, economic, or legal harm.[1] When respondents complete an interview, they should be no worse off than when they started it. Ideally, the interview experience is so smooth and easy that respondents barely remember participating one week later.

The second principle is informed consent. Respondents must be told about the survey's purpose, who is conducting the research, how they were selected, how many minutes the survey is expected to last, that the survey is either anonymous or confidential, and that their participation is voluntary. They also have the right to skip any question or stop the interview entirely. You convey this information to each respondent in the first few carefully scripted sentences of an interview. If a respondent asks more detailed questions about the survey, you must be prepared to answer them. Precontact letters also convey informed consent language, but often respondents who receive them still want, or need, you to assure them on these issues.

The third principle involves special populations. Adults with mental or emotional handicaps and children cannot give informed consent. Gaining informed consent from prisoners and seriously ill people is tricky because they may feel coerced into participating. Your employer will train you in particular procedures for interviewing special populations.

Anonymity Versus Confidentiality

Before going any further, we need to define the difference between anonymity and confidentiality. When you conduct an *anonymous* telephone survey, you have no idea who your respondents are, where they live, or what they do. Moreover, you have no way to find out any information about them (unless you exert unusual effort). This is a compelling aspect of random-digit-dial (RDD) telephone surveys. A computer generates the telephone numbers you call, without regard to anyone's identity. Many respondents feel comfortable participating in telephone surveys when they understand that their participation is anonymous.

> **Anonymity.** Respondents' identities are not known and cannot be determined. **Confidentiality.** Respondents' identities are known or can be learned, but their privacy is guaranteed.

In a *confidential* survey, interviewers know respondents' identities, but promise that no one will link their identities to their answers. This promise covers not only data collection—your job. It also covers how your employer creates data files for analysis, reports the survey results, and archives the data for future use. The promise of confidentiality means that respondents' identities will be kept secret through all phases of the survey process and forever after. Researchers maintain confidentiality and anonymity by stripping names, telephone numbers, and any other identifying information from the study's sample and data files.

Sometimes respondents waive confidentiality for specific purposes. For example, in longitudinal studies, which gather data multiple times from the same individuals over time, respondents grant researchers permission to recontact them. This means that their names and how to contact them must be kept somewhere in order to reach them for the next interview. However, survey research organizations keep such identifying information separate from the data, in a secure place accessible only to one or two senior research staff, such as a locked file cabinet, a password-protected computer area, or a safe deposit box in a bank.

> Interviewers are obligated to honor respondents' confidentiality in all situations, public and private.

After a respondent agrees to participate in an interview, you will learn information about that person's values, opinions, beliefs, and personal characteristics as he or she answers questions. Talkative respondents may also tell you information extraneous to the interview, concerning work, home, family, activities, or other facets of their lives. Interviewers must treat all this information in a strictly confidential manner. The respondent's agreeing to an interview establishes a relationship of trust between that person and you, the interviewer. You are obligated to honor that trust.

Human nature causes interviewers to want to share touching, amusing, or tragic stories about respondents. However, you should do so only in your place of employment with your coworkers, supervisors, and similar employees. Never share stories about your respondents with friends or family members. How would a respondent standing behind you in the grocery store checkout line feel overhearing you tell your spouse about a ridiculous interviewing episode? Sometimes respondents reveal things to interviewers that they have never mentioned to anyone else before. How would it affect survey research in general if a respondent told only one interviewer about a particular episode in her life, and later heard it repeated in community gossip?

You must treat all respondent-related information as privileged, private, confidential, classified, and top secret. The only legitimate use of an individual respondent's answers to survey questions is in creating the survey data set. Any other use of that information is prohibited. If you find yourself keenly interested in the individual persons whom you interview, beyond the interviews themselves, interviewing is not an appropriate job for you.

Your employer will also treat each respondent's answers as privileged information when staff members compile the survey data set, analyze the results, and write reports. As soon as data collection is completed, all information that links interviews to respondents is removed and filed in such a way that reestablishing the correspondence between the identifying information and the interview is impossible. In the case of longitudinal studies, in which respondents grant permission to be recontacted, only those who maintain security could link identifying information to the data if needed. Once a longitudinal study is completed, all such information is destroyed.

> It is unethical to photocopy, borrow, or take your survey employer's records, reports, or other documents unless you have approval in advance.

In addition, the survey sponsor or client has the right to use the data first. Any disclosure or use of the data before the survey organization gives it to the sponsor or without the sponsor's permission is considered unethical and is prohibited. Finally, it is unethical to remove or photocopy your employer's records, reports, or documents without prior approval, preferably written approval.

The Role of Professional Associations

Ethics emerged as an especially hot topic among professional survey researchers in the 1980s and 1990s, when unscrupulous telemarketing firms hijacked telephone survey methods to engage in deceptive practices with respondents. Survey researchers' professional associations fought hard to distinguish legitimate from illegitimate telephone survey research, conveying this information to state and federal governments, the media, and the public. In order for the reputation of professional survey research to remain uncontaminated, telephone interviewers must always act in the ethical manner described here.

Professional associations both guide and protect survey researchers' ethical conduct. People who work in specialized occupations, industries, and businesses often form professional associations. Their members convene at meetings to share experiences, learn what's new, certify or license new entrants in the field, and particularly important, keep each other in line. Professional associations are one way to keep imposters, swindlers, and quacks from tarnishing the reputations of those doing excellent work in a specialized field of work.

A professional association's most important feature is its code of ethics. Ethical codes formally define the standards, norms, values, and best practices in the field. Associations update and adapt their ethical codes to keep abreast of changing conditions. Professional associations require members to subscribe to and uphold the group's code of ethics as a condition of membership. Members who violate these standards of moral conduct risk private chastisement, public censure, and expulsion from the professional association. A code of ethics is the defining feature of professionalism.

You will enjoy a more professional experience as a telephone interviewer if your employer belongs to one of the professional associations listed in Exhibit 3.1. Each of these groups guides the broad field of survey research in a different way. By visiting these associations' Web sites, you can see if your employer is listed as a member in good standing. The following paragraphs briefly describe each of the major professional associations connected to survey and public opinion research.

The American Association for Public Opinion Research (AAPOR) was founded in 1947 to represent professional public opinion researchers and to protect and strengthen the credibility of survey research. This cross-disciplinary group comprises about 1,800 members from academia, federal and state government, private research institutes, businesses, and the news media. It includes people who primarily collect survey data, those who primarily analyze and report it, and those who do both. It publishes a scholarly journal, *Public Opinion Quarterly*, that promotes scientific research on the survey process. Members network formally and informally at annual conferences, on an e-mail listserv, and in regional chapter

EXHIBIT 3.1. MAJOR U.S. SURVEY-RELATED PROFESSIONAL ASSOCIATIONS AND THEIR WEB SITES.

American Association for Public Opinion Research, *http://www.aapor.org*
American Evaluation Association, *http://www.eval.org*
American Marketing Association, *http://www.marketingpower.com*
American Statistical Association, Survey Research Methods Section, *http://www.amstat.org/sections/srms*
Council for Marketing and Opinion Research, *http://www.cmor.org*
Council of American Survey Research Organizations, *http://www.casro.org*
Council of Professional Associations on Federal Statistics, *http://members.aol.com/COPAFS/index.htm*
International Field Directors and Technologies Conference, *http://capps.wsu.edu/IFD&TC*
Marketing Research and Intelligence Association, *http://www.mria-arim.ca*
Marketing Research Association, *http://www.mra-net.org*
National Council on Public Polls, *http://www.ncpp.org*
National Network of State Polls, *http://survey.rgs.uky.edu/nnsp*
Professional Marketing Research Society, *http://www.pmrs-aprm.com*

meetings. Its code of ethics guides the professional conduct of those performing a large portion of scientific survey research in the United States and internationally.

Membership in the American Statistical Association's Survey Research Methods Section overlaps with AAPOR membership, especially for those who conduct basic research on the survey process. Members engage in theoretical and applied research on all aspects of survey sampling, ethics, error, and data analysis. This group also disseminates information on survey methods in its "What Is a Survey?" booklet (*http://www.whatisasurvey.info*).

Over 150 organizations and firms fund the Council for Marketing and Opinion Research (CMOR) to promote and protect survey research as an industry. CMOR tracks legislation that could harm survey data collection, and lobbies legislative representatives on behalf of scientific survey research to prevent restrictive legislation, such as that related to telemarketing and Do Not Call lists. CMOR also conducts research on respondent cooperation with surveys, both to encourage best practices among survey researchers and to improve public understanding of the importance of polling and surveys.

The Council of American Survey Research Organizations (CASRO) is a membership organization whose goals cooperatively overlap CMOR's. It provides guidelines on survey data collection, data processing, and reporting; offers specific recommendations on how to meet legislated privacy requirements in conducting surveys; suggests contract language; conducts research on how people feel about surveys (such as the 1999 CASRO Poll About Polls); produces member reports on industry financial, compensation, and Internet data; oversees proposed changes in government policies and laws that could affect its members; and publishes an annual journal.

The Council of Professional Associations on Federal Statistics (COPAFS) represents various federal agencies that collect and publish statistics, such as the Bureau of Justice Statistics, Bureau of Labor Statistics, Bureau of Transportation Statistics, Economic Research Service, Energy Information Administration, National Agricultural Statistics Service, National Center for Education Statistics, and National Center for Health Statistics. All of these agencies rely on surveys and censuses to create their statistics. COPAFS helps these agencies obtain timely, relevant, confidential, and high-quality data. It also serves as a go-between for the agencies that produce and distribute statistical data on the one hand and those who use their data on the other hand.

The National Council on Public Polls (NCPP) represents a relatively small group of private research firms and media giants who aim to improve professional standards for public opinion pollsters and educate politicians, the media, and the general public about how pollsters conduct polls and interpret the results. It sponsors tutorials and issues press releases. An example of NCPP's work is "20 Questions a Journalist Should Ask About Poll Results."[2]

The National Network of State Polls (NNSP) archives state-level survey data that researchers can access electronically for free. NNSP members share survey questions, methods, and results. Of particular value is NNSP's database of survey questions.

The International Field Directors and Technologies Conference (IFD&TC) is not a professional association per se, but an annual conference for people in charge of gathering survey data, including interviewer supervisors, field directors, operations managers, and computer-assisted telephone interviewing (CATI) programmers. They meet formally and informally each year to exchange information about their practices, share information about emergent trends, and discuss how to improve all aspects of hands-on data collection.

The American Evaluation Association (AEA) is an international professional association of researchers who specialize in evaluating programs, products, personnel, organizations, technology, and the like. Its members often use surveys to assess evaluation targets' strengths and weaknesses and to improve evaluation effectiveness.

The American Marketing Association's 38,000 members use polls, surveys, and focus groups to design, promote, and sell products. Unlike the results of the research conducted by most AAPOR, CMOR, CASRO, NCPP, and NNSP members, the results of most market research are proprietary and never made public. The American Marketing Association's code of ethics is straightforward, exhorting members to "do no harm," "foster trust in the marketing system," and "improve consumer confidence in the integrity of the marketing exchange system." The Marketing Research Association differs in that it offers certification "to recognize the unique qualifications and expertise of marketing and opinion research professionals." In Canada the Marketing Research and Intelligence Association and the Professional Marketing Research Society perform similar functions for their members.

Codes of Ethics

Although each of the professional associations just described has its own ethical code, AAPOR's Code of Professional Ethics and Practice and CASRO's Code of Standards and Ethics for Survey Research are the standards in the field. When ethical issues arise, professional survey researchers usually turn to one of these codes first to determine what behavior is acceptable and what is unacceptable. Because telephone interviewers serve as the "face" of survey research to respondents, it is essential that you and your colleagues understand your ethical obligations.

AAPOR's code, Exhibit 3.2, is organized around three dimensions of professional behavior: how researchers conduct surveys, their obligations to people involved in surveys (respondents, clients, the media, and others in the profession), and how they report survey results. It promises that AAPOR members will not engage in sugging, frugging, and push polls. Particularly important, AAPOR's code promises that even if legal proceedings demand that researchers reveal a respondent's identity, members will not do so. Like journalists, survey researchers will go to jail before violating a promise of confidentiality.

Read through AAPOR's ethical code now. Expect to be tested on its main themes before you are allowed to begin interviewing. Section II-D applies particularly to telephone interviewers.

CASRO's ethical code, Exhibit 3.3, is organized around responsibilities to respondents, clients, and the media. It is more detailed than AAPOR's code. It also differs by explicitly addressing Internet-based surveys. In this code the preamble, Section A-1, Section A-3-a, Section A-3-b, and Sections B-1 and B-2 apply most to telephone interviewers. Read it now, and review it later on your own time, because you are likely to be quizzed on it before you begin working.

The AAPOR and CASRO codes of ethics speak to professionals in the field of survey research. Principle investigators, researchers, programmers, analysts, report writers, and all others involved in the processes of survey data collection, analysis, and reporting mutually understand and share the values expressed in these codes. Survey researchers who fail to abide by these agreements can be barred from their profession and personally humiliated.

These ethical codes do not, however, speak to survey respondents. Most respondents know little about how professional survey researchers regulate themselves. However, most respondents care a great deal about how telephone survey research affects them. As a telephone interviewer, you are the researchers' bridge to respondents. In that role, you need to be able to communicate generally survey researchers' obligations to respondents. You must also be able to answer respondents' specific questions about ethical issues. This will be an ongoing part of your job.

To address survey respondents' major concerns, CMOR has developed the respondents' *bill of rights* shown in Exhibit 3.4. In a straightforward manner, it explains to respondents how AAPOR's and CASRO's ethical codes bear directly on them. Although different ethical codes may state the same points in different

EXHIBIT 3.2. AAPOR CODE OF PROFESSIONAL ETHICS AND PRACTICES.

We, the members of the American Association for Public Opinion Research, subscribe to the principles expressed in the following code. Our goals are to support sound and ethical practice in the conduct of public opinion research and in the use of such research for policy- and decision-making in the public and private sectors, as well as to improve public understanding of public opinion and survey research methods and the proper use of public opinion and survey research results.

We pledge ourselves to maintain high standards of scientific competence and integrity in conducting, analyzing, and reporting our work; in our relations with survey respondents; with our clients; with those who eventually use the research for decision-making purposes; and with the general public. We further pledge ourselves to reject all tasks or assignments that would require activities inconsistent with the principles of this code.

The Code

I. Principles of Professional Practice in the Conduct of Our Work
  A. We shall exercise due care in developing research designs and survey instruments, and in collecting, processing, and analyzing data, taking all reasonable steps to assure the reliability and validity of results.
    1. We shall recommend and employ only those tools and methods of analysis that, in our professional judgment, are well suited to the research problem at hand.
    2. We shall not knowingly select research tools and methods of analysis that yield misleading conclusions.
    3. We shall not knowingly make interpretations of research results that are inconsistent with the data available, nor shall we tacitly permit such interpretations.
    4. We shall not knowingly imply that interpretations should be accorded greater confidence than the data actually warrant.
  B. We shall describe our methods and findings accurately and in appropriate detail in all research reports, adhering to the standards for minimal disclosure specified in Section III.
  C. If any of our work becomes the subject of a formal investigation of an alleged violation of this Code, undertaken with the approval of the AAPOR Executive Council, we shall provide additional information on the survey in such detail that a fellow survey practitioner would be able to conduct a professional evaluation of the survey.

(continued)

EXHIBIT 3.2. *(CONTINUED)*

II. Principles of Professional Responsibility in Our Dealings with People

A. The Public:

1. When preparing a report for public release we shall ensure that the findings are a balanced and accurate portrayal of the survey results.

2. If we become aware of the appearance in public of serious inaccuracies or distortions regarding our research, we shall publicly disclose what is required to correct these inaccuracies or distortions, including, as appropriate, a statement to the public media, legislative body, regulatory agency, or other appropriate group, to which the inaccuracies or distortions were presented.

3. We shall inform those for whom we conduct publicly released surveys that AAPOR standards require members to release minimal information about such surveys, and we shall make all reasonable efforts to encourage clients to subscribe to our standards for minimal disclosure in their releases.

B. Clients or Sponsors:

1. When undertaking work for a private client, we shall hold confidential all proprietary information obtained about the client and about the conduct and findings of the research undertaken for the client, except when the dissemination of the information is expressly authorized by the client, or when disclosure becomes necessary under the terms of Section I-C or II-A of this Code.

2. We shall be mindful of the limitations of our techniques and capabilities and shall accept only those research assignments that we can reasonably expect to accomplish within these limitations.

C. The Profession:

1. We recognize our responsibility to the science of survey research to disseminate as freely as possible the ideas and findings that emerge from our research.

2. We shall not cite our membership in the Association as evidence of professional competence, since the Association does not so certify any persons or organizations.

D. The Respondent:

1. We shall avoid practices or methods that may harm, humiliate, or seriously mislead survey respondents.

2. We shall respect respondents' concerns about their privacy.

3. Aside from the decennial census and a few other surveys, participation in surveys is voluntary. We shall provide all persons selected for inclusion with a description of the survey sufficient to permit them to make an informed and free decision about their participation.

4. We shall not misrepresent our research or conduct other activities (such as sales, fund raising, or political campaigning) under the guise of conducting research.

EXHIBIT 3.2. *(CONTINUED)*

5. Unless the respondent waives confidentiality for specified uses, we shall hold as privileged and confidential all information that might identify a respondent with his or her responses. We also shall not disclose or use the names of respondents for non-research purposes unless the respondents grant us permission to do so.

6. We understand that the use of our survey results in a legal proceeding does not relieve us of our ethical obligation to keep confidential all respondent identifiable information or lessen the importance of respondent anonymity.

III. Standards for Minimal Disclosure

A. Good professional practice imposes the obligation upon all public opinion researchers to include, in any report of research results, or to make available when that report is released, certain essential information about how the research was conducted. At a minimum, the following items should be disclosed.

1. Who sponsored the survey, and who conducted it.

2. The exact wording of questions asked, including the text of any preceding instruction or explanation to the interviewer or respondents that might reasonably be expected to affect the response.

3. A definition of the population under study, and a description of the sampling frame used to identify this population.

4. A description of the sample design, giving a clear indication of the method by which the respondents were selected by the researcher, or whether the respondents were entirely self-selected.

5. Sample sizes and, where appropriate, eligibility criteria, screening procedures, and response rates computed according to AAPOR Standard Definitions. At a minimum, a summary of disposition of sample cases should be provided so that response rates could be computed.

6. A discussion of the precision of the findings, including estimates of sampling error, and a description of any weighting or estimating procedures used.

7. Which results are based on parts of the sample, rather than on the total sample, and the size of such parts.

8. Method, location, and dates of data collection.

From time to time, AAPOR Council may issue guidelines and recommendations on best practices with regard to the release, design and conduct of surveys.

As revised in 2005.

Source: American Association for Public Opinion Research, 2005, *Code of professional ethics and practices*, retrieved November 2006 from *http://www.aapor.org/pdfs/ AAPOR_Code_2005.pdf.*

EXHIBIT 3.3. CASRO CODE OF STANDARDS AND ETHICS FOR SURVEY RESEARCH.

Introduction

This Code of Standards and Ethics for Survey Research sets forth the agreed upon rules of ethical conduct for Survey Research Organizations. Acceptance of this Code is mandatory for all CASRO Members.

The Code has been organized into sections describing the responsibilities of a Survey Research Organization to Respondents, Clients and Outside Contractors and in reporting study results.

This Code is not intended to be, nor should it be, an immutable document. Circumstances may arise that are not covered by this Code or that may call for modification of some aspect of this Code. The Standards Committee and the Board of Directors of CASRO will evaluate these circumstances as they arise and, if appropriate, revise the Code. The Code, therefore, is a living document that seeks to be responsive to the changing world of Survey Research. To continue to be contemporary, CASRO advocates ongoing, two-way communication with Members, Respondents, Clients, Outside Contractors, Consultants and Interviewers.

(Please also refer to other CASRO Publications which may provide detail relevant to many sections of the *Code of Standards and Ethics*.)

Responsibilities to Respondents

Preamble

Researchers have professional and legal responsibilities to their respondents that are embodied in the procedures of a research study. Underlying these specific responsibilities are four fundamental ethical principles:

Respondents should be:

    a. willing participants in survey research;
    b. appropriately informed about the survey's intentions and how their personal information and survey responses will be used and protected;
    c. sufficiently satisfied with their survey experience;
    d. willing to participate again in survey research.

A. Confidentiality
    1. Since individuals who are interviewed are the lifeblood of the Survey Research Industry, it is essential that Survey Research Organizations be responsible for protecting from disclosure to third parties—Clients and members of the Public—identity of individual Respondents as well as Respondent-identifiable information, unless the Respondent expressly requests or permits such disclosure.

EXHIBIT 3.3. *(CONTINUED)*

2. This principle of confidentiality is qualified by the following exceptions:

a. A minimal amount of Respondent-identifiable information will be disclosed to the Client to permit the Client: (1) to validate interviews and/or (2) to determine an additional fact of analytical importance to the study (including the practice of appending Client-owned database information to the Survey Research Organization's data file as an analytic aid). Where additional inquiry is indicated, Respondents must be given a sound reason for the re-inquiry; a refusal by Respondent to continue must be respected.

Before disclosing Respondent-identifiable information to a Client for purposes of interview validation or re-inquiry, the Survey Research Organization must take whatever steps are needed to insure that the Client will conduct the validation or recontact in a fully professional manner. This includes the avoidance of multiple validation contacts or other conduct that would harass or could embarrass Respondents. It also includes avoidance of any use of the information (for example, lead generation) for other than legitimate and ethical Survey Research purposes or to respond to Customer/Respondent complaints. Assurance that the Client will respect such limitations and maintain Respondent confidentiality should be confirmed in writing before any confidential information is disclosed.

Where Respondent-identifiable data is disclosed to Clients so that the Survey Research Organization may analyze survey data in combination with other Respondent-level data such as internal customer data, Respondent-level data from another survey, etc., it is understood that the information will be used for model building, internal (Survey Research Organization) analysis, or the like and not for individual marketing efforts and that *no action can be taken toward an individual Respondent* simply because of his or her participation in the survey. To assure Client compliance, the Survey Research Organization must obtain written confirmation from the Client before releasing any data. (A suggested CASRO Client agreement clause is available.)

Further, with respect to such research uses as Database Segmentation and/or Modeling (see preceding paragraph), specific action(s) may not be taken toward an individual Respondent as a result of his/her survey information and participation beyond those actions taken toward the *entire database population group* the Respondent *by chance* has been selected to represent. In order for such specific action, the following two elements must be met:

The Respondent has first given his/her permission to do so, having been told the *general purpose and limitations* of such use; and the research firm has obtained *a written agreement from the Client* assuring that no other use will be made of Respondent-identifiable information.

(continued)

EXHIBIT 3.3. *(CONTINUED)*

Predictive equations which integrate a segmentation scheme into a Client database may be applied so long as *no action is taken toward an individual Respondent* simply because of his or her participation in the survey. Respondents must be treated like all other individuals in the database according to the segment(s) to which they belong or have been assigned.

b. The identity of individual Respondents and Respondent-identifiable information may be disclosed to other Survey Research Organizations whenever such organizations are conducting different phases of a multi-stage study (for example, a trend study). The initial Research Company should confirm in writing that Respondent confidentiality will be maintained in accordance with the Code.

c. In the case of research in which representatives of the Client or others are present, such Client representatives and others should be asked not to disclose to anyone not present the identity of individual Participants or other Participant-identifying information except as needed to respond, with the Participant's prior specific approval, to any complaint by one or more of the Participants concerning a product or service supplied by the Client.

3. The principle of Respondent confidentiality includes the following specific applications or safeguards:

a. Survey Research Organizations' staff or personnel should not use or discuss Respondent-identifiable data or information for other than legitimate internal research purposes.

b. The Survey Research Organization has the responsibility for insuring that Subcontractors (Interviewers, Interviewing Services and Validation, Coding, and Tabulation Organizations) and Consultants are aware of and agree to maintain and respect Respondent confidentiality whenever the identity of Respondents or Respondent-identifiable information is disclosed to such entities.

c. Before permitting Clients or others to have access to completed questionnaires in circumstances other than those described above, Respondent names and other Respondent-identifying information (for example, telephone numbers) should be deleted.

d. Invisible identifiers on mail questionnaires that connect Respondent answers to particular Respondents should not be used. Visible identification numbers may be used but should be accompanied by an explanation that such identifiers are for control purposes only and that Respondent confidentiality will not be compromised.

e. Any Survey Research Organization that receives from a Client or other entity information that it knows or reasonably believes to be confidential, Respondent-identifiable information should only use such information in accordance with the principles and procedures described in this Code.

EXHIBIT 3.3. *(CONTINUED)*

f. The use of survey results in a legal proceeding does not relieve the Survey Research Organization of its ethical obligation to maintain in confidence all Respondent-identifiable information or lessen the importance of Respondent anonymity. Consequently, Survey Research firms confronted with a subpoena or other legal process requesting the disclosure of Respondent-identifiable information should take all reasonable steps to oppose such requests, including informing the court or other decision-maker involved of the factors justifying confidentiality and Respondent anonymity and interposing all appropriate defenses to the request for disclosure.

B. Privacy and the Avoidance of Harassment

1. Survey Research Organizations have a responsibility to strike a proper balance between the needs for research in contemporary American life and the privacy of individuals who become the Respondents in the research. To achieve this balance:

a. Respondents will be protected from unnecessary and unwanted intrusions and/or any form of personal harassment.

b. The voluntary character of the Interviewer-Respondent contact should be stated explicitly where the Respondent might have reason to believe that cooperation is not voluntary.

2. This principle of privacy includes the following specific applications:

a. The Research Organization, Subcontractors and Interviewers shall make every reasonable effort to insure that the Respondent understands the purpose of the Interviewer-Respondent contact.

(1) The Interviewer/Research Company representative must provide prompt and honest identification of his/her research firm affiliation.

(2) Respondent questions should be answered in a forthright and non-deceptive manner.

b. Deceptive practices and misrepresentation, such as using research as a guise for sales or solicitation purposes, are expressly prohibited.

c. Survey Research Organizations must respect the right of individuals to refuse to be interviewed or to terminate an interview in progress. Techniques that infringe on these rights should not be employed, but Survey Research Organizations may make reasonable efforts to obtain an interview including: (1) explaining the purpose of the research project; (2) providing a gift or monetary incentive adequate to elicit cooperation; and (3) re-contacting an individual at a different time if the individual is unwilling or unable to participate during the initial contact.

d. Research Organizations are responsible for arranging interviewing times that are convenient for Respondents.

e. Lengthy interviews can be a burden. Research Organizations are responsible for weighing the research need against the length of the interview and Respondents must not be enticed into an interview by a misrepresentation of the length of the interview.

f. Research Organizations are responsible for developing techniques to minimize the discomfort or apprehension of Respondents and Interviewers when dealing with sensitive subject matter.

g. Electronic equipment (taping, recording, photographing) and one-way viewing rooms may be used only with the full knowledge of Respondents.

(continued)

EXHIBIT 3.3. *(CONTINUED)*

3. Internet Research
   a. The unique characteristics of Internet research require specific notice that the principle of Respondent privacy applies to this new technology and data collection methodology. The general principle of this section of the Code is that Survey Research organizations will not use unsolicited emails to recruit Respondents for surveys.
      (1) Research organizations are required to verify that individuals contacted for research by email have a reasonable expectation that they will receive email contact for research. Such agreement can be assumed when ALL of the following conditions exist:
         (a) A substantive pre-existing relationship exists between the individuals contacted and the Research Organization, the Client or the list owners contracting the research (the latter being so identified);
         (b) Individuals have a reasonable expectation, based on the pre-existing relationship, that they may be contacted for research;
         (c) Individuals are offered the choice to be removed from future email contact in each invitation; and,
         (d) The invitation list excludes all individuals who have previously taken the appropriate and timely steps to request the list owner to remove them.
      (2) Research organizations are prohibited from using any subterfuge in obtaining email addresses of potential Respondents, such as collecting email addresses from public domains, using technologies or techniques to collect email addresses without individuals' awareness, and collecting email addresses under the guise of some other activity.
      (3) Research organizations are prohibited from using false or misleading return email addresses when recruiting Respondents over the Internet.
      (4) When receiving email lists from Clients or list owners, Research Organizations are required to have the Client or list provider verify that individuals listed have a reasonable expectation that they will receive email contact, as defined, in (1) above.
4. Privacy Laws and Regulations
   a. Research Organizations must comply with existing state, federal and international statutes and regulations governing privacy, data security, and the disclosure, receipt and use of personally-identifiable information (collectively "Privacy Laws"). Some of the Privacy Laws affecting Survey Research are limited to specific industries (for example, financial and health care industries), respondent source (for example, children), and/or international venues.
   b. In instances in which privacy laws apply to Survey Research operations for specific industries or respondent source, Research Organizations will:
      (1) Always enter into a confidentiality or "chain of trust" agreement when receiving and using legally-protected, personally-identifiable information from a source other than the data subject, insuring that the Research Organization will protect the information and only use it for the purposes specified in the agreement;

EXHIBIT 3.3. *(CONTINUED)*

(2) Always require subcontractors and other third parties to whom they disclose personally-identifiable information to enter into confidentiality or "chain of trust" agreements that require such party(ies) to provide the same level of security and limitations of use and disclosure as the Research Organization;

(3) Always store or maintain personally-identifiable information in a verifiably secure location;

(4) Always control and limit accessibility to personally-identifiable information;

(5) Always use reasonable efforts to destroy personally-identifiable information once the survey is complete and validation has been conducted, unless the personally-identifiable information relates to Respondents in panels, to ongoing studies, or for some other critical research reason, or the research Client is legally or contractually obligated to require its service providers to maintain such information for a certain period of time and contractually imposes this requirement on the Research Organization;

(6) Never knowingly receive, use or disclose personally-identifiable information in a way that will cause the Research Organization or another party to violate any Privacy Law or agreement.

c. In order to conduct international research that requires either transmitting or receiving personally-identifiable information of Respondents, Research Organizations must comply in all material respects with international privacy laws and regulations, by, in the case of data transfers with a person or entity in the European Union, either (i) certifying their compliance with the privacy provisions described in the U.S. Safe Harbor Principles of the European Union Directive on Data Protection or (ii) satisfying an alternative method of complying in all material respects with the Directive. The EU Safe Harbor privacy principles are contained in the CASRO Model Privacy Policy and are as follows:

(1) Notice: A description of what information is collected, how it is collected, its purpose, and its disclosure to third parties.

(2) Choice: A statement of and procedures for allowing individuals to choose not to participate in the research and/or to have their personal information used or disclosed to a third party.

(3) Onward Transfer: A statement that personal information will be transferred only to third parties who are also in compliance with the Safe Harbor Principles.

(4) Access: Procedures to provide individuals with access to their personal information in order to correct, amend, or delete that information where it is inaccurate.

(5) Security: A description of the reasonable precautions taken to protect personal information from loss, misuse and unauthorized access, disclosure, alteration, and destruction.

(6) Data Integrity: A statement that information will be used consistent with the purpose for which it was collected.

(7) Enforcement: A description of internal and external mechanisms for assuring compliance, and addressing and resolving disputes and complaints.

(continued)

EXHIBIT 3.3. *(CONTINUED)*

d. Research Organizations will, to the extent required by law or as necessary to fully and completely comply with the principles set forth in the section of this Code entitled Responsibilities to Respondents, adopt effective and comprehensive legal and operational policies, such as those set forth in CASRO's Privacy Protection Program, which will be updated as necessary to conform with additions to and changes in Privacy Laws.

Responsibilities to Clients

A. Relationships between a Survey Research Organization and Clients for whom the surveys are conducted should be of such a nature that they foster confidence and mutual respect. They must be characterized by honesty and confidentiality.
B. The following specific approaches describe in more detail the responsibilities of Research Organizations in this relationship:
    1. A Survey Research Organization must assist its Clients in the design of effective and efficient studies that are to be carried out by the Research Company. If the Survey Research Organization questions whether a study design will provide the information necessary to serve the Client's purposes, it must make its reservations known.
    2. A Research Organization must conduct the study in the manner agreed upon. However, if it becomes apparent in the course of the study that changes in the plans should be made, the Research Organization must make its views known to the Client promptly.
    3. A Research Organization has an obligation to allow its Clients to verify that work performed meets all contracted specifications and to examine all operations of the Research Organization that are relevant to the proper execution of the project in the manner set forth. While Clients are encouraged to examine questionnaires or other records to maintain open access to the research process, the Survey Research Organization must continue to protect the confidentiality and privacy of survey Respondents.
    4. When more than one Client contributes to the cost of a project specially commissioned with the Research Organization, each Client concerned shall be informed that there are other Participants (but not necessarily their identity).
    5. Research Organizations will hold confidential all information that they obtain about a Client's general business operations, and about matters connected with research projects that they conduct for a Client.
    6. For research findings obtained by the agency that are the property of the Client, the Research Organization may make no public release or revelation of findings without expressed, prior approval from the Client.
C. Bribery in any form and in any amount is unacceptable and is a violation of a Research Organization's fundamental, ethical obligations. A Research Organization and/or its principals, officers and employees should never give gifts to Clients in the form of cash. To the extent permitted by applicable laws and regulations, a Research Organization may provide nominal gifts to Clients and may entertain Clients, as long as the cost of such entertainment is modest in amount and incidental in nature.

EXHIBIT 3.3. *(CONTINUED)*

Responsibilities in Reporting to Clients and the Public

A. When reports are being prepared for Client confidential or public release purposes, it is the obligation of the Research Organization to ensure that the findings they release are an accurate portrayal of the survey data, and careful checks on the accuracy of all figures are mandatory.

B. A Research Organization's report to a Client or the Public should contain, or the Research Organization should be ready to supply to a Client or the Public on short notice, the following information about the survey:

1. The name of the organization for which the study was conducted and the name of the organization conducting it.
2. The purpose of the study, including the specific objectives.
3. The dates on or between which the data collection was done.
4. A definition of the universe that the survey is intended to represent and a description of the population frame(s) that was actually sampled.
5. A description of the sample design, including the method of selecting sample elements, method of interview, cluster size, number of callbacks, Respondent eligibility or screening criteria, and other pertinent information.
6. A description of results of sample implementation including (a) a total number of sample elements contacted, (b) the number not reached, (c) the number of refusals, (d) the number of terminations, (e) the number of non-eligibles, (f) the number of completed interviews.
7. The basis for any specific "completion rate" percentages should be fully documented and described.
8. The questionnaire or exact wording of the questions used, including Interviewer directions and visual exhibits.
9. A description of any weighting or estimating procedures used.
10. A description of any special scoring, data adjustment or indexing procedures used. (Where the Research Organization uses proprietary techniques, these should be described in general and the Research Organization should be prepared to provide technical information on demand from qualified and technically competent persons who have agreed to honor the confidentiality of such information.)
11. Estimates of the sampling error and of data should be shown when appropriate, but when shown they should include reference to other possible sources of error so that a misleading impression of accuracy or precision is not conveyed.
12. Statistical tables clearly labeled and identified as to questionnaire source, including the number of raw cases forming the base for each cross-tabulation.
13. Copies of Interviewer instructions, validation results, code books, and other important working papers.

C. As a *minimum*, any general public release of survey findings should include the following information:

1. The sponsorship of the study.
2. A description of the purposes.
3. The sample description and size.
4. The dates of data collection.

(continued)

EXHIBIT 3.3. *(CONTINUED)*

5. The names of the research company conducting the study.
6. The exact wording of the questions.
7. Any other information that a lay person would need to make a reasonable assessment of the reported findings.

D. A Survey Research Organization will seek agreements from Clients so that citations of survey findings will be presented to the Research Organization for review and clearance as to accuracy and proper interpretation prior to public release. A Research Organization will advise Clients that if the survey findings publicly disclosed are incorrect, distorted, or incomplete, in the Research Organization's opinion, the Research Organization reserves the right to make its own release of any or all survey findings necessary to make clarification.

Responsibility to Outside Contractors and Interviewers

Research Organizations will not ask any Outside Contractor or Interviewer to engage in any activity which is not acceptable as defined in other sections of this Code of Standards and Ethics for Survey Research or related CASRO publications.

Source: Council of American Survey Research Organizations, 2006, *Code of standards and ethics for survey research*, retrieved November 2006 from *http://www.casro.org/codeofstandards.cfm*.

EXHIBIT 3.4. SURVEY RESPONDENTS' BILL OF RIGHTS.

Your participation in a legitimate marketing or public opinion research survey is very important to us, and we value the information you provide. Therefore, our relationship will be one of respect and consideration, based on the following practices:

- Your privacy and the privacy of your answers will be respected and maintained.
- Your name, address, phone number, personal information, or individual responses won't be disclosed to anyone outside the research project without your permission.
- You will always be told the name of the person contacting you, the research organization's name and nature of the survey.
- You will not be sold anything, or asked for money, under the guise of research.
- You will be contacted at reasonable times, but if the time is inconvenient, you may ask to be recontacted at a more convenient time.
- Your decision to participate in a study, answer specific questions, or discontinue your participation will be respected without question.
- You will be informed in advance if an interview is to be recorded and of the intended use of the recording.
- You are assured that the highest standards of professional conduct will be upheld in the collection and reporting of information you provide.
- Marketing and opinion research is an important part of our democratic society, allowing people to express their views on political and social issues, as well as on products and services.

Source: Council for Marketing and Opinion Research, 2005, *What your rights are if you are interviewed*, retrieved February 2007 from *http://www.youropinioncounts.org/index.cfm?p=rights*.

ways, CMOR's respondents' bill of rights summarizes the profession's commitments well.

> CMOR's "bill of rights" explains to respondents how survey researchers' ethical codes affect them.

No one expects you to memorize and recite the respondents' bill of rights. Instead, in Chapters Five, Six, and Seven you will learn and memorize a few sentences that succinctly summarize it and that effectively answer most respondents' concerns.

Many survey organizations also have their own internal ethical pledges, statements, or codes by which each employee must abide. Before you can start your job, your employer may ask you to sign such a pledge, promising to uphold your role in the ethical conduct of telephone survey research. If you bend or break any aspect of your employer's ethical standards, you will probably be fired on the spot or at least suspended without pay for some period. Exhibit 3.5 provides an example of a pledge of professional ethics for a fictitious "Survey Research Laboratory." The contents of this oath have been gleaned and adapted from the pledges of several survey organizations.

Federal Government Requirements

The federal government works to ensure the ethical treatment of humans in research in two basic ways, through *institutional review boards* (IRBs) and through the Office of Management and Budget (OMB). Interviewers will not interact with an IRB or the OMB directly. But their requirements may dictate that you recite specific (and perhaps awkward) language from interview scripts to ensure informed consent.

Institutional Review Boards

The federal government requires that all organizations receiving federal funding and conducting research related to humans establish an IRB. These boards protect the rights, well-being, and dignity of human subjects who participate in research—all sorts of research, from surveys to tests of tongue tissues. An IRB typically comprises five to eight people who are concerned with ethics and who voluntarily review and decide whether to approve research projects in their

EXHIBIT 3.5. EXAMPLE OF AN INTERVIEWER PLEDGE OF PROFESSIONAL ETHICS.

The rights of human subjects are a principal concern of the Survey Research Laboratory (SRL). SRL is a member of the American Association for Public Opinion Research (AAPOR) and abides by its Code of Professional Ethics and Practices, which is printed on the other side of this page. Read SRL's statement of its ethical commitments and your ethical obligations as an SRL interviewer below. Read AAPOR's code of ethics on the reverse. If you are prepared to maintain these ethical standards in all aspects of your work as an SRL interviewer, please sign and date this pledge. Keep a copy for your employment records.

The Organization's Commitments

SRL only undertakes research that contributes to scholarly knowledge and to society in general. SRL does not conduct research that it judges to be trivial, unethical, of limited importance, or secretive. SRL does not engage in fundraising, selling, or push polls. SRL does not conduct surveys if the same data are available elsewhere or could be collected in a better way. The results of SRL's research are returned to the public in news releases, magazine articles, journal articles, books, civic lectures, papers presented at professional meetings, and classrooms.

SRL takes great care to ensure that respondents' rights are protected at each stage of the survey process. Researchers analyze the data in groups and statistical categories. The results are presented in aggregate statistics. No individual can be identified in the survey data or reports; only numbers identify individual interviews. All information that might link a respondent to a particular interview is stripped from the data. In the case of longitudinal studies (in which respondents agree to be recontacted), identifying information and linking records are kept in secure files, accessible to only a few persons.

Your Obligations

As a telephone interviewer for SRL, part of your job is to explain to respondents their rights, assure them that SRL will protect their rights, and always act in a manner that protects their rights. You must treat as confidential all information obtained in your interactions with respondents, concerning any aspect of their lives, even if it was offered spontaneously and is unrelated to the survey.

As a professional interviewer, your only proper relationship with respondents is to conduct interviews in the manner in which SRL has trained you. If you depart from your role in any way, you can undermine an entire study, weaken SRL's reputation, cause regulatory sanctions, and invite legal action. You must consistently resist the temptation to offer respondents counsel, comfort, or consorting opportunities. Likewise, you must never seek counsel, comfort, or opportunities to socialize. You must prevent respondents from attempting to sell or recommend goods or services to you. Likewise, you must never attempt to sell or recommend goods or services, or otherwise exploit the interview situation for personal benefit. If a respondent asks for help, you must summon your supervisor or write separate notes that will allow another appropriate person to decide the most ethical way to proceed.

EXHIBIT 3.5. *(CONTINUED)*

SRL monitors interviewers' work. If you violate your obligations in any way, you may be dismissed at once.

Signing this pledge indicates that you understand both SRL's ethical policies and AAPOR's code of ethics and that you will support and practice them in all situations related to your interviewing work.

_____   _____

Print and sign your name   Date

Please keep a copy of this document for your records.

organizations. Specifically, IRBs enforce those sections of the Code of Federal Regulations that contain rules for the protection of human subjects.[3]

As this code relates to survey research, IRBs require that researchers gain informed consent from respondents by conveying key information about the survey (topic, sponsor, time, voluntariness, confidentiality or anonymity, and so forth) and by receiving the respondents' agreement to proceed with the interview. However, IRBs vary in how they require that researchers do this, depending on their organizational cultures. For example, IRBs in medical colleges tend to regard survey research quite differently from IRBs in policy-related research organizations.

Interviewers involved in surveys funded by the National Institutes of Health (NIH) may need to complete a special training requirement on the protection of human subjects. If you do this, you can receive a certificate demonstrating it. NIH policy requires all "key personnel" on a grant or contract to demonstrate their understanding of human subjects protection. The extent to which interviewers are considered key personnel is not yet clear under this policy and it may vary across organizations.

The NIH offers a free, two-hour, online tutorial (through its National Cancer Institute), which presents information about the rights and welfare of human participants in research and satisfies the NIH protection of human subjects training requirement for obtaining federal funds (see *http://cme.cancer.gov/clinicaltrials/ learning/humanparticipant-protections.asp*). Upon successfully completing the course, you receive the option of printing a certificate of completion or sending an electronic notice of your completion to your employer. You may also obtain certification through the NIH Office of Human Subjects (at *http://www.nihtraining. com/ohsrsite/cbt/cbt.html*). This exam takes about one hour. Before doing either of these on your own, however, be aware that your employer may have its own requirements vis-á-vis NIH certification; follow those instructions first.

Office of Management and Budget

In addition to an IRB's approval, every survey that is sponsored by the federal government must receive clearance from the OMB. Section 3506 of the Paperwork Reduction Act of 1995[4] requires the OMB to provide interested federal agencies and the public with an opportunity to comment on surveys.

A key function of the OMB is to protect the public from redundant surveys: for example, making sure that two widely disparate federal agencies do not conduct essentially the same survey unknowingly. In this way, the OMB minimizes the public burden of surveys. The OMB also invites comments on other ways to minimize respondent burden, such as asking the National Park Service to count the number of wilderness passes sold instead of asking people if they have visited National Park wilderness areas. The OMB also endeavors to ensure that federal agencies conduct only surveys having practical purposes, consistent with agency functions, and of the highest quality.

Unethical Pseudosurveys and Laws Protecting Your Work

Legitimate, scientific telephone survey research was tarnished in the 1980s and 1990s when telemarketers adopted survey methods for fraudulent purposes. Telemarketing is not a legitimate form of survey research. Rather, it is what professional survey researchers call *sugging*—selling under the guise of survey research—or *frugging*—fundraising under the guise of survey research.

In sugging and frugging, telemarketers would call households, posing as survey interviewers and sounding quite reasonable. But after asking a few questions in the pseudosurvey, the caller would launch into a sales pitch for a vacation package, a plea for a donation to a seemingly genuine charity, or a breathless announcement that you had just won a (bogus) sweepstakes (if you first send in $100). Telemarketing contributed heavily, and understandably, to respondents' refusals to participate in scientific telephone survey research in the 1990s.

Do Not Call Lists

After a groundswell of consumer complaints and evidence that people had been bilked out of billions of dollars, the U.S. Congress passed the 1991 Telephone Consumer Protection Act[5] and also the 1995 Telemarketing and Consumer Fraud and Abuse Prevention Act. In addition, the Federal Trade Commission established the Telemarketing Sales Rule.[6] All have been subsequently updated several times. Part of the Telemarketing Sales Rule established the National Do Not Call (DNC) Registry, which went into effect October 1, 2003. Telemarketers still play dirty tricks, however, such as calling from outside U.S. boundaries.[7]

> Do Not Call lists *exclude* unsolicited telephone calls solely for research purposes.

These are the primary federal laws and rules affecting unsolicited telephone calls. What is most important for our purposes is that these regulations do not affect calls made for research purposes only. The public, however, often has a hard time distinguishing between research calls and telemarketing. Part of your job will involve clarifying these differences for respondents. Many telephone books have a page describing these laws and regulations, stating that they exclude public opinion research. You may find it helpful with certain respondents to direct them to such a page in their local telephone book.

Some survey research organizations also maintain internal DNC lists. When a respondent clearly tells an interviewer to never call again for any reason, his or her telephone number is placed on a special DNC list just for that organization. Because such a respondent is often angry or abusive, or may credibly threaten legal action, no interviewer wants to speak with them again anyway. Survey organizations typically keep telephone numbers on their internal DNC lists for two to three years before trying them again. Why try these numbers again at all? Because people tend to move. When they do so, telephone companies reassign their telephone numbers to others, and the new persons may be more amenable to survey participation. Of course, if the same people as before still have these numbers, they are put back onto the internal DNC list. Chapter Six discusses internal DNC lists in more detail.

In the long run, DNC lists should prove good for telephone interviewers' work. Roughly sixty million telephone numbers are now in the National Do Not Call Registry. Presumably, these people have had several years without annoying and misleading telemarketing calls. Even though consumers were initially confused about what types of calls the national DNC list covers,[8] eventually many potential respondents should be able to differentiate telemarketers from legitimate interviewers and, thus, be more amenable to telephone data collection. The advent of push polls, however, could add more years to respondents' learning curve.

Push Polls

In the late 1990s, telemarketing techniques moved to election campaigns in the form of *push polls*. In this type of pseudo-poll, callers posing as interviewers phone thousands of potential voters, supplying them with false or deceptive information about a candidate or ballot measure to see how that information influences voters' choices. A push poll "interview" might go something like this:

Question: In the upcoming election, do you plan to vote for John Doe or Joe Schmoe for the U.S. Senate?

Answer: John Doe, of course.

Question: Would you vote for John Doe if you knew that he has missed twenty-five out of the last thirty votes in the Senate?

Answer: Well, that seems irresponsible, but I would need to know why he missed them.

Question: Would you vote for John Doe if you knew he is a lifetime member of the American Rifle Association?

Answer: What difference does that make?

Question: Would you vote for John Doe if you knew he had smoked marijuana in college?

Answer: Didn't we all? So what?

Question: Would you vote for John Doe if you knew he had a child out of wedlock with his mistress of ten years?

Answer: Hey, what is this all about? Who did you say you work for?

These pseudo-polls are typically run out of a large telephone bank, with hundreds of callers making thousands of calls. Some push polls seek to uncover an opposing candidate's weaknesses among voters. But others do not even bother to record respondents' answers because their goal is not to measure public opinion but to manipulate it. Their calls try to push voters away from a certain candidate by planting false or misleading information about the candidate's integrity and suitability for elected office and by creating negative feelings. Push polls are a form of telemarketing because, essentially, they sell propaganda under the guise of a legitimate election poll.[9]

Respondents find such lines of questioning offensive, but few can distinguish a push poll from a legitimate election poll. Many state legislatures and the U.S. House of Representatives have sought to make push polling illegal. But the task has been difficult because push polls can be considered a form of free speech, which is protected under the First Amendment to the U.S. Constitution. Many professional associations representing legitimate polling organizations have issued public statements condemning push polls, for example, AAPOR,[10] the National Council on Public Polls,[11] and Public Opinion Strategies, a private polling firm.[12]

Research on Survey Research

When sugging and frugging flourished in the 1990s, more and more people refused to participate in genuine research because they could not distinguish authentic research from telemarketing. Even then, however, research on survey research showed that most survey respondents believe that scientific telephone surveys are valuable and important. This means that your work as an interviewer is regarded as valuable and important by a substantial segment of the population.

At the height of public rage about telemarketers, a 1995 national survey conducted by CMOR found that 86 percent of Americans agreed that survey research serves a useful purpose, 76 percent agreed that surveys are useful for government officials to learn how the public feels about important issues, 65 percent said that responding to surveys is in their best interest, and 64 percent found responding to surveys interesting.[13] Fewer respondents, 58 percent, believed that research firms maintain confidentiality. This is an important issue, and our professional associations are working to improve this perception.

> Most adults regard surveys as useful, important, and interesting.

The same survey found that 73 percent of respondents disagreed that responding to surveys is a waste of time, and 67 percent disagreed that surveys are an invasion of privacy. In addition, three-quarters of respondents said that they find television and newspaper stories about survey results interesting, and 64 percent of them like to compare their own opinions with those reported in surveys. Fully 74 percent said that bias in surveys depends on the particular survey.

A Gallup survey in 1996 found that a large majority of Americans consider polls a good thing for the country.[14] They believe that the nation would be better off if its leaders followed the views of the public more closely. They also believe polls work for the best interest of the public at large. In addition, the survey found that 55 percent of Americans read survey results in newspapers and magazines, with 31 percent saying they read survey results closely.

With these opinions, why were so many people refusing to participate in legitimate surveys? The 1996 Gallup survey found that four-fifths of respondents had received a telemarketing call in the preceding year. Nearly half (48 percent) had responded to a poll that turned out to be a sales pitch. The CMOR survey in 1995 found that 55 percent of respondents believed that the terms *survey* and *poll* were used to disguise a sales pitch. However, just 5 percent said surveys are a waste of time, just 6 percent said survey questions were too personal, and just 10 percent said they did not want to be bothered.

The main reasons people did not participate in legitimate surveys, the CMOR survey found, concerned issues that well-trained interviewers can address. Forty-nine percent of respondents said that they did not have time when they were called. Similarly, 20 percent said that they were just called at a bad time. And 21 percent said they were not interested in the survey topic.

In 2000, 2001, and 2002, the University of Oregon Survey Research Laboratory found that between 84 and 88 percent of Oregonians believed that "participating in telephone surveys, like the one you just completed" is important. In 2001 and 2002, just 27 and 29 percent, respectively, believed that participating in telephone surveys would "not at all" affect their lives.[15]

The findings in the 1990s indicated that telephone interviewers had to work hard to distinguish themselves from telemarketers. They did so by emphasizing that their surveys were scientific in nature, that randomly selected respondents represent hundreds of others like them, that their instruments were carefully pretested for validity and reliability, and that named survey sponsors were legitimate. Yet, response rates continued to decline.[16] Since then, call screening devices have become more pervasive, making it even harder for interviewers to get through to respondents. As fewer people participate, survey results become less representative, and the cost of contacting respondents increases. Survey researchers hope that the trend will reverse as the general public becomes accustomed to the DNC lists.

Summing Up

In studying this chapter, you have learned the basics of survey ethics. You know that survey respondents must be fully informed about the nature of the survey in which you ask them to participate, including how their personal information and answers will be protected. The essential elements of informed consent should become second nature to your work. You should also understand why codes of ethics exist, as well as the role of professional associations and IRBs in guiding and protecting your work. You now know about telemarketers' devastating effect on telephone survey research in the 1990s, and the legislation it spawned. Despite the telemarketers' short invasion into the field, however, most respondents understand and appreciate the need for legitimate surveys and polls.

What this chapter has not given you are examples of the kinds of ethical situations you can encounter and how to handle them. These examples will emerge in Chapters Five, Six, and Seven, where you will learn what to do if a respondent admits to committing crimes or breaks down emotionally in an interview. By the time you finish your interviewer training, you will recognize when you have encountered an ethical problem, know the ethically sound course of action to take, and be inspired to systematically follow through with your decision. Because your interactions with survey respondents occur in a matter of minutes, not hours or days, your ethical behavior vis-á-vis respondents must become instinctive.

> You are responsible for knowing your job's ethical requirements and for obeying them, even in stressful situations.

Be aware that ignorance is not a sufficient excuse for unethical work. Even if you unknowingly or unwittingly engage in unethical practices, you may still be held responsible for your behavior. It is your responsibility to know the ethical requirements of your job and to obey them, even in stressful situations.

Nevertheless, if you believe you have witnessed or overheard unethical behavior on the job, exercise caution. You could be wrong; remember that you can hear only one side of the conversation in a telephone interview. Accusations sometimes damage the would-be whistle-blower as much as the accused. Do not approach a coworker with your concerns; such action can create gossip. Follow your employer's work policies to determine to whom you should express your concerns—typically a supervisor or senior staff member.

A professional association of interviewers? Finally, I urge you, the interviewers, to organize your own professional association and develop your own code of ethics. This will benefit all of you in two ways. It will raise your visibility as a group and give you the tools to self-regulate your performance. Too many investigators take your work for granted, overlooking your crucial link between the data they analyze and the respondents who willingly supply those data because of the skilled and systematic manner in which you perform your work. In addition, too many interviewers do not take their work as seriously as they should, failing to appreciate their important role in social science research and public policymaking.

A professional association of interviewers would draw attention and respect to your specialized expertise. Your own professional association could guide and protect your work by creating an environment of authority for interviewers. It could ensure interviewer quality by implementing a certification program and by exercising a code of ethics that excluded or censured those who falsify or otherwise undermine data quality. This in turn would help to develop interviewers' dignity and pride in their work. A professional organization of interviewers could help to improve survey research and public opinion polling generally, operating side by side with the other professional associations in the field.

CHAPTER FOUR

WHAT TO EXPECT IN TELEPHONE INTERVIEWER TRAINING

This chapter is intended to give you an idea of what to expect in telephone interviewer training. Most survey research organizations offer three basic types of training: general, project specific, and refresher. Here you will learn about the kinds of activities in which you will participate, the people you are likely to meet, how long your training will take, and what the training schedule may be like.

General Telephone Interviewer Training

A medium-sized survey research organization is likely to conduct general telephone interviewer training a few times each year, over several days, for ten to fifty interviewers. Often the organization schedules the general training sessions three to ten days before starting one or more new or large telephone survey projects for which it needs more interviewers than it currently employs. You can expect to receive pay for training, because your employer is investing in your skill development, which benefits both it and you.

Activities and Trainers

Your activities during the general training period may include introductions to key members of the survey research organization's staff, listening to lectures, and role-playing with other interviewers (that is, taking turns pretending that one of you is an interviewer and the other is a respondent). You are likely to be tape-recorded as you conduct interviews. You may listen to the tape with an instructor to learn how to better control your voice or handle specific problems. Some employers show new interviewers videos that describe the organization and its workplace policies, present interviewing techniques, or discuss human subjects' protections. Expect solemn discussions about confidentiality and ethical issues. You may need to sign a pledge of confidentiality. You will probably spend several hours learning how to use the computer-assisted telephone interviewing (CATI) software and practicing with it.

Many survey employers give their new interviewers pop quizzes and discuss the results to make sure everyone is learning correctly. Before you conduct a real survey interview, expect to be tested, using a real or fictitious survey instrument, on things like accurately reading the script, probing, and using the CATI system. Of course you should also be prepared to fill out the paperwork necessary to become an employee of the organization. Usually this means that you should bring your Social Security card and two other forms of official identification.

Various people in the organization are likely to conduct these activities. For example, a director or president might present the organization's history, mission, goals, accomplishments, and internal structure. The person responsible for the CATI system may be the one who gives you hands-on training in how it works. Interviewer supervisors may work with you one on one for teaching and testing. Someone in charge of personnel may handle the paperwork and explain scheduling and pay. Someone else may lay down the law about workplace rules, behavior expectations, and disciplinary procedures. The trainees themselves may be divided into teams or pairs to conduct certain learning activities.

This *Handbook* is just one part of your training, but it will serve as a reference throughout your telephone interviewing career.

In most survey research organizations, general telephone interviewer training activities are varied and not boring. Expect to meet a lot of new people. Expect to learn a lot of new things. Expect to get worn out. Take copious notes. To do well, set aside time to study at home, using both this *Handbook* and background materials from your employer.

The length of the general training period varies across organizations and by the number of trainees. (Training ten new interviewers requires less time than training fifty.) Because the training activities are intense and exhausting, organizations often spread them over several days, working three to five hours each day. Your training may take place on evenings and weekends, the same times in which the most productive interviewing work occurs. Altogether, your general training may last as long as eight to twenty-five hours. If you miss any part of those training hours, for any reason, most survey research organizations will release you without payment for the part of the training you completed.

Testing

As your general training nears its end, your employer will test your new skills. A conventional test goes something like this. First, you will be trained on a real survey or a short, fictitious survey that your employer has specially designed to check the full range of necessary skills. (Most real surveys do not include the entire range of question and answer types, but a fictitious survey will.) After studying the instrument and practicing with it, you will administer the survey from a regular interviewing station, but the telephone number you call will ring in another room in the organization, not in a real household. A *confederate respondent* (a person involved in the interviewer training process who role-plays certain types of respondents) will pick up the telephone and answer your questions from a standard script. The entire test interview will take five to ten minutes. It may be tape-recorded.

You will probably conduct multiple interviews with multiple confederate respondents, who may act as a harried young mother, a retiree, or a traveling salesman. Each respondent type will have a different set of scripted answers. Each trainee will receive identically scripted answers from each confederate, to ensure comparability in the test results.

The confederates may also be your testers, or the tester may eavesdrop on your interviews, or both. The testers will score you on how well you conducted the interviews, including your telephone etiquette, tone of voice, pace, probing, and enunciation. In addition, your CATI keystrokes will be checked to make sure you entered all data correctly. Exhibit 4.1 lists the interviewing behaviors on which new interviewers are most often tested at this stage. Later on, you will probably also be tested on assigning call disposition codes and leaving proper messages for subsequent interviewers.

The testers will then compare their scores on your interviews. You must consistently display each of the ideal interviewing behaviors in Exhibit 4.1 to score well. Later one or more testers will debrief you on your interviewing strengths and areas needing improvement. A tester may use one of your tape-recorded interviews as a training device. That is, as you listen to a tape together, the tester will point out instances of proper interviewing behavior and offer suggestions in the places where you erred or could improve.

EXHIBIT 4.1. INTERVIEWING BEHAVIORS LIKELY TO BE TESTED.

Uses courteous telephone manners.
Answers respondents' initial concerns properly.
Uses appropriate phrases to gain cooperation from reluctant respondents.
Reads the entire interview script exactly as written.
Interviews directly, without extra chatty words.
Probes when necessary, without leading respondents.
Gives neutral feedback, as appropriate.
Maintains a suitable conversational pace.
Enunciates all words clearly.
Speaks with a pleasant, professional, confident, and assertive tone of voice.
Speaks without a timid, inappropriately apologetic, or overfriendly affect.
Avoids awkward pauses and "empty air."
Properly sidesteps answering questions about self when asked.
Records answers exactly and accurately.

Very few interviewers-in-training fail their general interviewer training and are fired at this point. But you may be sent back for more training and then retesting. Yet passing your general training does not mean that you are ready to start interviewing immediately. Next you must participate in project-specific training. In addition, many survey organizations require a probationary employment period before they invite new interviewers to stay.

Probationary Employment Period

Your first few interviewing shifts are likely to serve as a probationary employment period. Many survey research organizations set aside approximately twenty to thirty hours of interviewing, or the first four to six work shifts, as a temporary employment phase for new interviewers. During this time, your supervisors will scrutinize the quality of your work, and the organization will carefully evaluate your suitability as an interviewer. Of course during this period you also should decide whether this particular organization, and telephone interviewing in general, is right for you.

The length of the probationary period varies across organizations. It may also vary by less predictable factors, such as how many telephone surveys the organization has in the field at the time, whether a specific survey finished earlier than planned, and whether a large survey was postponed. These structural factors are beyond your control but can influence your ability to complete your trial period in a timely manner.

You must complete your probationary period within two months in most survey research organizations. If you do not, you may be asked to repeat the general training. Similarly, an experienced interviewer who has not worked at all for six months, no matter what the reason, usually must repeat the general interviewer training or an intensive refresher training before commencing the job again. The reason for this is that new skills decay quickly if people do not use them shortly after general training. To get work hours, you must attend project-specific training sessions and then sign up for work shifts. If structural reasons prevent you from getting the hours you need in two months (for example, a survey's start date is delayed) but your performance to date is excellent, sometimes employers will make an exception.

At the end of the probationary period a supervisor will discuss your performance with you, in a manner similar to the test interviews at the end of general training. At this time, you can also raise your questions and concerns. If your work habits, attendance, and performance have measured up to the organization's standards during this period, you will be invited to continue. Some organizations also give a token raise to interviewers who have successfully completed their trial period. If you have shown any marginal work habits (such as repeated lateness), these will be discussed, and your probationary period may be extended.

Successfully completing the probationary period does not guarantee continued employment for a certain number of hours per week or a specific period of time. Nor does it mean that an employer can discharge interviewers only for cause. In many survey research organizations interviewing hours are unpredictable, and in most private firms employees can be released at the employer's discretion, for no apparent reason.

Project-Specific Training

Project-specific training (sometimes called *interviewer briefing*) refers to the preparation interviewers receive to work on a particular survey. In order to conduct interviews for a particular survey, you must sign up for and participate in its training session. Survey research organizations require interviewers to attend these project-specific training sessions because each survey is unique in its goals, target population, topics, and details. Only with this training can you learn each project's background and receive comprehensive instructions on how to collect the survey data accurately.

Project-specific training sessions are typically scheduled one or two days before a new survey goes into the field. Often they are held on evenings and weekends, when most interviewers can attend. Some organizations always schedule their project-specific training sessions for the same time and day of the week (say, Thursday at 5:00 PM), so that interviewers can plan for them, even though there may only be one or two project-specific trainings in an average month. Depending on a survey's length and complexity, project-specific training can last from two to twenty hours. Most sessions, however, average three to five hours.

Preferably, all persons involved in a survey will attend the project-specific training sessions. In addition to the interviewers, these people typically include the principal investigator or client, project director, programmers, interviewer supervisors, coders, and research assistants.

There is no right or wrong way to conduct project-specific training sessions. Some survey organizations conduct them right at the interviewer stations, focusing mainly on the CATI aspects. Others conduct them lecture style, with the key staff speaking up front and interviewers taking notes (like students), with the CATI training given later. I prefer to use multiple methods—a combination of lecture, discussion, and round-robin activities (described later in this chapter), followed by CATI training with interviewers randomly assigned into pairs. Your employer may use all the methods described here or just some of them. No matter the method, project-specific training should give you the detailed tools to administer a particular survey with optimum accuracy and efficiency.

Preliminary Activities

Project-specific training sessions usually start with five or ten minutes of rustling around, that is, distributing materials, completing forms, setting up equipment, writing on the blackboard, and arranging chairs. Each person should receive paper copies of the survey instrument, the precontact letter (if appropriate), and *answers to common questions* (a sheet of paper containing interviewers' scripted answers to respondents' usual questions about a survey, sometimes called a *fallback sheet*). A sign-in sheet should be distributed to ensure that each interviewer present receives pay for this training session.

A *schedule request form* is likely to be distributed, asking what shifts you will be available to work on this survey and how many hours you can commit to work each week that the survey is in the field. (See Exhibit B.1 in Appendix B for an example.) Fill in the form, and return it to the person who schedules interviewers' work. Be sure to bring your personal calendar to these training sessions to help you both to fill in this form and to record later the work shifts to which you are assigned.

During this settling-in period a supervisor or project director may call your attention to upcoming surveys and their anticipated project-specific training dates by writing the study names and dates on a blackboard or projecting them on a screen. Record these dates on your personal calendar too.

Ideally, at the start of project-specific training you will be introduced to the study's principal investigators or clients, and they will explain what the survey is about and why it is important. They will not, however, reveal their hypotheses to you, because doing so could unconsciously influence how you ask a question or use a probe. You will learn about the type of sample you will be working from (random-digit-dial, randomly chosen from a list, or just a list). You will also find out the survey geography (national, regional, state, county, or local), whether you will have respondents' names, the types of respondents to expect, and any special circumstances or unusual conditions about the survey.

Reviewing the Precontact Letter and Answers to Common Questions

The next step in project-specific training is to review the precontact letter, if one has been sent, as well as the answers to common questions. A precontact letter lets respondents know that they have been randomly selected for a survey, explains the survey's purpose and why each respondent is important, and tells them that a professional interviewer will be calling. Most precontact letters also include all needed human subjects' protection language.

The sheet of answers to common questions contains much of the same information found in the precontact letter, but interviewers deliver it orally and exactly as written. These answers are intended to lessen respondents' concerns about the survey sponsor, the nature of the survey, how respondents were selected, and related issues. It varies somewhat from project to project, just as projects vary. This sheet, as well as the precontact letter (if one has been sent) should be posted in each interviewing station for interviewers' easy reference. You should memorize these answers.

> From this point onward, the *Handbook* uses the Transportation Needs and Issues Survey as its example survey.

Exhibit 4.2 provides an example of answers to common questions, taken from the Transportation Needs and Issues Survey.[1] This survey will serve as an example throughout the rest of this *Handbook*. Exhibit 4.3 provides CASRO's list of similar answers to respondents' questions. During project-specific training, you will review these (or something similar) line by line. Even though they will be posted in your interviewing station, you should endeavor to memorize them. Doing so will allow you to answer respondents' issues and concerns smoothly, quickly, and conversationally. Pausing or tripping over your tongue while attempting to answer respondents' concerns may make respondents hesitant to participate. So learn these answers well.

EXHIBIT 4.2. ANSWERS TO RESPONDENTS' COMMON QUESTIONS ABOUT THE TRANSPORTATION NEEDS AND ISSUES SURVEY.

What is the purpose of this (survey/study)? How will the data be used?

- The survey's purpose is to learn what Oregonians think about traffic congestion, highway construction, and how well the state is maintaining roads and bridges.
- The survey results will be used to help the Oregon Department of Transportation plan for the future.
- Citizens' opinions are very important to the Oregon Department of Transportation.

How did you get my telephone number? How was I chosen for this survey?

- This is a random sample survey.
- All Oregon households have an equal chance of being selected for the survey.
- It was strictly by chance that your telephone number was chosen.
- Only a few households are being asked to participate, so your answers are very important.

Who is (sponsoring/paying for) this survey?

- The Oregon Department of Transportation.

I am not a good person for you to talk to because (I don't drive/I have only lived here 2 weeks/I am not involved/I am too old/I am too young/I am too busy/I don't know anything about highways or bridges).

- Every person randomly chosen for this survey is important, whether you are typical or not.
- It is very important to hear from people who do not drive, because many questions are about alternative forms of transportation.
- As we talk, I am sure you will find you have answers to the questions.
- Even people who just moved here are important for us to talk to.
- Let's try a few questions and you will see that the survey applies to you as much as to anyone else.

How long will the survey take?

- The survey will take approximately sixteen to twenty minutes, depending on your answers.
- I can talk fast if you are in a hurry.
- We can complete part of it now and I can call back tomorrow to finish the rest.

Is this survey (confidential/anonymous)?

- Yes, most definitely. This survey is completely anonymous.
- I do not know your name, and I have no need to know it. All we want is your opinions.
- When the interview is completed, your telephone number is automatically stripped from your answers and destroyed.
- All results of the survey are released in the form of percentages and averages.
- It is not possible to identify any individual person or response in the results. Anonymity is very important to the Survey Research Laboratory.
- We are very careful to protect individuals' anonymity.

EXHIBIT 4.2. *(CONTINUED)*

What if I do not want to answer a question?

- None of the questions in this survey are personal or sensitive in nature. But you may feel free to skip any question you wish.
- You may also terminate the survey at any time.

How much does the survey cost?

- I really do not know. But I can tell you that the Survey Research Laboratory is non-profit.

How can I be sure that this is real/legitimate?

- You may talk with my supervisor *[name]*; (she/he) is right here.
- You may call our Human Subjects Compliance Office at *[telephone number]*.
- You may call *[client name]* in ODOT at *[telephone number]*, or e-mail him at *[name]*@state.or.us.

Who is in charge of this survey? May I talk to (her/him)?

- Our director, *[name]*, would be happy to talk with you. You may call her at *[telephone number]*. If she is not in her office, leave a message and she will call you back as soon as possible.

How do I know you will not use my telephone number for something else?

- The Survey Research Laboratory does not sell telephone numbers. We report to the vice president for research at the *[organization name]*. Our research is subject to the strictest ethical standards. All of our surveys are reviewed by the Committee for the Protection of Human Subjects at *[organization name]*. Strict records are kept about the promises we make to the people who agree to take part in our research. If we violate any of our promises, we may be subject to civil or criminal liability. For these reasons, we take our promises of anonymity very seriously.

What is the Survey Research Laboratory?

- It conducts surveys with researchers at *[organization name]*. The laboratory is used for surveys like this one, in order to find out how people feel about issues and to train students in survey methods. The laboratory operates under the vice president for research at the *[organization name]*.

You can't call me because … (I signed up for the Do Not Call registry/I have a black dot next to my number in the telephone book.)

- We are calling to conduct research. Research is exempt under the Do Not Call laws, because your answers are anonymous and no attempt will be made to sell you anything. Your opinions are important in helping ODOT make decisions that can affect you.

Phoning

- Let phones ring 8 times before giving up (about 35 seconds).
- Leave no messages on answering machines unless instructed.

EXHIBIT 4.3. CASRO'S SUGGESTED RESPONSES TO RESPONDENTS' QUESTIONS AND COMPLAINTS.

A survey research call is not a commercial or telemarketing call

- We are not selling anything.
- We are only asking for your opinions.
- Our democracy relies on an informed public, and much of that information comes from surveys. Society needs survey research to enable government, the news media, business, and social service organizations to understand the experiences, views, and needs of the nation in critical areas of health, the economy, security, politics and much more.

Survey research calls are exempt from do not call laws

- We are specifically not included in do not call laws because we do not mislead, we care about your privacy, and we try to talk to you when it is convenient for you.
- In fact, we support these laws to protect your privacy.

Survey researchers respect your privacy

- Your name and number and specific opinions will be kept anonymous.
- Your answers will be combined with others and statistically analyzed to determine the population's overall opinions.
- We respect your right not to be interviewed, if you say no.

Survey researchers regulate themselves

- SRL's privacy policy is available on this Web site [*URL*] or by calling [*telephone number*].
- We belong to CASRO—the Council of American Survey Research Organizations—and must follow its Code of Ethics, which protects your privacy and your confidentiality and prohibits any abuse or harassment of our respondents (http://www.casro.org).

Source: Adapted from Council of American Survey Research Organizations, *The Legal Status of Telephone Interviewing vs. Telemarketing*, p. 4. Available February 24, 2007, from www.nustats. com/Telephone%20Interviewing.pdf.

Reviewing the Survey Instrument

You will spend most of your project-specific training time reviewing the survey instrument. Survey research organizations vary a great deal in how they present the instrument to interviewers. Some survey organizations begin the instrument review with a quick read-through of the instrument. For example, a project director or a supervisor poses as an interviewer and someone unfamiliar with the instrument pretends to be a respondent. They read the entire survey aloud. During this exercise, I suggest that you close your eyes and listen in a general way, to get a sense of how the instrument flows conversationally. This step works well only with surveys lasting less than ten minutes.

Some organizations project the CATI version of the instrument on a screen, just as interviewers will see it on their monitors while working, and explain it question by question. Although this saves paper and printing costs, the disadvantages are that interviewers do not have their own copies on which to write notes, and in a darkened room, no one sees whether some interviewers are nodding off. Most organizations provide each interviewer with a paper copy of the instrument, sometimes including the CATI computer code, and then interviewers and trainers talk it through, as a group. Having your own copy is useful not only for note taking but also because you can take it home for practice and review. Many interviewers also find that the CATI code is not hard to follow, and having your own copy allows you to track the instrument's skip logic most clearly.

Other places introduce the survey instrument by having the project director or someone very familiar with the instrument read it aloud at a lectern, making comments as she or he goes. Interviewers make notes on their copies and raise questions where needed. This process can be deadly dull, especially with a long instrument.

Certain well-funded organizations have specialized personnel who prepare detailed, three-ring binders of documents (often called the *Q by Qs*, or *question by question instructions*) for interviewers' project-specific training. In such documents the left-hand page typically contains each question, exactly as it appears to interviewers on the computer screen. The right-hand page contains detailed instructions about that question, including why it is necessary, how it fits with other questions, how to ask it, how to handle problems you might encounter, and any skip logic that flows from it. This approach standardizes explanations best, and interviewers can take additional notes on their own copies.

When a survey organization lacks the resources to create a Q by Q document for each survey, my favorite way to review the instrument is to make it a round-robin type of activity, in which everyone present participates—not just the interviewers but also the principal investigators, project directors, programmers, and other noninterviewers. This activity is easiest when the room has a table large enough for everyone to sit around it or the room has movable chairs that can be arranged so that everyone sits in a circle. Moving clockwise around the circle, Person A starts by reading the survey introduction, Person B reads the first question, Person C reads the next question, and so on, moving sequentially through the instrument and sequentially around the room. With a long instrument each person may read several questions going around the circle multiple times. Keeping the process casual allows anyone to request a pause in order to ask about something that seems unclear. Oftentimes the project director or principal investigator will interrupt the question-reading process to present the rationale for a particular question, to explain some skip logic, or to discuss a rare problem revealed in pretesting. Inevitably, an eagle-eyed interviewer will find a misspelled word or a missing comma, no matter how thoroughly pretesters reviewed and revised the instrument before it got to this stage. Although these interruptions usually prove helpful for interviewers, too many picky, redundant, or unnecessary questions will slow the review process. The round-robin approach keeps all participants awake and on their toes. In my experience the principal investigators almost always depart from this process commenting on the interviewers' savvy perspicacity.

CATI Training

Part of project-specific training also involves interviewers sitting at interviewing stations and going through the CATI version of the instrument. Ideally, interviewers should do this right after you have reviewed the instrument as a group, while it is still fresh in your minds. I recommend randomly assigning interviewers to pairs. Each takes a turn acting as the interviewer while the other role-plays a respondent. (Often role-playing respondents will challenge you much more than the average real respondent.) Pairing with an interviewer you do not know is preferable to working with a buddy when studying the CATI version of the instrument, because buddies tend to repair or cover for each other's interviewing weaknesses. For long instruments or those with complex skip logic, interviewers should repeat this role-playing exercise several times, with role-playing respondents acting out different character types, to familiarize interviewers thoroughly with the different paths through the interview script.

As you work through the instrument in CATI, you may find little things that will help you, as an interviewer, read a question more easily on the screen. For example, a hard return (to break the line) placed at the end of a certain clause in a question might help you read it more conversationally, or more space placed between the question and the answer categories might help your eyes move more efficiently over the computer screen. Request that the CATI programmer make these changes. Such seemingly little things can sometimes make a big difference in the quality of data collection, but few CATI programmers understand interviewers' experiences well enough to anticipate them.

If your first interviewing shift on a survey is more than one day after project-specific training, you should review the CATI version of the instrument again. If possible, repeat the role-playing process once or twice instead of just reading through the instrument on the computer screen.

Scheduling Work Shifts

Data collection usually starts the day immediately after training. (If you have an afternoon training session, it may even start that evening.) Thus interviewers need to know their upcoming work schedules right away. Efficient survey organizations distribute schedule request forms at the start of project-specific training sessions and assign a scheduler to make up the interviewers' work schedules while project-specific training is in progress. Starting data collection while training is fresh in interviewers' memories helps them to apply successfully what they have just learned.

For interviewers to be paid for project-specific training, most survey research organizations require that they work on the survey for a minimum number of hours. If you fail to work the minimum hours, you will be paid for your interviewing hours only and not for project-specific training. The minimum hours of work vary. Some organizations require interviewers to work at least the same number of hours as the length of the project-specific training session, typically three to five hours. Others require twice the number of project-specific training hours, typically six to ten interviewing hours. Some require a flat number of interviewing hours (for example, eight hours).

Avoiding Predictable Problems During Project-Specific Training

Certain problems predictably emerge at project-specific training sessions. You can avoid incurring the wrath of all those participating by following a few simple courtesies. You already know them, but all trainers have seen people who ignore them, so I will go over them here.

Arrive to project-specific training on time. If for some reason you cannot, slip into the training room quietly and unobtrusively. Do not, for example, allow the door to bang shut announcing your late appearance. If you will be more than ten minutes late or if you must leave more than ten minutes early, for whatever reason, do not attend at all. If you know in advance of a schedule conflict, let your employer know right away. But do not be surprised if you are asked to wait until the next training session, because people who enter the training room late or leave early inevitably miss important details and disrupt others' concentration. Makeup training may be available, depending on the number of interviewers working and how quickly the project is going, but do not count on it.

Do not interrupt the training sessions in any way, for yourself or others. When training begins, immediately stop chatting with your friend or neighbor. Speak only when called on. Do not engage in sidebar conversations, and never ask your neighbor for clarifications. If you missed or did not understand something, raise your hand immediately and ask. Undoubtedly other interviewers also did not hear or understand and will appreciate your asking. If you need to borrow a pen, paper, tissue, or whatever, ask a neighbor before training, not during it. Turn off your cell phone and put it away. Take notes by hand, and leave your laptop computer at home.

Resist the temptation to engage in excessive *wordsmithing*—offering suggestions about how to improve question wording—during project-specific training. Instead, write down your suggestions and share them with the project director or principal investigator afterward. Realize that most instruments have been carefully designed and thoroughly pretested. Moreover, project-specific training generally takes place only after the client has given the instrument final approval. Question wording that seems awkward to you may be required for comparability to other surveys. Changing a gendered question to gender-neutral phrasing may seem necessary to you, but it is no small matter for the investigators and programmers. Usually, only obviously missing words and errors in spelling, grammar, and punctuation can be changed at interviewer training. Other changes must be approved by the client, which can delay a project from going into the field.

Similarly, resist the temptation to present your shift-scheduling problems in front of everybody else. Meet with the scheduler after project-specific training to discuss and resolve the issues. If you have an issue to discuss with one of the trainers, also wait until after training. Above all, do not interrupt or try to speak with the people conducting the training sessions about your personal issues while they distribute training materials, set up a video, or engage in similar activities. Because they are otherwise occupied, they will not remember later what you said.

Do not leave and reenter the training room because you are thirsty or need to use the restroom. Walking across the room as you exit and reenter distracts everyone else. Bring a covered beverage to training sessions. If you forget, being thirsty for an hour might help you to remember the next time. Empty your bladder before training or hold it for a scheduled break or until the training ends. Breaks will be built into long training sessions. Also fill your stomach before training. The smells and sounds of your eating will distract others and interfere with your ability to concentrate. Never openly read a newspaper, write a letter, trim your nails, rearrange your backpack, stand to dress or undress, or engage in other irrelevant activities during training. It is disrespectful.

As I mentioned, most interviewers do not need these reminders about basic civility in the workplace. But I raise these issues because I have witnessed some interviewers do each of them during project-specific training sessions. Needless to say, incivility may result in discontinued employment.

Homework

Before you start interviewing for a survey, you must have answers to all respondents' possible concerns on the tip of your tongue. Reserve at least thirty minutes at home to memorize the answers to common questions for this survey. Know the survey sponsor, the expected length of the interview task, whether respondents' identities will be kept confidential or anonymous, and how respondents were selected. Be able to offer a few short sentences on why the survey is important and what topics it includes. You will learn details about how to answer respondents' objections in Chapter Six.

If you have more than one day before your first work shift on this survey, review and study the interview script at home. Enlist a few family members or friends to act as respondents—either acting as themselves or role-playing a different type of person. Some friends and relatives really enjoy doing this. Be sure, however, that they understand the purpose of their participation—namely, to help you learn the interview script. Many people want to help by suggesting ways to reword the questions. Explain that revisions are not possible at this stage of the survey process.

Refresher Training

Refresher training sessions generate from three general conditions. First, the survey organization employing you expects a gap of several weeks between telephone interviewing projects and wants to prevent interviewers' skills from rusting. A week or so before a new project commences, trainers or supervisors schedule four or five hours to refresh interviewer skills, often on a Saturday or Sunday when the most interviewers can attend. During the session, interviewers review the more difficult skills, such as refusal conversion, certain types of probing, avoiding bias, and the technical details that are easy to forget, such as call disposition codes. This may be accomplished lecture style, in small groups, or with a combination of these methods. Snacks may be provided as an incentive.

Second, certain interviewers repeatedly err in some technique or skill. Interviewer supervisors should invite them in for a one- to two-hour session of intensive remedial work. This will probably involve one-on-one work with a supervisor or trainer in relearning basic skills, role-playing, and testing.

Third, some survey organizations set aside five to eight minutes just before a work shift begins for mini-training sessions in which supervisors present reminders about a particular facet of interviewing. The topics are changed each day or each shift. They address such matters as telephone etiquette, tone of voice, pace, enunciation, reading questions completely, probing, scheduling callbacks, handling respondents' objections ("it is not legal for you to call me"), avoiding bias in feedback to respondents, leaving helpful notes for the next interviewer's callback, and the like. At the same time, interviewers are briefed about the progress of surveys in the field.

> Structured conversations ensure that interviewers administer a survey properly to all respondents.

The types of refresher training detailed so far involves trainers or supervisors. However, some well-established survey research organizations have put their refresher training onto interactive CD-ROMs for interviewer self-administration. The advantages of self-training include conserving trainers' and supervisors' costly labor in repetitive activities and saving their time for individualized assistance. The potential disadvantages are plain. Self-training is not customized to each interviewer's unique lapses or blunders, and supervisors may not be immediately on hand to answer questions or provide specialized assistance, feedback, and guidance.

Summing Up

Data from surveys are only as good as the interviewers who collect them. Conducting an interview is not like carrying on a casual conversation. Rather, you will learn to carry out structured conversations, to ensure that the survey instrument is administered properly to all respondents. This will involve many hours in classrooms and call center settings and many hours of peer coaching and self-study, potentially using a combination of paper, computer, tape-recorded, video, and CD-ROM tools. You will learn the basic definitions and concepts that underlie survey research as well as the procedures for conducting interviews. You will learn to use proper interviewer telephone etiquette, control your voice, handle uncooperative or reluctant respondents, and avoid biasing respondents' answers. For each project in which you participate, you will learn the survey instrument in detail, going through it question by question in conversation, in practice, and on a computer. Interviewer training, you will find, is continual and practical. Ultimately, you will know not only the best practices for conducting telephone interviews, but also how to apply these practices to widely varying survey topics and with vastly varying respondents.

CHAPTER FIVE

CALLING

At this point you should understand the overall survey process and your role as a telephone interviewer in that process. Now we get to the nuts and bolts of your job—actually calling and interviewing people. This chapter and the next are organized chronologically, presenting your activities in the same way you will conduct interviews. This chapter is devoted to calling and call dispositions. The next chapter is devoted to interviewing itself.

The section on call disposition codes may seem overwhelming at first. Know in advance that most survey research organizations use just a subset of these codes and that they will all appear on your computer screen as part of the computer-assisted telephone interviewing (CATI) system.

Getting Ready

Each time you arrive for an interviewing shift, your employer will have a short protocol for you to accomplish before you begin calling. A typical start might go like this: you will punch a time clock or sign in noting the time, check your mailbox or cubby for memos, stash your coat and personal items, and review a whiteboard for progress on surveys in the field. A supervisor will greet you and the others working that shift, give updates on each survey's status in the field, and assign you and the other interviewers to workstations and the survey(s) on which you will work. Some survey organizations set aside three or four minutes for a mini-training session before you start calling.

After you sit down at your workstation to begin interviewing, most CATI systems require you to type in your identification number and password. Next, select the survey on which you will work. CATI will open that survey and present a call screen for the first respondent you are to call. For a random-digit-dial (RDD) survey, the call screen will show each case's telephone number. For a list sample survey, the call screen may also show the intended respondent's name and, sometimes, database information about the respondent. For example, if you are calling members of an organization, the call screen might show each person's title and years of affiliation with the organization.

> Carefully review each respondent's call history before dialing the telephone.

The call screen will also show each respondent's call history, or allow you to easily access it, depending on the type of CATI system you use. The call history shows the record of all calls made to each respondent, displaying the dates and times of days of all previous calls, their call disposition codes, and explanatory notes from prior interviewers about their experiences when they called. Review this history carefully. How many times has an interviewer called this number before and at what times and on what days? Examine the prior call dispositions. Has any interviewer reached a person yet? Review messages left by previous interviewers. Has the respondent expressed reluctance or interest? Is a wife screening calls for her busy husband? The call history will help you plan a callback strategy for approaching the respondent; Chapter Six will offer detailed tips on these techniques.

Note that you do not select the respondents or telephone numbers you want to call. Rather, the CATI system is preprogrammed to rotate the cases to interviewers in a logical manner. The general principle is to rotate cases through blocks of time on weekdays, weeknights, and weekends in such a way as to optimize the likelihood that a real person will pick up the telephone. For example, when cases have been called on weekdays but never reached, CATI at some point will automatically move them to weeknights. Likewise, it will move cases not reached on weeknights to weekends and those not reached on weekends to weekdays or weeknights.

CATI can also bring up scheduled callbacks and direct particular respondents to particular interviewers. For example, when respondents say they are too busy now but will gladly take the interview at a particular time on a particular day, CATI will bring up those cases at the scheduled times—if interviewers have recorded them properly in the CATI system. CATI can also assign particular cases to interviewers with special skills, such as Spanish speakers or those with excellent refusal conversion skills. If a pressing situation arises, most CATI systems allow a supervisor to direct a particular case to a particular interviewer at that moment.

Dialing

Figure 5.1 outlines the typical procedures for dialing telephone numbers. The procedure depends on who dials (you or the computer), how the call is dialed (manually or by pressing a key on the keyboard), and whether the call will be local or long distance. Most survey organizations choose one mode of dialing that you will use consistently. However, even if you routinely use an automated

FIGURE 5.1. TYPES OF TELEPHONE CALLS, BY TYPE OF DIAL AND TYPE OF CALL.

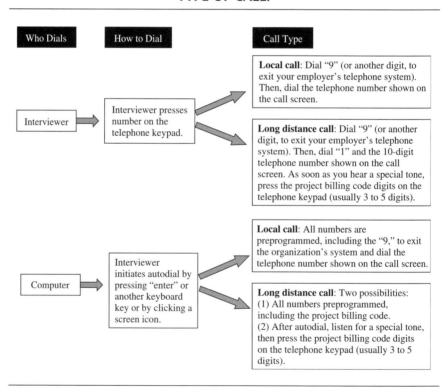

computer dialing feature, you may sometimes need to manually dial a telephone number yourself, so be sure to learn that procedure. Your CATI system may also require you to click a button on your computer screen with your mouse to indicate whether you will be autodialing or manually dialing the number.

Next, determine whether the call you will make is local or long distance. (You will probably already know this from project-specific training.) For long distance calls many survey research organizations assign a project-specific long distance code number, which ensures that the long distance charges are billed to the proper survey in the field. Some organizations program these billing codes (also known as access codes) into the autodial; otherwise, you have to type them in yourself. If the latter is the case, be sure you have the billing code handy for the particular survey on which you are working *before* you need it. After dialing the long distance number, yourself or with autodial, wait to hear a special tone. In the ten to twenty seconds that tone lasts, type in your survey's billing code.

With manual dialing, most organizations require you to punch a single telephone digit in order to exit the organization's telephone system, usually a 9. Then, for local calls, you punch the seven-digit or ten-digit telephone number into the telephone keypad. Most local areas in the U.S. use seven-digit telephone numbers. But certain rapidly growing areas, such as the Denver-Boulder area in Colorado, require ten-digits for local calls. If this is a local call, the respondents' telephone should start ringing. For long-distance calls, dial 1 before the ten-digit telephone number.

Most survey organizations recommend that interviewers let the telephone ring eight times, which takes about thirty-two seconds (four seconds per ring). Some survey research organizations will ask you to let the telephone ring up to fifteen times (about one minute) if you are working with an elderly sample or if no one has answered the telephone after several dial attempts and no answering device has picked up.

> Let telephones ring eight times before assigning a call disposition code.

The explosion of telephone numbers for modems, fax machines, and other nontalking purposes in the last fifteen years has increased the potential number of fruitless dial attempts that telephone interviewers make in RDD surveys. Although it is possible to buy lists of RDD samples that exclude nonresidential and non-working numbers, not all survey organizations do so because purged lists can be costly and often they are not up to date. When interviewers are calling a non-purged list for an RDD survey, a lot of their effort in the first few days involves sifting the nonresidential and nonworking telephone numbers from that randomly generated list. Few calls will result in interviews. After those first few days, dialing becomes more productive.

For example, in a statewide RDD survey I conducted in 2003, interviewers made 23,680 dial attempts to reach the target sample size of 1,014 completed interviews. In other words, interviewers averaged 23 calls per completed interview. For that survey, a list of 5,230 RDD telephone numbers was generated. Of those, fully 3,027 were nonworking or disconnected numbers, fax or modem or data lines, or nonresidential numbers. Interviewers made 3,245 dial attempts to determine the status of those 3,027 numbers, meaning that most of them were settled with one call. Once they were weeded out, interviewers focused on the remaining 2,203 telephone numbers. People at 210 numbers refused; they received 1,036 calls overall (about 5 each). The 1,014 telephone numbers that resulted in completed interviews received 3,139 calls (about 3 each), but 91 eligible respondents were never interviewed because they were "too busy," "not home now," or sick when called. Fully 16,260 dial attempts resulted in no answers, busy signals, and answering machines. In the end, 888 telephone numbers were left in these unknown categories. Altogether in this survey, a person answered the telephone on just 24 percent of all dial attempts. This is fairly typical for an RDD survey with a nonpurged sample.

Call Disposition Codes

Every time you call a telephone number for a survey, you must assign either a *final* or an *in-progress* call disposition code before you can go to the next case. The final codes indicate that an interview has been completed, the respondent has refused, or no interview is possible. The in-progress codes indicate that an interview has not yet been completed and offers information about why it is incomplete. Most CATI systems automatically assign just two of the call disposition codes, one for completed interviews and one for partially completed interviews. You are responsible for the assigning the rest.

These codes may vary somewhat from survey to survey. Because these codes appear automatically on your computer screen with a short description, and because some survey organizations number their codes differently from the code numbers shown here, you do not have to memorize the code numbers themselves. However, you must remember what they mean and when to use them. In addition, Tables 5.1 and 5.2 show all possible final and in-progress call disposition codes, respectively. Many survey organizations use a simpler subset of these lists.

You do not have to memorize each disposition code, because CATI shows them with short descriptions on your computer screen. However, you must understand which codes to use and when to use them.

Final Call Disposition Codes

Final call disposition codes are essential for calculating a survey's response rate, cooperation rate, refusal rate, and similar measures. After data collection is completed, researchers calculate these rates by examining the final call disposition code for every single telephone number in the survey. These rates are important for two basic reasons. They provide information about the extent to which a sample survey may be generalized to a population. They also signify the overall quality of the completed survey project. For example, researchers regard a survey with an 80 percent response rate as more reliable than one with a 33 percent response rate.

Until 2000, survey research organizations used their own final call disposition codes and had their own algorithms for calculating response rates, guided by professional associations' recommendations. The call disposition codes were similar across organizations, yet they differed enough that accurate comparisons of one survey to another were impossible. After years of assessment, AAPOR published *Standard Definitions: Final Dispositions of Case Codes and Outcome Rates for Surveys* in 2000.[1] Most survey research organizations and CATI software systems have adopted these definitions, or a close version of them, for coding call dispositions and for calculating response rates.

Table 5.1 outlines the final call disposition codes for RDD telephone surveys. Because list sample surveys use very similar codes, Table 5.1 also comments on how to use these codes for list surveys. In order to understand the code explanations in Table 5.1, you must be familiar with the acronyms and abbreviations commonly used in survey research. To review these acronyms and abbreviations see Table 1.2 in Chapter One.

To learn these disposition codes, first glance over the entire table. Notice that the call dispositions are divided into four broad categories: (1) interviews, (2) eligible cases that did not result in interviews, (3) noneligible cases, and (4) cases of unknown eligibility. Table 5.2 provides a fifth broad category, in-progress codes. Within each broad category, subgroups indicate the different circumstances that may arise with each dial attempt. Each call disposition is assigned a unique code number. At the end of data collection, researchers want as many cases as possible in the first category (completed interviews) and as few as possible in the fourth category (cases of unknown eligibility) and fifth category (cases in-progress).

Skimming over Table 5.1 will help you determine the general structure of the call disposition codes. As you do so, note the *general codes*, which are subdivided into more detailed codes. For example, code 2.1 is a general code for all types of refusals and break-offs. (A *break-off* occurs when respondents refuse partway through the interview to continue it, which is rare.) Respondent refusals by themselves may be assigned code 2.11, while break-offs may receive code 2.12. Respondent-level refusals can be further subdivided into household-level refusals (code 2.111) and refusals by the actual person who is supposed to be interviewed (code 2.112). Some surveys and survey organizations do not require such fine differentiation and will ask you to use only the general code, 2.1. Similarly, Table 5.1 shows three possible specific codes for language barriers—2.331, 2.332, and 2.333—but one more general code, 2.33, will suffice in many circumstances. Your survey employer will explain during interviewer training which level of code is required.

Next, read through the entire list of codes carefully. Pay special attention to the column entitled "explanation, usage, and instructions." For example, study how household-level refusals (code 2.111) differ from respondent refusals (code 2.112).

Several hours of interviewer training will probably be devoted to studying these codes. You might have to pass a quiz on them before you are allowed to start interviewing. Flag Table 5.1 and keep this *Handbook* in your workstation so that you can check the definitions until you are completely sure you know how to use the codes. If you still cannot find an appropriate code, ask a supervisor for help.

Note too that some CATI systems cannot display all possible call disposition codes on one computer screen. You may need to use your computer mouse to scroll up and down your screen to see the entire list.

> Review Table 1.2, "Commonly Used Acronyms and Abbreviations in Survey Research," before studying Table 5.1.

Remember that some survey research organizations use the same definitions and concepts as those in Table 5.1 but assign different code numbers to them. In addition, some surveys require more precise differentiation than others. Call disposition codes can also vary from survey to survey, because some require survey-specific codes and some codes are not necessary for all surveys; for example, not all surveys have a screener—code 3.2.1. Again, these details will become clear in interviewer training.

TABLE 5.1. AAPOR FINAL DISPOSITION CODES FOR RDD TELEPHONE SURVEYS, WITH EXPLANATIONS AND INSTRUCTIONS FOR USE.

Code Group	Call Disposition	Code #	Explanations and Instructions for Use
1. Interview			An Iw was completed, wholly or partially. Your SRO will determine the threshold of # of Qs answered for partials to be considered complete Iws.
	Complete	1.1	R has answered all Qs in the survey; the Iw is complete. Most CATI systems record this call disposition code automatically when you complete an Iw and enter your Ir ID#.
	Partial	1.2	R began Iw but did not answer all Qs. This may occur b/c R had to stop partway through Iw or b/c the TP disconnected; a CB to complete Iw could not be made before data collection halted.
			If R refused partway through Iw, use code 2.12 for break-off.
			Most CATI systems record this call disposition automatically when all Qs were not answered. Upon restart, CATI automatically picks up at the next Q for Ir to read.
			Some CATI systems record a partial Iw when Irs fail to enter their Ir ID# after all Qs asked.
2. Eligible, Noninterview			A potential R is known to be at the TP# but no Iw was completed, despite repeated CBs.
	Refusal and break-off	2.1	General code for informed dissent or R refused partway through Iw. Examples explained below.
	Refusal	2.11	Final refusal codes. Using this group of final refusal codes will cause CATI to remove the TP# from calling queue. Use code 5.11 until you are certain you have a final refusal or R credibly threatens legal action. Some SROs require Irs to have supervisor permission to code a final refusal.

(continued)

TABLE 5.1. *(CONTINUED)*

Code Group	Call Disposition	Code #	Explanations and Instructions for Use
	Household-level refusal	2.111	For use in surveys of HHs in which any willing adult can take Iw.
			For surveys of selected individual Rs, use this code as a last resort. A protective GK, a recorded msg, or a paid go-between should not refuse on an eligible R's behalf; R must give informed dissent.
			TP blocking device with recorded msg indicates HH will *never* accept calls from this SRO. Interpreted as HH-level refusal, even though Ir never talked to R.
	Known R refusal	2.112	Ir reads introduction, R understands survey purpose, hears informed consent language, hears Ir is not selling, and still refuses; that is, R gives informed dissent. CBs with ref conversion techniques by different Irs on different days of week and times of day have not worked.
	Break-off	2.12	R began Iw but refused partway through. CBs with ref conversion techniques by different Irs on different days of week and times of day have not worked.
	Noncontact	2.2	General code for Rs not reachable due to schedule, call screening, or nonresponse to msg.
	R never available	2.21	See code 5.24. Examples: • KA informs Ir that R is out of town survey dates and cannot be reached. • KA informs Ir that R has long, unpredictable hours (for example, medical student or flight attendant). CBs and attempts to schedule Iw at odd hours did not work.

TABLE 5.1. *(CONTINUED)*

Code Group	Call Disposition	Code #	Explanations and Instructions for Use
	Telephone answering device	2.22	General code for recorded or automated msg which confirms residential HH or HH with home business. Irs may or may not have left msg.
	Message left	2.221	Scripted msg(s) left by Ir for R did not yield completed Iw despite CBs. See code 5.35.
	No message left	2.222	Irs hang up TP before R's recorded msg ends.
	Other	2.3	General code for various other call outcomes with eligible R.
	Dead	2.31	R has died. CATI will remove this TP# from the calling queue.
	Physically or mentally unable or incompetent	2.32	R's condition temporary (cold, flu, fever, drunk, stoned) but no CB before survey was completed. See code 5.21.
			KA explained R terminally ill, too chronically ill, too senile for the task while survey was in the field, or tragic circumstances.
			Hearing-disabled Rs not interviewed with alternate resources, like TTY.
	Language problems	2.33	General code for language barrier preventing Iw.
	Household-level language problem	2.331	No one in HH speaks English or other languages on Ir staff. Communication impossible.
	R language problem	2.332	R does not speak English.
	No interviewer available for needed language	2.333	Failed attempts to locate translator on Ir staff, in HH, or elsewhere.

(continued)

TABLE 5.1. *(CONTINUED)*

Code Group	Call Disposition	Code #	Explanations and Instructions for Use
	Miscellaneous	2.35	Rarely used code. Examples: • If Ir knows R personally or by reputation, the case must be passed to another Ir to ensure confidentiality. Schedule quick CB with explanatory msg for next Ir. • Duplicate TP#. R claims to have already completed Iw and accurately repeats subject matter. Usually a result of sample problems or multiple TP lines within HH. Apologize. Make sure TP# is removed from call queue. • KA says R has taken a vow of silence.
3. Unknown Eligibility, Noninterview			Unable to determine whether TP# represents a HH or whether known HH contains an eligible R.
	Unknown if housing unit	3.1	General code for inability to determine if TP# represents an HH.
	Not attempted or worked	3.11	TP# was never called before data collection ended. The presence of Rs and their eligibility is unknown.
	Always busy	3.12	Busy signal. CATI automatically schedules CBs every few minutes, but busy signal persists. No Ir spoke with a person.
	No answer	3.13	TP rings more than 8 times with no answer by person or TAM. CATI automatically schedules CBs at different times of day and days of week. No Ir has spoken with a person.
	Telephone answering device (DK if residential)	3.14	TP consistently answered by TAM, but msg does not indicate HH, business, or other. Leave msg if instructed. Schedule CB as instructed.

TABLE 5.1. *(CONTINUED)*

Code Group	Call Disposition	Code #	Explanations and Instructions for Use
	Telecommunication technological barriers, such as call blocking	3.15	TP call is met with call screening, call blocking, or other telecommunication technology that creates a barrier. Attempts to get through were fruitless. See code 5.14.
	Technical phone problems	3.16	Odd line sounds, no connection. TP company msg indicates circuit overload, bad TP line, TP company equipment switching problems, and so forth. Ir cannot hear R or vice versa. Line quality is too poor to conduct Iw. CBs to code 5.14 did not determine whether this is an eligible HH or has an eligible R.
	Household #, eligible R unknown	3.2	Survey-specific code for targeted sample. Ir determines this TP# is residential, but existence of eligible R unknown. Schedule CB 3–5 days ahead (depending on # of weeks survey will be in the field) at a different time of day. Hope to get R upon CB to ask screening Qs.
	No screener completed	3.21	See code 3.2. If you see this code in the CB queue, review refusal conversion skills for getting past GK.
	Other	3.9	Rarely used code. Example: no adult in HH at time of call. Try to obtain information on when adults will return and schedule CB for that then.
4. Not Eligible			CATI removes these TP#s from the calling queue when Ir assigns these codes. Follow instructions carefully to be sure no R is available or appropriate. Some circumstances may result in Iws.
	Out of sample area	4.1	Screening Qs reveal HH TP# outside geopolitical sample area. Occurs most often with RDD samples of small areas. Offer sincere thank-you and good-bye.

(continued)

TABLE 5.1. *(CONTINUED)*

Code Group	Call Disposition	Code #	Explanations and Instructions for Use
	Fax/data line	4.2	Loud beeping or squealing sound. Do not use this code if KA says HH fax/modem line is also used for regular calling.
	Nonworking or disconnected number	4.3	General code for TP# problems. Not to be confused with technical TP problems (3.16).
	Nonworking number	4.31	Nothing happens after you dial; no dial tone or busy signal. Manually redial TP# twice before using this code.
	Disconnected number	4.32	Operator msg says TP# is disconnected. For a list sample or a poverty sample, you may be asked to CB a week or two later, to verify that it is still disconnected.
	Temporarily out of service	4.33	Operator msg says TP# is temporarily out of service, for example, due to a storm. Schedule CB 3–5 days ahead (depending on # of weeks survey will be in the field).
	Special technological circumstances	4.4	General code for changed TP#s, CPs, pagers, and call forwarding. Many situations can result in completed Iws, so read instructions carefully. For unusual circumstances, ask supervisor before proceeding.
	Number changed	4.41	Operator msg says this TP# is no longer in service and gives a new TP#. Or, for list sample, KA says R no longer lives there but offers R's new TP#. Write down new TP# and call it immediately. If R available, verify former TP# and location; if same location as original #, proceed with Iw. If new location inside survey's geographical boundaries, proceed with Iw. If new location outside survey boundaries, explain ineligibility and thank R for assistance. For other situations, check with supervisor. Be sure to record new TP# and circumstances in Ir msg box. Give new TP# to supervisor.
	Cell phone	4.42	KA says this is a CP. If CPO HH, attempt Iw. If not, apologize for calling the wrong TP#.

TABLE 5.1. *(CONTINUED)*

Code Group	Call Disposition	Code #	Explanations and Instructions for Use
	Call forwarding	4.43	General CF code. Rarely can Irs hear automatic CF because connection usually takes just a few seconds more. If you suspect CF, ask R. If somehow you know CF, determine from where to where.
	Residence to residence	4.431	If CF from HH to HH, from HH to CP, from HH to nonresidence, or within HH, proceed with Iw attempt. Basically, the CF still represents R's home TP#.
	Nonresidence to residence	4.432	If CF from nonresidence (such as R's business) to residence, the case is not eligible.
	Pagers	4.44	Pager #s are indicated by an oral msg asking you to leave your TP#. Do not do it.
	Nonresidence	4.5	General code for nonresidences. A real person or a clear recorded msg must confirm that this is a business, government agency, nonprofit, or other nonresidence.
	Business, government office, other organization	4.51	If this is a business located in a home, and TP# is used solely for business, use this code. If TP# is used for both home and business, attempt Iw.
	Institution	4.52	Person or msg clearly indicates this is a jail, monastery, home for disabled teens, convalescent home, sanitarium, or other institutional setting. If list sample, ask to speak with R. If RDD sample, apologize and hang up.
	Group quarters	4.53	Person or msg clearly indicates this is a sorority, fraternity, commune, campground, cowboy bunkhouse, room shared by several migrant farmworkers, military barracks, or other noninstitutional group quarters. If list sample, ask to speak with R. If RDD sample, apologize and hang up.

(continued)

TABLE 5.1. *(CONTINUED)*

Code Group	Call Disposition	Code #	Explanations and Instructions for Use
	No eligible R	4.7	Survey-specific code for targeted sample. No HH member meets survey's requirements. For example, no commuters or no likely voters. May be automatically assigned by CATI when survey skip logic discovers ineligible R. May also be used with advance permission in certain unusual situations, such as no one in HH age 18+.
	Quota filled	4.8	Survey-specific code for targeted sample. Automatically assigned by CATI when survey skip logic discovers no more Rs like this needed.

Source: Adapted from American Association for Public Opinion Research, 2006, *Standard definitions: Final dispositions of case codes and outcome rates for surveys,* retrieved November 2006 from *http://www.aapor.org/pdfs/standarddefs_4.pdf*.

In-Progress Call Disposition Codes

In-progress (or temporary) call disposition codes, shown in Table 5.2, are for interviewers; they are not for calculating response rates and refusal rates. They tell you the outcome of each prior call to a respondent that did not result in a final call disposition. At the end of a survey, any cases that still have these temporary codes will be assigned an appropriate final disposition code.

In-progress codes are for interviewers because you will use them, along with prior interviewers' messages, to develop strategies for approaching respondents in callbacks. The information in these codes and in interviewer messages is important because interviewers often call a telephone number several times before they actually speak with a person or reach the intended respondent.

AAPOR offers no recommendations on in-progress call disposition codes. Table 5.2 offers several examples, such as "potential refusal," "phone slam," "respondent not home, call back," and "respondent too busy now, call back later." Your employer is likely to use temporary call disposition codes that are similar to these, but they may not be identical.

Again, read each call disposition code carefully, with special attention to the explanations and instructions for use. Note that the in-progress codes offered here

TABLE 5.2. IN-PROGRESS OR TEMPORARY CALL DISPOSITION CODES FOR TELEPHONE SURVEYS.

Code Group	Call Disposition	Code #	Explanations and Instructions for Use
5. In-progress or temporary codes			These in-progress call disposition codes all require Ir CBs before a final call disposition code is assigned.
	Potential refusal	5.1	General code for initial refusal, break-off, or use of technological devices to force refusal.
	Initial refusal	5.11	Initial or "soft" refusals require CBs. See Table 6.2 for examples. A protective GK, recorded msg, or paid go-between cannot refuse on an eligible R's behalf. R must give informed dissent.
			• Ir reads the introduction, R understands survey purpose, hears informed consent language, hears you are not selling, and gives a soft refusal, such as "I'm too busy." Refusal conversion tactics might work. Schedule CB 3–5 days ahead (depending on number of weeks the survey will be in the field) at a different time of day. Hope to get R at a better time or in a better mood. If you see this code in the CB queue, read prior Ir's comments carefully, and review refusal conversion skills.
			• For HH surveys in which any willing adult can be Iwed, try to determine availability of other adults in HH. Schedule CB for a different time of day and different day of week, hoping to catch another adult then.

(continued)

TABLE 5.2. *(CONTINUED)*

Code Group	Call Disposition	Code #	Explanations and Instructions for Use
			• For surveys of selected individuals, if a GK tries to refuse on R's behalf, explain that only Rs themselves can refuse. Try to determine when you can best reach R. If GK will not give such info, schedule CB for a different time of day and different day of week, hoping to catch R then.
			• R refuses partway through Iw. Schedule CB for 1–2 days hence with a different Ir who should use ref conversion techniques.
	Phone slam	5.12	R or KA hangs up before you finish reading the survey introduction. This is not a refusal, because person does not know your call's purpose. R cannot give informed dissent without hearing all elements of informed consent. Schedule CB 3–5 days ahead (depending on number of weeks survey will be in the field) at a different time of day. Upon CB, hope to get different person. CB too soon risks angry R. *Not to be confused with initial refusal!*
	Break-off	5.13	R begins Iw but refuses partway through or TP disconnects. For disconnect without warning, CB immediately and apologize for bad connection, even though it may have been deliberate. For refusal partway through, try to make appointment to finish the next day or another day and time convenient to R. Try to determine reason for break-off. Leave detailed msg for next Ir. Upon CB, CATI should restart where break-off occurred.
	Technological barrier	5.14	TP call is met with call screening, call blocking, or other telecommunication technologies that create a barrier or seek to refuse the call outright. Seek clues to determine whether this is a residential #. Examples:

TABLE 5.2. *(CONTINUED)*

Code Group	Call Disposition	Code #	Explanations and Instructions for Use
			• An automated voice allows you to type in your TP# or leave a short msg. Ask supervisor whether to leave msg or schedule CB.
			• TP blocking device stops nonapproved names and TP#s in incoming calls. But recorded msg indicates it might accept call later and requests that you state name and purpose. Leave scripted msg only if instructed by supervisor. Schedule CB a few days ahead to give R time to check out your SRO.
			• Answering service. R pays private operator to screen calls. If instructed by supervisor, read survey introduction to operator, request permission to conduct Iw, and say you will CB. Schedule CB for 1–2 days later. If possible, leave toll-free TP# for R to CB to arrange Iw.
			• Sometimes TP lines seem to cross. For example, in a list sample survey, you call the given TP# and ask for named R; KA says no such person has ever lived there and they have had this TP# for years. In verifying the TP#, you find that the TP# you dialed does not match the TP# of that HH. Apologize and redial. If you get the same person again, apologize sincerely and explain seemingly crossed TP lines. Schedule CB for a few days ahead, with clear explanation for next Ir. If the same thing happens again, assign code 3.16 and schedule CB beyond survey dates.
	Temporary delays	5.2	General code for illness, busy-ness, and other conditions causing temporary delay.
	R too ill/CB	5.21	If R's condition is temporary (cold, flu, fever, drunk, or stoned) and will feel better before survey is completed, schedule CB a few days ahead.

(continued)

TABLE 5.2. *(CONTINUED)*

Code Group	Call Disposition	Code #	Explanations and Instructions for Use
			If R's condition permanent or will extend through survey duration, use code 2.32 and schedule CB beyond survey dates.
			For hearing-disabled Rs, use public TTY service if available in your state (for example, Oregon Relay 1-800-735-1232). If not, use code 2.32 and schedule CB beyond survey dates.
	R not home/CB	5.22	Specified R is not home. Schedule CB at a time when R will be home. If no window of time was specified, follow your SRO's CB rules.
	R too busy now/CB	5.23	Specified R is too busy now. Schedule CB at a time frame that R specifies. If R did not specify a window of time, follow your SRO's CB rules. *Note*: Some R's say "too busy" as a polite "no," but we do not understand that.
	R too busy always/CB	5.24	KA informs Ir that R has long, unpredictable hours (for example, medical student or flight attendant). Try to determine when R will be in to schedule CB. Offer to CB at odd hours. Stress that you can schedule Iw at R's convenience. Try scheduling CBs at extreme hours within calling hours.
	Definite appointment	5.25	R requests that an Ir CB at a specified time on a specified day.
	Indefinite appointment	5.26	R is likely to be home during a block of time on a given day. Leave a clear, detailed msg for the next Ir.
Other		5.3	General code for cases requiring CBs.
	Tracking, attempting to locate	5.31	Usually used with list samples. KA (such as parent) is checking for new #, getting permission to give out new #, or gives Ir information to locate R's new TP#. Leave clear explanation in msg box for next Ir. If KA is doing the work, schedule CB for less than 7 days hence. Express gratitude.
	Language problems	5.32	Language barriers. Ask what language R speaks, try to decipher it, or make an educated guess. Record language in msg box so that CB can be assigned to an appropriate bilingual Ir.

TABLE 5.2. *(CONTINUED)*

Code Group	Call Disposition	Code #	Explanations and Instructions for Use
			Some SROs allow bilingual adult family member to translate. If so, determine whether or when that person will be available and schedule Iw accordingly. Ask supervisor whether child (less than age 17) may translate on adult's behalf.
	Technical phone problems	5.33	Examples include: • Odd line sounds, no connection. • TP company msg indicates circuit overload, bad TP line, TP company equipment switching problems, and so forth. • Person answers, but cannot hear Ir or vice versa. • Person answers, but line quality too poor for Iw. Redial TP# twice before assigning this code. Schedule CB for 2–3 days hence to determine whether this is a residential TP# with an eligible R.
	Screening Qs needed	5.34	Survey-specific code for targeted sample. Ir has determined this TP# is residential, but has not conducted screening Ir to determine whether it contains an eligible R, possibly due to GK. If you see this code in the CB queue, review refusal conversion skills for getting past GK. Hope to get R upon CB to conduct screener. See codes 3.2 and 3.21.
	Left message for R	5.35	If instructed by supervisor or in project-specific training, Irs read scripted msg about survey into R's TAM. May also be used if R scheduled Iw for a certain time but did not pick up TP at that time; leave msg to let R know you tried. Only leave scripted, approved msg. Schedule CB for next day or two hence.

start with the numeral 5—to indicate the fifth broad category of possible call outcomes. To the extent possible, the in-progress code numbers correspond to the final call disposition codes.

All these call disposition codes can seem intimidating at first, but you will be surprised at how quickly they become second nature, especially given that most survey organizations use much-shortened sets of these codes. You will find that these codes, combined with previous interviewers' messages, are a great help as you scope out your next call. Again, you do not have to memorize each code number itself, because most CATI systems show short descriptors on the screen instead of, or in addition to, the actual numerical codes. You must, however, understand the situations in which to use each code.

When you are sitting at your interviewing station and looking over a case you are supposed to call, it can be daunting to see a previous initial refusal or repeated phone slams. Such cases challenge most interviewers in attempting to develop a callback strategy. Some interviewers are tempted to fake a call disposition code so that they do not have to talk with Mr. Rude again: for example, they might think of assigning a nonresidence code to the case instead of risking another phone slam. Do not be tempted. This is falsification. When supervisors discover it, as they inevitably will, interviewers who falsify are fired. A far better tactic is to accept the challenge of the job.

Your most difficult task will be persuading every single randomly selected respondent to participate in an interview, no matter how grouchy or skeptical he or she may seem at first. In fact, sometimes the respondents who initially refuse end up giving significantly longer and more detailed interviews than those who jump aboard eagerly at the first call. With practice you will be able to gain the confidence of skeptical people, busy people, and indifferent people. You will also develop a thick skin, knowing that grouches and cynics are not judging you as a person.

Leaving Messages for the Next Interviewer

Almost all CATI systems have a message box on the callback screen where one interviewer can convey to the next interviewer useful information learned about the respondent. These messages are as essential as the call disposition codes, if not more so, in helping the next interviewer figure out the best way to approach a potential respondent when calling the next time. Pass along to subsequent interviewers the kinds of messages that you wish they would leave you.

Your messages should include the sex or status of the person with whom you spoke (if you can determine it), as well as information on the best time to call back.

The space is limited, so use the acronyms and abbreviations in Table 1.2. Never make up your own acronyms. Here are some examples of useful messages: "Child said mom comes home from work at 5:30 PM"; "AF sounds drunk"; "Secretary GK for boss"; "MR is day sleeper; CB 2–3:30p weekdays"; "Death in family; CB in 3 weeks." Clear, detailed messages will assist the next interviewer in locating the proper respondent and understanding any conditions that might affect that person's ability to respond to the survey and the interviewer's ability to conduct it.

Do not leave messages that may seem cute but could be misunderstood. A humorous young interviewer who worked for me once left this message: "suspected child abuse in background." The next interviewer read it and wondered if we should call the child protection services. We later learned that the original interviewer had intended the comment to be funny. The kids in the background were whooping it up at a rambunctious indoor birthday party, and the mother had asked to be called back at another time. In some states suspected child abuse or elder abuse must be reported to authorities. This can create enormous problems for survey researchers and for respondents to whom we have promised anonymity or confidentiality. If you have solid evidence of abuse, tell your supervisor. Under no circumstances should you attempt to handle the situation by yourself.

Scheduling Callbacks

CATI is programmed to schedule callbacks automatically for certain call dispositions, such as those of unknown eligibility (codes beginning with 3). After talking with someone at the telephone number, the interviewer can schedule subsequent callbacks if they are needed to complete an interview. In scheduling each callback, you take into consideration your experiences with respondents or other informants at that telephone number.

Sometimes respondents request an exact time and day for an interview. If they do, make sure an interviewer on the project actually calls them then. It is extremely disappointing when a cooperative respondent waits for the call to come and gradually becomes less obliging when the call comes late or on the next day. Sometimes respondents suggest a vague block of time in the future ("call me back on Tuesday"). At other times, an informant may give you blocks of time when an interviewer is most likely to reach the intended respondent. Get as much detail as you can on the time of day, day of the week, and the actual calendar date. Keeping a calendar posted in the interviewing stations helps in scheduling interview appointments.

Every survey organization has its own rules for scheduling callbacks for certain call disposition codes. Some places, for example, instruct interviewers to wait a full week before calling back phone slams, initial refusals, and break-offs; others wait three days. Sometimes callbacks are scheduled within shorter time frames as the survey nears the end of data collection. Make sure that you know your employer's rules and follow them faithfully.

When scheduling a callback for an initial refusal or phone slam, be sure to vary the callback time. For example, if you received an initial refusal at 6:00 PM on Monday and your employer's rules are to wait at least seven days before calling again, schedule the callback for 8:00 PM the next Monday or noon the next Tuesday. Again, be sure to leave a clear, informative note for the next interviewer.

Also make sure that you schedule callbacks during your employer's calling hours. Most survey organizations do not call on Sundays mornings because that is a traditional time of worship for Christians. Some organizations do not call at all on Sundays. Traditionally, survey organizations also do not call on Christian holidays, that is, Christmas and Easter, or on certain other holidays, such as the Fourth of July and Thanksgiving. But they vary in their approaches to the holidays of other religions and to secular holidays such as New Year's Day, Martin Luther King Day, and Labor Day. In my experience, these latter holidays can be quite productive for interviewing, as can the days just before and just after religious holidays. The reasons seem to be that you can reach many people who would normally be at work, those people tend to be in a generous mood (especially in December), and some respondents treat interviewers sympathetically for having to work on a holiday.

The bottom line is this: know your employer's calling schedule and callback protocols in advance and then carefully arrange callbacks in accordance with those factors.

Common Mistakes in Scheduling Callbacks

Learn to use your CATI system's call scheduling accurately. New interviewers make three common call scheduling errors: (1) failing to specify AM or PM, (2) neglecting to indicate the time zone, and (3) counting forward to the wrong day of the week.

If a respondent asks to be called between "2:00 and 4:00 tomorrow," you can safely assume that he or she means PM. Surely no respondent would request a callback between 2:00 AM and 4:00 AM. However, if you forget to specify PM, CATI may default the case to AM. Because interviewers do not typically work then, a case like this will often be overlooked or it may get lost in the CATI system.

> The three cardinal rules of scheduling callbacks:
>
> 1. Check AM or PM.
> 2. Check the time zone.
> 3. Make sure you have the correct day of the week.

Forgetting about time zones is equally disastrous. More than once I have witnessed an interviewer working on the Pacific Coast calling a cooperative respondent for a scheduled interview at 8:30 PM only to find that the person actually lives in the Eastern U.S. time zone and thus is receiving the call at 11:30 PM. Such mistakes do not amuse respondents. A cooperative respondent can quickly become a final refusal. The interviewers who arranged the callbacks I witnessed forgot to indicate the time zone or just assumed it was the Pacific time zone. Always check your time zones when scheduling callbacks.

When a respondent asks to be called back in a certain number of days, count forward correctly and take into account the time of day you and the respondent spoke. For example, say that at 6:00 PM on Monday a potential respondent asks you to call back in three days. You should count forward three days: Tuesday would be Day 1, Wednesday would be Day 2, and Thursday would be Day 3. However, you also must take into account the time of day. If you schedule the callback for any time on Thursday, the person may be called on Thursday morning, which is not an entire three days from the original call. In this case you should schedule the callback in CATI for *later than* 6:00 PM on Thursday. To be completely sure, attempt to verify the day of the week with respondents and the time of day they would prefer the callback.

Effects of Telephone Answering Machines on Call Scheduling

The proliferation of different types of telephone answering machines and call screening devices has challenged survey researchers and changed the way in which we try to reach respondents. Estimates of the number of households with answering machines and caller ID varies from two-thirds to three-fourths of all households with phones. Estimates of the percentage of households that use these devices to screen incoming calls vary from 43 percent to 55 percent.

In order to enhance the chance of reaching respondents and gaining their cooperation in these circumstances, survey researchers use three basic strategies: (1) sending an explanatory precontact letter in advance, (2) calling more frequently, and (3) leaving messages. It is also helpful if the survey organization's name appears on households' caller ID, instead of "anonymous" or a blank.

> Vary the times of day and the days of the week when scheduling callbacks to reluctant households.

Experimental evidence shows that precontact letters enhance telephone respondents' cooperation most. Precontact letters explain that an interviewer will be calling, from where, and why. They present the survey's purpose, tell respondents how they were selected and why they are important, explain the elements of informed consent, and offer a telephone number for respondents to call or a Web site for them to visit if they have questions. Precontact letters contain much the same information as the introduction to a telephone interview does, but having it on paper allows respondents to study the details, think about their decision to participate, and decide in advance to participate. In this way, precontact letters can enhance the efficiency of telephone interviewing.

Precontact letters are most often sent in advance of confidential list sample surveys. For anonymous RDD surveys, sending precontact letters should be impossible. However, some vendors will, for a fee, match RDD telephone numbers to addresses. The process goes something like this: a survey research organization computer-generates a list of RDD numbers and e-mails it to the vendor; the vendor cross-checks the RDD telephone numbers with its own list of telephone numbers and matching addresses (which it has compiled from many sources); then the vendor e-mails the matched list back. The results are often messy, with multiple addresses for some telephone numbers and no addresses for others. A telephone number with no matching address could be a nonworking number—or not. For a higher fee, vendors will also supply the names that go with each address and telephone number. That practice, however, changes the survey from anonymous to confidential, and interviewers sometimes find that the names are embarrassingly out of date (for example, Mrs. Smith says that Mr. Smith died eight years ago).

Increasing the number of calls to households enhances the chance that someone will pick up the telephone rather than letting the answering machine do it. Every survey organization has its own rule for the minimum number of callbacks interviewers must make to each telephone number. Some specify twenty or more callbacks if human contact has been made at some point or if a telephone answering machine clearly indicates a residence. Others require just three to eight calls. The survey research industry has no firm rules or recommendations on how many dial attempts each number should receive. Calling fewer times enhances the efficiency of interviewers' time but it can undermine coverage rates. Calling many times risks potential respondents' ire. Some people feel harassed when they see eleven interview attempts on their caller ID over a two-day period, even though they have not spoken with an interviewer.

The efficacy of leaving messages on respondents' telephone answering machines is less clearly established. Survey researchers have not agreed on what to say or on what call attempt to leave such messages (the first call? the second? the fifth?). A script for an interviewer to read into an answering machine might look something like this:

Hello, this is [organization name] *calling. We are conducting an anonymous nationwide survey about your views on transportation issues. We will be calling you back and hope you will help us with this important survey. If you have questions, please call us at 1-800-xxx-xxxx. Thank you.*

The toll-free callback number helps to affirm the authenticity of the survey research organization.

A remarkable number of screening households can be reached using one or more of these three strategies. Once respondents know that a survey is legitimate, many choose to participate because it is fun or challenging, they feel a sense of civic duty or altruism, or they are lonely and enjoy the human contact. As DNC lists become established, more potential respondents should be able to distinguish a scientific survey from sugging or frugging.

Summing Up

Calling is one of an interviewer's most pervasive activities. You will call many more numbers than you will conduct interviews. You might even spend more time dialing and recording call disposition codes than talking at certain stages of the data collection process. The essential skills that you must learn from this chapter are how to operate the telephone system for local and long distance calls, how to apply call disposition codes, what to say in brief messages for the next interviewer, and when to schedule callbacks. Next, you will learn how to speak with respondents.

CHAPTER SIX

INTRODUCING THE STANDARDIZED INTERVIEW

After all that dialing, at last someone answers their phone. This chapter explains what to do next—how to introduce the interview and gain respondents' voluntary participation. As in the preceding chapter, we will move more or less chronologically through your tasks in the first minutes of contact with respondents and their households. (For ease of presentation, the discussion in this and the following chapters focuses on conducting household surveys, but telephone surveys of organizations and named individuals will follow similar protocols.) These few crucial moments with respondents include your initial "hello," the survey introduction, and respondent selection procedures. This chapter also includes detailed suggestions on how to address respondents' concerns before the interview begins and how to avoid refusals. We start, however, with much more basic skills that all interviewers need to develop, namely how to control their voices.

Controlling Your Voice

When someone picks up the telephone and you begin to speak, the only things your listener has at that moment to judge the survey are the words you speak and how you say them. Characteristics of your voice can determine a respondent's decision to participate. Your voice can also help you control the interview once it begins. Very few new interviewers have a perfect voice for interviewing. Rather, they develop their interviewing voices with practice. No matter if your voice is high pitched or low pitched, no matter if you have some type of accent or marbles in your mouth, you can and must learn to control the tone of your voice, the rate at which you utter words, and your volume.

Your tone of your voice should be at once pleasant, friendly, and sincere, yet businesslike, direct, and slightly distant. An overly interested, sympathetic tone may make you sound as though you want to be the respondent's new best friend, which you actually do not, and cannot, want. An overly practiced, rapid delivery may make you sound like a slick salesperson, which you are not. The guidelines that follow will help you train your voice to convey professionalism and confidence.

Know What You Will Say

Essential to voice control is knowing in advance what you are going to say. Memorize your introductory script and all the variants you may need to answer respondents' questions. You must answer respondents' questions without pause or hesitation. Never, ever giggle nervously; never say "um," "uh," or "ah"; and do not audibly flip through papers or reach for your sheet of answers to common questions. Such interviewer behaviors suggest inexperience, which may raise doubts in respondents' minds and possibly create bad feelings about you, whom you represent (your employer and the survey sponsor), the survey itself, and the prospect of doing the interview.

> When uttering statements, your voice pitch should descend. When uttering questions, your voice pitch should rise, but just a little.

Another problem may occur with certain respondents who think they can take advantage of an inexperienced interviewer; they agree to do the survey, but they tease and attempt to sidetrack you throughout, making you wonder later if their answers were real. To avoid these problems, practice, practice, practice—during training sessions, with a buddy, and alone at home. If you regard your work seriously, your respondents will too because it will be apparent in your voice. Again, memorize your script.

Enunciate Each Word Clearly

Enunciate. Pronounce each syllable, word, and phrase clearly and exactly. Do not slur. Do not run sentences together. The questions and probes that constitute a professional interview represent decades of experimentation and experience. They have been created and repeatedly pretested with care by a professional staff. Your job is to read them exactly as they are written, articulately. Most general population surveys are written at about the tenth-grade level, so the average respondent should be able to understand the meaning of the words you say, if you say them clearly.

Manage Your Voice

Learn to manage the pitch, modulation, timbre, and volume of your voice. Your voice pitch should generally go down as you read a statement. It should rise just slightly when you read a question. Have you ever noticed that some people always seem to speak in questions, even when they utter statements? The pitch of their voice rises at the end of each sentence, even if they are not asking a question. (Think of the character Cher as played by Alicia Silverstone in the movie *Clueless*. Cher would speak that previous sentence as though it were punctuated this way: "The pitch of their voice rises? at the end of each sentence? even if they are not asking a question?") This style of speech conveys immaturity, inexperience, and a lack of confidence. It is especially deadly in the opening exchanges of an interview.

Figure 6.1 illustrates how a poorly trained interviewer's voice pitch rises and falls during the opening sentences of a list sample interview. The script reads: "Hello. May I please speak with Jane Doe? Thank you." However, as the graph line illustrates, this interviewer reads "hello" as a question. The interviewer's voice then peaks two more times. A voice that rises three times while uttering ten words suggests that the speaker questions his or her own ability and self-worth.

Read the sentences in Figure 6.1 aloud yourself, as they are graphed and as if you were speaking on a telephone. Listen to your voice. When you say, "Hello," hear how your voice goes up on the second syllable. When you say, "May I please speak with Jane Doe?" hear how your voice rises when you say "I" and "Doe." With the word "thank," your voice returns to its opening pitch. With "you," it drops lower. This is the *Clueless* way to speak with respondents. It lacks modulation and control. It suggests uncertainty, lack of skill, and an inappropriate sense of self-apology.

Now examine Figure 6.2 for comparison. It graphically illustrates how a well-trained telephone interviewer's voice rises and falls with the first sentences in a list sample interview. The interviewer says "Hello" as a statement. The falling pitch on the second syllable suggests confidence. The interviewer's voice rises slightly when saying "May I," and then steadily declines until the word "Jane," suggesting that the interviewer is in control. The voice rises slightly for

FIGURE 6.1. DIAGRAM OF POOR VOICE PITCH.

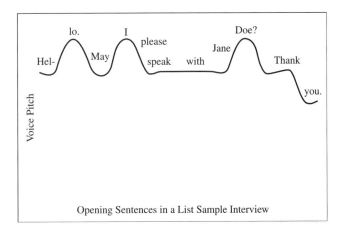

Opening Sentences in a List Sample Interview

FIGURE 6.2. DIAGRAM OF BETTER VOICE PITCH.

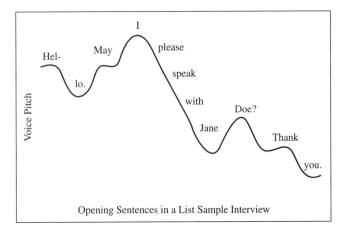

Opening Sentences in a List Sample Interview

the final word in this sentence, "Doe," indicating that a question has been asked. For the statement "Thank you," the interviewer's voice pitch is lowest on the word "you," and it is substantially lower than his or her opening voice level. A well-modulated voice pitch like this indicates that interviewers know what they are doing, and that they are knowledgeable and secure in their skills.

Practice reading the words in Figure 6.2 aloud, modulating your voice in the recommended way. The pitch of your voice should rise, just slightly, only at the end of questions. For statements, your pitch should be lower at the end of the sentence than it was at the beginning. Tape-record yourself while role-playing with another interviewer. Listen to each sentence you utter. Draw a line to show how your voice's pitch changes. Practice, practice, practice until your voice naturally modulates in the manner suggested here. People who routinely speak in a monotone, or who seem to be reading a book aloud instead of conducting a conversational interview, rarely make good interviewers.

Excellent interviewers also attend to the quality of sound in their voices, focusing on timbre and volume. Speaking from the chest creates a more attractive voice than the shallow sound of speaking through the mouth or nose. The volume of an interviewer's voice should be normal, neither too loud nor too soft. The best indicator of your voice's volume comes from listener feedback.

Pay attention to the feedback you receive from others about how loudly or softly you speak. Some people shout and some whisper without knowing it. People who are slightly hard of hearing, due to natural aging or overexposure to loud machinery or music, have a tendency to shout. Some people "swallow" their sentences, that is, they start out talking at a normal volume and then speak more softly at the end, especially when they are uncertain or shy. Your respondents should not have to ask you to "speak up." They also should not have to hold their telephones five inches from their ears to hear you properly.

The people involved in your interviewer training will tell you if you need to raise or lower your voice. Then practice with a tape recorder until an appropriate volume and resonance becomes second nature to you.

Control Your Speaking Pace

Finally, the pace at which you speak should be normal or slightly brisk, unless a respondent requests otherwise or active listening indicates that you should change pace. For example, if someone asks you to repeat a question more than once, you should slow down. (This may be necessary, with the elderly, who are more often hard of hearing.) With people who say they are busy, speed up. Several interviewer training manuals say that interviewers should speak about two words per second, but the origin of that maxim is unclear. One important difference between ordinary conversation and an interview is that the time between your utterances and your respondent's replies should be as short as possible. If you pause even slightly in the introduction, some respondents will use it as an excuse to refuse.

> Minimize the time between your utterances and your respondent's replies.

With practice these speaking strategies will become habitual. Your voice will combine with the survey instrument's words in your own unique way to communicate a skilled and capable impression to respondents. These skills in turn will enhance your productivity. You will also learn to adapt your volume and your pace of speaking easily for particular respondents, especially elderly persons and non-native English speakers. You will know from your respondents' cues the directions in which to alter your speech; many people will be too shy to ask you outright to do so. Of course you should also display excellent telephone etiquette on all occasions. "Please" and "thank you" carry a lot of weight.

A Person Answers the Telephone

When somebody finally picks up the telephone, you have two immediate tasks: (1) determine whether this is a residential telephone number, and if so, (2) make sure you are speaking with an adult.

Usually it is easy to determine whether you have reached a nonresidential telephone number, because most people answering the phone for an organization or business start by stating the place's name: for example, Jaleno's Pizza or Roosevelt Middle School or First Congregational Church. Reply by first confirming that you have reached a business, school, church, or other type of organization, and then apologize. For example:

Oh, is this a business?
Yes, this is Jaleno's Pizza.
I am sorry. I must have called the wrong number. Good-bye.

> Note: All text read by interviewers is indicated in italics.

If you get an organization's answering machine, it too typically names the place. Assign the appropriate call disposition code and immediately move on to your next case.

The boundary between residential and nonresidential telephone numbers is sometimes blurry, particularly for self-employed persons and those who operate businesses from their home. If a potential respondent says that you have called their home business telephone number, ask whether it is dedicated solely to their business; if so, treat it as you would any other business. If this telephone line is used both for the respondent's work and regular household activities (that is, if friends, relatives, bill collectors, and business clients all call the same telephone number), treat the person as a potential respondent and go right into the survey introduction.

Similar issues arise in households with telephone numbers dedicated solely to a fax, modem, or other data purpose. Often such telephone numbers can be used for conversational purposes if the residents want to do so (they can hear the telephone ring), but they do not usually choose to do so. When they do answer such a telephone line, they may protest because they are not accustomed to using it. Treat this telephone number as representing a residence anyhow and jump right into the introduction. Telephone numbers dedicated to children's use should also be regarded as regular residential lines even though the family might not think of them that way.

Random-digit-dial (RDD) sampling procedures should prevent you from reaching cell or mobile telephones. If you are working from a list sample (for example, a list of the parents of high school seniors with the telephone numbers parents supplied to the school), you are more likely to reach a cell phone. You usually will not be able to tell when respondents take your call on a cell phone unless they volunteer that information. If they do tell you that, apologize (because each minute on a cell phone may cost the respondent money), explain how you got this telephone number, and then determine whether this is a cell-phone only household. For example:

I am sorry to have reached you on your cell phone. I am calling from [organization] *to conduct a survey with the parents of seniors at Elmtown High School, and this is the telephone number the school provided. Is this your household's only telephone number, or do you also have a regular telephone line in your home on which I could call you back?*

If the household has a landline, attempt to get the number. If this is a cell-phone-only household, attempt to conduct the interview. Volunteer to speak quickly to keep it as short as possible. Even though each minute may cost some respondents, many will be happy to speak with you. If not, use call disposition code 4.42 and immediately move on to the next case. For an RDD sample, cell phones are ineligible unless they represent cell-phone-only households.

Once you are sure you have a residential telephone number, your next step is to speak with an adult aged eighteen or older. Even in the rare instances in which you conduct telephone interviews with minors, you still must talk with a parent first. If a child or someone who sounds like a teenager answers the telephone, do not read the full survey introduction. Instead lead up to the introduction, with this:

Hello, I am calling from [organization]. *I need to speak to someone who is 18 or older. Would that be you?*

The minor hands the telephone over to a parent, or a young adult self-identifies as an eligible respondent. Then give the full introduction.

If the person who answers the telephone self-identifies as a guest of the household, ask to speak with an adult household member. If one is not available, ask:

What would be a convenient time to call back to speak with (her / him)?

Respondent Selection

You finally have a residence and an adult is on the telephone. Your next step—selecting a respondent—depends on the type of sample for your survey. You will work with three basic sample types: (1) list, (2) RDD–any adult, and (3) RDD–randomly selected adult. Part of your job will be to select the *units of analysis,* that is, the individuals that you intend to interview. Sometimes these units of analysis (or *cases*) are individuals speaking about themselves. At other times individuals speak on behalf of their families or households. In yet other types of surveys, the units of analysis are firms or organizations that individuals speak on behalf of. With any of these sample types, you may use screening questions to select a respondent.

List Samples

When working with list samples, you will ask for the survey respondent by name as soon as someone answers the telephone. For example:

May I please speak with Mary Smith?

As soon as the named person gets on the telephone, go right into the survey introduction. If the named person is not available, ask for a good time to call back to reach the person, and then schedule the callback appropriately. You may need to read part of the survey introduction in order to gain cooperation. Be sure to leave the next interviewer a message indicating the type of person with whom you spoke (a knowledgeable adult, a child, or someone else) and anything said about the respondent. Remember, no one may substitute for the named person.

RDD Samples–Any Adult

For some RDD samples, the unit of analysis is the household. This means you can speak with any knowledgeable adult who is willing to speak on behalf of the household. These are easy. Launch immediately into the introduction, as if you know that the person is interested and willing to participate. If the person says he or she is too busy or not interested, say,

I can speak with any adult at this telephone number. Please give the telephone to another adult in your home who is (is not busy/is interested).

If another person is not available at the moment, arrange a callback for a time he or she will be there. Also, try to obtain that person's first name or initials so that the next interviewer knows whom to ask for when calling back:

So that we know whom to ask for when we call back, what is that person's first name?

Do not press if the person who answered the telephone resists naming the other person. Again, you may need to read part of the survey introduction in order to gain cooperation.

RDD Samples–Randomly Selected Adult

For other RDD samples the unit of analysis is the individual. In other words, not only is the household randomly selected but an adult within the household is also randomly selected. You perform the task of randomly selecting an adult within each household. Luckily, almost 40 percent of all U.S. households have just one adult living in them.

The most typical way of randomly choosing an adult to complete the survey is to use the *most-recent-birthday* technique. In the population as a whole, birthdays are randomly distributed across the calendar year. Thus, choosing the person who most recently celebrated a birthday is a form of randomization. When using this method, the survey introduction contains a sentence something like this:

I need to talk with the adult in your household who most recently had a birthday. Would that be you?

Avoid sentences like this:

I need to talk with the adult in your household who most recently celebrated *a birthday.*

They invite smart alecks to remark:

Everyone here is too old to *celebrate* birthdays.

If the adult who most recently had a birthday is unavailable, arrange for a callback, using the procedures outlined above for RDD–any adult samples.

A much more difficult random selection method, especially on the telephone, is a series of questions that helps you build a household roster, that is, a list of all persons living there, usually with indicators of their age, sex, and sometimes first name or initials. Then you follow your employer's instructions on which adult to select. This is difficult to accomplish because you have explained in the introduction that the survey is about, for example, health or transportation or schools, but before you even ask a question on the topic, you have to ask unrelated questions that some respondents regard as unnecessary and even invasive. Moreover, the person who trusts you enough to give you that information may not be the one randomly selected. The most-recent-birthday technique is far easier to implement; some respondents even regard it as amusing.

Each survey research organization has its own, slightly varying procedures for randomly choosing an adult in a household to interview. For example, some organizations have interviewers read the entire survey introduction and then ask the questions to randomly choose an adult. Others have interviewers read part of the introduction, saving the whole introduction for the chosen respondent. You are responsible for learning and following your employer's protocol.

You still might be puzzled about why you have to randomly select an adult in the household. Would it not be easier on everyone just to interview the person who wants to participate? Of course, it would be easier on you, but a group of volunteers may differ systematically from all adults in the target population. Only a random sample of adults can accurately represent all adults in the target population (just as a spoonful of beans tells the cook whether the entire pot of beans is thoroughly cooked). Remember, telephones are attached to households, not persons, so an RDD sample is really a sample of households. In order to obtain a random sample of persons, you must perform another round of randomization at the level of the individual. That task, your task, is an essential step when researchers need a random sample of adults.

Screening Questions

With any of the three types of samples just described, interviewers may need to ask a *screening question,* that is, a question that determines who is eligible to participate in the survey. A screening question could, for example, reasonably start an election survey of registered voters only. In such a case the screening question might ask:

Are you registered to vote?

Similarly, a transportation survey might focus only on those with driver's licenses:

Do you have a current driver's license?

Only persons answering yes to the screening question continue with the survey. Others receive a polite, scripted thank-you and good-bye. Anytime researchers wish to study the members of registered lists, such as voters and drivers, obtaining a list sample is not difficult, especially with confidentiality guaranteed. In such cases the interviewer asks for a named person, and the screening question serves to verify that person's status. For an RDD–any adult survey, if you do not get a yes to the screening question, survey guidelines should allow you to ask to speak with another potential respondent in the household. For an RDD survey with a randomly selected adult, you will need to say good-bye and dial a new number.

Screening questions always belong at a survey's beginning. In some cases the screening question is placed among the first few sentences and before the more complicated protection of human subjects language. The idea here is to waste as little of potential respondents' time as possible. In other cases, an institutional review board (IRB) may demand that the screening question occur after a respondent has given informed consent for the survey.

Some complex survey designs of rare populations require interviewers to conduct short screening interviews. In these *screeners,* as they are sometimes called, the entire short interview is designed to seek people with certain characteristics. For example, in one survey in which I participated, it took over 15,000 screeners to locate 200 dual-career couples without children. (This was in the 1970s, when such couples were rarer.) To meet the study specifications, the couple had to have been married a certain number of years, each spouse had to work more than half time, and neither could have children from this marriage or any other marriage. Couples with the necessary characteristics were invited to participate in face-to-face interviews at a later date.

The Survey Introduction

The survey introduction is one of the most important parts of interviewing, for it determines whether you get a foot in the door. In just a few moments you must convey all the elements of informed consent, address respondents' concerns, and avoid an initial refusal. This section begins with an example of a real survey introduction, explains the elements of introductions and why they are present, offers suggestions on how to handle respondents' common questions and objections, and clarifies effective ways to prevent refusals. It also explains the nature of your brief relationship with a respondent and how to control it with your words, voice, and the attitude you convey. Read this section carefully because the quality of the introduction can make or break the entire interview.

> The quality of a survey's introduction can make or break the entire interview.

Each survey's introduction is designed to provide a clear and efficient way of introducing the interviewer and the survey's objective to respondents. The introduction aims to convey the survey's legitimacy, convince respondents that their participation is worthwhile, and obtain respondents' informed consent. Each survey's introduction will vary just as each survey's topic differs. Survey introductions also vary across organizations partly due to custom and partly because IRBs differ in their interpretations of laws protecting human subjects and thus in their requirements for what you should say. There is no single, correct way to phrase a telephone survey introduction, but they all contain common elements.

Exhibit 6.1 contains the opening script for the Transportation Needs and Issues Survey, which the author wrote for the Oregon Department of Transportation in 2003. Look at it now. First, note the words in uppercase letters. These are question names, interviewer instructions, and answer categories. By custom, interviewers never read aloud words that appear in uppercase letters. (Also, in this script "1" and "Ctrl/End" refer to coding keystrokes.)

Note the words and phrases in Exhibit 6.1 that appear in parentheses and brackets. This material is called *fill*. Words and phrases in parentheses represent obligatory fill. Interviewers must read one of the words or phrases offered, exercising their judgment to choose the fill that best suits their respondent. Words and phrases in square brackets are a type of fill offering optional language that interviewers may choose to use at their discretion, to help remind respondents and keep them on track. (Square brackets may also contain generic terms, such as

EXHIBIT 6.1. EXAMPLE OF A SURVEY INTRODUCTION.

Q:HELLO1
Hello. The Oregon Department of Transportation has asked the Survey Research Laboratory at [*organization*] to conduct a 16 to 20 minute survey with adults [age 18 or over] about transportation issues in your area. (This is/I am) _____, and I want to assure you that I am not selling a thing, and that this survey is completely anonymous and voluntary. [Please do not even tell me your name.]
1 R ON TELEPHONE
CTRL/END → SCHEDULE CALLBACK

Q:HELLO2
Do you have any questions about the survey before we begin?
1 NO QUESTIONS OR QUESTIONS ANSWERED, OK TO BEGIN SURVEY
HAS QUESTIONS → REFER TO "ANSWERS TO Rs' COMMON QUESTIONS"

Q:COOPERAT
We appreciate your cooperation. [I would like to begin the survey now.]
1 OK
CTRL/END NO

organization, that are to be replaced with specific names, such as your employer's organization name. These terms appear in a typeface that differs from the surrounding typeface.) Chapter Seven discusses how to use parenthetical and bracketed language in more detail.

Read the question named HELLO1 in Exhibit 6.1. In just a few sentences it tells the respondent who you are, why you are calling, where you are calling from, on whose behalf you are calling (the client or sponsor), the survey's purpose, the approximate interview length, your name, and that participation is anonymous and voluntary. These are the key elements of informed consent. When interviewing, read the survey introduction verbatim, pronounce the words clearly, and do not rush. If a respondent interrupts you, make sure that you cover each element of informed consent before going to the next computer-assisted telephone interviewing (CATI) system screen.

Our professional ethics require that we obtain each respondent's informed consent before beginning the interview. The second question, HELLO2, does so by asking the respondent if he or she has any questions. If the person has none, the interviewer acknowledges this in COOPERAT and proceeds with the interview. If the person does have questions, the interviewer must address them and then, in most cases, return to HELLO2 and COOPERAT before embarking on the interview. The only exception occurs when a respondent asks to "try out a few questions" before starting the interview.

You may have noticed that the survey introduction in Exhibit 6.1 does not start with a statement like this:

Hello. My name is [name], *and I am calling from* [organization].

That kind of introduction harkens back to the days of suggers and fruggers, who used similar first sentences. Another key sentence to avoid is:

How are you doing this (morning / afternoon / evening)?

This is a line used by salespeople and fundraisers in their second or third sentence. Instead, the introduction in Exhibit 6.1 starts with the name of the survey sponsor and the place from which you are calling and then goes right into the length and nature of the task. In my experience, conveying these four key elements in the first few seconds of the conversation is most effective for gaining respondents' immediate attention and cooperation.

Precontact Letters

Sometimes the principal investigators for a survey decide to send a *precontact letter* to respondents in advance of the survey, especially if the survey contains sensitive subject matter. Precontact letters contain all of the introductory language that interviewers would normally say—and more. They describe the survey, explain its benefits to society, tell how respondents were chosen, explain why each respondent is important, present all the informed consent language that respondents need to know, and provide a way for respondents to ask questions, such as a toll-free telephone number or e-mail address. They are printed on official letterhead, are usually hand signed, and have pretty stamps affixed to their envelopes. (Often interviewers who are between surveys are enlisted to help with the signing, stuffing, stamping, and mailing of precontact letters.)

Precontact letters help respondents make informed consent decisions and generally answer all their survey-related questions in advance. Some respondents scrutinize the letter carefully and will call or e-mail to get their questions answered in advance, to let the survey organization know the best times to reach them, or to make an interview appointment. Some cranks and hard refusals call in or e-mail their refusal to participate, thereby saving a lot of interviewer effort. Of course some people glance at the precontact letter, toss it away, and by the time an interviewer calls, have only a vague memory of having received it.

Surveys with precontact letters generally have shorter introductions, simplifying interviewers' tasks. These introductions are scripted so that interviewers first identify themselves, their employer, and the survey. Then they verify that the respondent received the letter and read it. If the respondent answers yes to the verification question, the interviewer asks a question like HELLO2 and proceeds with the interview. However, if a respondent does not remember the precontact letter, threw it away, or did not receive it, the interviewer may need to read it aloud or read another introductory script.

Addressing Potential Respondents' Questions and Concerns

Some respondents will have no questions in response to HELLO2 and will plunge into the survey immediately. Most respondents ask one or two token questions. They are basically cooperative, but you should treat them carefully. If you fumble now, their willingness may evaporate quickly. Usually only a few respondents have serious problems or concerns about the survey's legitimacy, their own privacy, and other issues. They might not be able to articulate their concerns clearly, yet they stubbornly will not participate until they are fully satisfied by your answers.

> Respondents' questions do not necessarily signify reluctance. Rather, their questions show that they have engaged with your request and taken it seriously.

Most potential respondents' questions are simple and directly related to the survey. Do not interpret their questions as indicating an attitude of unwillingness or opposition. On the contrary the people who have engaged with your survey request and taken it seriously are the ones who ask questions. Respondents' questions signal that you have your foot in the door.

Table 6.1 lists respondents' most common questions and concerns; interviewers' short, direct answers; and explanations of the reasons that you should use those answers. Again, the Transportation Needs and Issues Survey serves as an example. However, your answers will vary somewhat for each survey.

Listen to potential respondents carefully as they verbalize their issues. Answer only what respondents ask, and do so clearly and concisely. Tailor the information you provide to what respondents actually request, not to what you think they want to hear.

This stage is so important that you should memorize the exact phrases and sentences on the sheet of answers to common questions that was handed out at project-specific training and that you should have posted at your interviewing station for easy reference. These short answers contain more detail about the survey's purpose and sponsor, how respondents or their telephone numbers were

TABLE 6.1. HOW TO ADDRESS RESPONDENTS' QUESTIONS AND CONCERNS.

Respondent's Question	What to Say and Why
What is the purpose of this survey? How will the data be used?	R wants more detail about the survey topics. Do not go into detail about every topic in the survey. Two or three short sentences of increasing specificity should suffice. Read the first sentence from the answers to common questions. If R says nothing, go on to the second sentence, and then the third if necessary.
	The survey's purpose is to learn what Oregonians think about traffic congestion, highway construction, and how well the state is maintaining roads and bridges. The survey results will be used to help the (Oregon Department of Transportation/ODOT) plan for the future.
	It includes questions about gas taxes, traffic congestion, safety, bridges, how you usually travel, and how satisfied you are with Oregon highways.
	It can also help to emphasize that public opinion is important to the survey sponsor.
	Citizen's opinions are very important to [client name].
Who is (sponsoring/paying for) this survey?	You have already mentioned this in the introduction, but say it again. If the survey has multiple sponsors, naming the first two or three should suffice. In some market research studies, knowing the survey sponsor in advance could bias respondents' answers, but you should be able to tell them at the end.
How long will the survey take?	Answer with an exact number of minutes, usually based on estimates from pretesting. If the instrument has substantial skip logic, offer a range.
	The interview takes about eleven minutes.
	The interview will take approximately 16 to 20 minutes, depending on your answers.
	If you run out of time now, I can call back tomorrow to finish the rest.
	A few potential respondents can focus and answer questions as quickly as you can ask them. Use the *fast talk* strategy only with busy people who are willing at the moment and you might never catch them again.
	I can speak quickly to make the interview go faster.
Is this survey (confidential/anonymous)?	Your answers should be consistent with the type of survey and sample.
	Yes, most definitely. This survey is completely [anonymous/confidential].

(continued)

TABLE 6.1. *(CONTINUED)*

Respondent's Question	What to Say and Why
	I do not know your name, and I have no need to know it. All I want is your opinions.
	As soon as we are done with the interview, your telephone number is automatically erased.
	All results of the survey are released in the form of percentages and averages. It is not possible to identify any individual person or response in the results.
	[Confidentiality/anonymity] is very important to [organization].
	We are very careful to protect people's [confidentiality/anonymity].
How much does this survey cost?	You will never know the survey's actual budget.
	I just do not know.
	If your firm is employee owned or nonprofit, some Rs to like hear it.
	I can tell you that [organization] is nonprofit.
	It is best for you to deflect such questions by emphasizing the survey's importance.
What if I do not want to answer a question?	Human subjects' regulations require interviewers to allow Rs to skip any question they wish or terminate the Iw at any time. Saying just the first sentence below usually suffices.
	None of the questions in this survey are personal or sensitive in nature, but you may feel free to skip any question you wish.
	The second sentence below invites Rs to refuse the Iw altogether. Avoid using it, even if it is true.
	You may also terminate the survey at any time.
	Once an Iw is underway, few Rs ever skip a question or stop the Iw altogether, because most become invested in the task. But Rs like to know that they can.
How can I be sure that this is a legitimate survey?	You should have handy the names, TP numbers, and e-mail addresses of your SRO's key personnel and a client representative. Most Rs know nothing about IRBs or the OMB, and most SROs would prefer that their personnel rather than their IRBs explain human subjects protections. However, most IRBs want to be available to Rs.
	You may talk with my supervisor, [name]; (she/he) is right here.
	Please visit our Web site at www.[organization].org.

TABLE 6.1. *(CONTINUED)*

Respondent's Question	What to Say and Why
	You may contact [client name] *in* [client's organization] *at* [telephone number], *or e-mail him at* [e-mail address]. *You may call our Human Subjects Compliance Office at* [telephone number].
Who is in charge of this survey? May I talk to (her/him)?	A professional in your SRO should be available to take such calls. Few Rs actually call, but they find satisfaction in knowing that they can.
	Our director, [name], *would be happy to talk with you. You may contact her at* [telephone number]. *If she is not in her office, leave a message and she will call you back as soon as possible. Or feel free to send her an e-mail message at* [e-mail address].
What is the [organization name]?	You should have a two- or three-sentence blurb that describes your SRO. Many people will be happy to just look at your SRO's Web site.
	We conduct research projects mainly for state and local governments. We have been in existence for 15 years now and have conducted about 300 survey projects altogether. We conduct only valid, scientific surveys. We do not engage in selling or fundraising. Please visit our Web site at www.[organization].*org.*
How was I chosen for this survey?	Your answers should be consistent with the type of sample the survey is using. However, the first answer below applies to most surveys. Most Rs will be satisfied with the first and second answers below.
	This is a random sample survey. It was strictly by chance that your telephone number was chosen. Our computer creates a list of random telephone numbers. We do not know who they belong to until we call. [We often call telephone booths, businesses, and nonworking numbers before reaching a household like yours.] All households in [your area/place name] *have an equal chance of being selected for this survey.*

selected, whom to call if respondents wish to verify your legitimacy, and what your organization is all about.

Having the survey details on the tip of your tongue will prevent you from falling into the abyss of tongue-tied conversational gaps. Practicing answers to respondents' common questions aloud at home or with another interviewer will boost your self-assuredness. Your employer understands that the survey introduction is the one place you may need to innovate slightly in order to completely satisfy your respondent's questions and concerns, but you should minimize any deviations from scripted language.

At this early stage of the survey process, allow no pauses in your answers or in your exchanges with a respondent. Keep the interchange going. Once the interview is underway and your respondent is committed to the task, you can use short gaps of silence effectively to probe. But in the first three minutes, especially with a reluctant respondent, pauses convey the sense that you are uncertain about how to answer the respondent's questions, that you are intimidated, or that you do not really know what you are doing. Worse, pauses allow respondents a brief window in which to refuse.

> Listen to reluctant respondents carefully. Answer immediately; allow no pause between their questions and your answers. Answer only what they ask. Incorporate their words into your answer. Address their issues in short, concise statements.

Some potential respondents do not have easy questions for you following the survey introduction. You can sense by their manner that they are about to hang up the telephone or refuse outright to participate. You need to pay close attention to the resistant respondent, identify the source of his or her opposition, and then handle the issue knowledgeably and without pausing. The best way to accomplish these tasks is by practicing active listening.

Active Listening

Active listening refers to the act of closely attending to what a person says, hearing his or her verbal cues, and combining them with your other knowledge and experience to determine what the person means. With practice, active listening enables you decide what to do next quickly and instinctively. Fatigue and distraction are the most obvious barriers to active listening. You can learn how to avoid respondents' refusals by practicing active listening in two domains: in project-specific interviewer training and in your interactions with respondents.

You cannot actively listen in project-specific training sessions if you arrive weary or if you must fend off a coworker trying to engage you in a whispered sidebar conversation. In these situations you will probably miss something important that can later cause you embarrassment. Indeed, you should feel mortified if you ask the trainer a question that another interviewer asked five minutes before. In project-specific training, active listening involves not just learning about the study generally, reading question by question through the instrument, and practicing on CATI. Active listening also involves combining the project-specific training with your entire previous interviewer experience, to determine how this survey extends, differs from, or rearranges your previous interviewing knowledge. In turn you will learn how to perform on this survey excellently.

Interviewers in action should exercise active listening at all times in their communications with respondents. From the first hello, you need to hear and note everything on the other end of the telephone line. In addition to the words respondents say, you should notice respondents' breathing, grammar, partial sentences, pauses between words and sentences, and background noises. Your interviewing station should be designed to help you focus, with sound-reduced walls that also impede your view of potential distractions. Active listening is the first step in tailoring, or individualizing, what you say in reply to each respondent's needs and characteristics. Active listening will also help you to answer only what respondents ask.

When actively listening, you should focus on exactly what respondents say and how they say it. Notice the words they use. Incorporating respondents' words and phrases into your replies is one way to tailor your answers and give respondents the consideration they are due. By incorporating their words, you affirm what they have said. Your answers should respond uniquely to what each individual uttered to you.

> When you use respondents' own words in your replies, you affirm what they said and meant. Answering their questions with generic or canned phrases makes respondents feel devalued and depersonalized.

In noticing how respondents say what they say, listen to their tone. Address a cautious, negative, or suspicious tone directly, by saying,

I can certainly understand how you might feel that way.

Then address the specific issues they raise, without hesitation or fumbling. But do not adopt their negative tone yourself; it is self-defeating. Your words and how you utter them must match. That is, if you tell respondents how important they are to a survey, the way in which you say it should make them feel important. If your answers sound generic or canned (as though you were reading aloud from a sheet of paper in a mechanical tone), your respondents will feel devalued and depersonalized.

Sometimes interviewers listen so carefully to reluctant respondents that they forget to listen to themselves. Project confidence. Your tone of voice should be positive, upbeat, steady, businesslike, and assertive. Your tone should convey your genuine interest in each respondent, and your words should address the precise reasons for their reluctance. Keep your comments and tone positive and assuring. Focusing on your objective—the completed interview—will help you avoid a defensive or apologetic attitude. Do not allow a respondent to annoy or goad you. Do not get sucked into a debate; it will alienate the respondent even more. Respondents should not have your behavior as a reason to refuse when they are called back or called for a different survey.

The longer you engage in the question-and-answer process with respondents, the more cues they will provide that help you tailor your answers. Moreover, the longer you and a respondent interact, the more the two of you become embedded in an exchange relationship. That embedding makes it less socially acceptable for respondents to refuse. In this way active listening helps prevent respondent refusals.

Initial (Soft) Refusals

An *initial refusal* refers to an excuse or objection that reluctant respondents utter during or after the survey introduction although they do not refuse outright to participate. To the extent possible, you want to avoid initial (or *soft*) refusals. If avoidance is not possible, you need to know how to prevent initial refusals from becoming final refusals. Interviewers can avoid initial refusals by assiduously following these steps:

1. Know the survey thoroughly, including its purpose, why that purpose is important, the general topics covered, the sponsor, how to contact the sponsor, the nature of the target sample, why that sample is important, how respondents were chosen, why each respondent's participation is necessary, and all elements of informed consent.

2. Memorize and drill the answers to common questions until they become second nature. This knowledge comes from project-specific interviewer training and your practice—at home, with other interviewers, and on the CATI system. Knowing a survey this well goes a long way in developing your self-confidence for each dial attempt.

3. Use a swift pace and a businesslike tone as you read the survey introduction, answer respondents' questions, and move into the first interview questions. Moving through these steps rapidly reduces the chance that respondents will refuse. But you must do this without making respondents feel rushed. Success

in this step can only be accomplished with the thorough knowledge, practice, and confidence that come from success in the first two steps.

Sometimes your strategies to avoid an initial refusal will seem useless. Respondents' questions are detailed, their attitude is suspicious, or they object to being called at all. Your job in such circumstances is to stay calm, actively listen to resistant respondents' words and affect, identify the sources of their opposition, and then handle their issues knowledgeably and without pausing.

> Never apologize for calling reluctant, resistant, suspicious, or hostile respondents. Listen to their issues. Provide the information they need. Make them feel that they are helping to do something important.

Do not take reluctant, resistant, or hostile respondents personally. Never apologize for calling. You are doing nothing wrong; your job and your request are legitimate. Their issues are about the task, not you. Respondents who object are essentially asking you to communicate more information. Answer their objections and excuses as if they were genuine requests for information. When people are presented with a good reason to complete a survey, they generally agree to participate. Even when respondents hang up, their initial refusals often leave open the possibility that they might later agree to participate.

By actively listening, you will be able to identify potential respondents' underlying issues and address them before the respondents hang up the telephone. Listen closely as they verbalize their issues. Determine their basic concern. Is the issue that they lack sufficient time? Have they never heard of the survey sponsor? Is the main issue about confidentiality? For inarticulate respondents, choose an issue that seems most salient. For grouchy respondents, attend to their words, not the emotion in them—and do not rise to the bait.

Table 6.2 provides numerous examples of respondents' excuses and objections that can result in initial refusals. Use this list to classify respondents' underlying issues. Once you have identified and classified reluctant respondents' concerns, you will then know which set of answers to use. With preparation and practice you will know almost instinctively the best sentences to use as replies. Answer with sincerity and directness in your manner of speaking.

Do not press reluctant respondents into deciding too quickly whether to participate. Let them keep asking questions or raising issues. As long as they ask questions and you answer them, the conversation continues. The longer it continues, the less likely they are to hang up. Pushing such respondents into participating more quickly than they are comfortable with increases the chance

TABLE 6.2. IDENTIFYING AND ADDRESSING RESPONDENTS' RELUCTANCE TO PARTICIPATE.

Respondents' Typical Excuses and Objections	What to Say and Why
I am not a good person for you to talk to because	Make R feel important and comfortable. Emphasize that R represents many others (find out how many, if possible).
I don't drive. I just moved here. I am not involved. I don't know anything about highways or bridges. I am too old. (And so forth.)	*Every person randomly chosen for this survey is important, whether you are typical or not. You represent roughly 800 people in your community.* *It is very important to hear from people who do not drive, because many questions are about alternative forms of transportation.* *Your opinions will help* [client] *make decisions about* [survey topic] *that can affect you.* *People who just moved here are especially important for us to talk to because your experiences are fresher.* *Older people's opinions are just as important to this survey as anyone else's.* *In order for the results to be representative, we have to be sure to get older people's opinions too. We really do want to know what you think.* *It is important to get everyone's opinions, not just younger people's.* *Let's try a few questions and you will see that the survey applies to you as much as anyone else.*
I am not interested in participating. I am not interested in that topic.	Stress how the survey could affect R, R's community, the state, or people like R. Some Rs are impressed if the survey covers controversial issues. *Before you hang up, let me tell you a little bit about the survey.* *You as an individual represent a large group of people like you in your community. It is important that your voices be heard on issues this survey covers.* *But we are interested in you, because you represent hundreds of others like you whose opinions need to be heard even if you are not very interested.* *Each patient randomly selected for this survey represents about 600 other patients treated at General Hospital.*

TABLE 6.2. *(CONTINUED)*

Respondents' Typical Excuses and Objections	What to Say and Why
	It is very important that we get the opinions of everyone we call, otherwise the results will not be very useful.
	The results of this survey will affect the state's priorities on funding for highways, roads, and bridges.
	We value your [input/experience/opinions] about [topic].
	I will bet that you will find many of these questions interesting.
That topic does not apply to me because I don't	Explain to R that the survey needs the entire spectrum of the population.
Have any problems with highways and bridges.	*We need to hear both from the people who complain about the state's roads as well as those who do not.*
Drive to work.	*It is important for us to know how everyone gets to work, not just those who drive.*
Have children at home.	*If we do not get information from you and people like you, we will not have anybody to compare the others to.*
Have health problems. (And so forth.)	*As we talk, I am sure you will find you have answers to the questions.*
	Let's try a few questions and you will see that the survey applies to you as much as to anyone else.
I am not very good at answering surveys.	Some Rs think of surveys as a test. Try to help R feel adequate for the task. The probes below are intended to explain that lack of knowledge on the topic can be just as important as expert knowledge and that this is not a test.
I don't know very much about the topic.	
	I am sure you will find it interesting, and we would really appreciate knowing how you feel about these topics.
	We need to hear from the entire range of people, from experts to those who do not know anything about it.
	The questions in this survey are quick and easy. You might even think it is fun.
	The questions are not hard. They are about how you feel about things, not about how much you know.

(continued)

TABLE 6.2. *(CONTINUED)*

Respondents' Typical Excuses and Objections	What to Say and Why
	We can pass over any question that you [cannot/do not want to] answer.
	We need input from everyone to get an idea of how much people do and don't know about the topic.
	We do not need specialists. We need to hear from real people on this topic too.
	I would like to point out that there are no right or wrong answers to the questions; we are only asking for your opinions.
	We need to hear about your experience, even if you went there just once.
	Some of the people I have already interviewed worried about the same thing at first, but once we got started they didn't have any problems answering the questions.
	That's why it is important for us to complete a survey with you. We are trying to find out how much people know—and do not know—about these issues.
	Maybe I could read just a few questions to you and you can see what they are like.
	This survey actually contains a variety of questions on several topics. Let's try a few. I am sure you will enjoy answering many of them.
The R objects to surveys in general.	Explain that this is a serious, scientific survey. Appeal to civic duty.
	But surveys are an important part of a democratic society, like voting. Without surveys, business, government, and the media would not know the people's opinions and wishes. Surveys give the information necessary to guide public policy and decision making on education, the economy, health, and public safety.
	This particular survey is especially important now because the state legislature is deciding how much funding to allocate to the state's highways, roads, and bridges. Your opinions will help tell them what the public wants.

TABLE 6.2. *(CONTINUED)*

Respondents' Typical Excuses and Objections	What to Say and Why
	We have found that people who do not want to participate in surveys differ significantly from those who do. That means that the opinions of people like you do not get represented in public decision making. Without your interview the results of this survey will not be scientifically sound.
I don't give out information over the telephone.	Many people said this in the 1990s because they got tired of being tricked by telemarketers.
Just send me a mail questionnaire; I don't do telephone surveys.	*I want to assure you that I am not selling a thing or asking for a donation. This is a scientific survey.*
	I appreciate your uneasiness about giving information out over the telephone. A lot of people feel that way. Why don't you take down our telephone number (1-800-xxx-xxxx)? You can check it out with a telephone operator or you can call us back to reassure yourself.
	Telephone surveys are faster and more cost effective than mail surveys, especially when they have just a few questions, like this one.
	[Client's name] has asked us to do this by telephone because this is the fastest way to do a survey and they need the information quickly.
	If we sent you this survey in the mail, you would no longer be anonymous. As it is, I do not know your name or where you live. Most people prefer to keep it that way.

(continued)

TABLE 6.2. *(CONTINUED)*

Respondents' Typical Excuses and Objections	What to Say and Why
That person is not home now, but I like doing surveys.	Most surveys are conducted with specific people or with a randomly selected person in a HH. Certain types of people more often volunteer for interviews than others, and research shows that volunteers do not accurately represent the others. Make no substitutions; they will compromise the survey's validity.
I know he will say no; he is too busy to participate. But I am happy to do it for him.	
She works nights and sleeps during the day. You'll never reach her. I will help out by doing it for her.	*You are generous to offer, but I would get fired if I let you do the interview. I am only allowed to interview the person who was scientifically selected for the survey. Will (she/he) be available tomorrow evening?*
	Telling KAs something about your job (getting fired) engages them in doing the right thing. Referring to science enhances the survey's legitimacy. Never accept a refusal by other. In a nice yet businesslike manner, tell KA that you really must explain the survey directly to R. Only then, if necessary, can you accept a refusal.
	I am sorry, but I really must speak with [name/her/him]. What would be the best time to reach [him/her]?
	Convince KA that interviewing R is so important you will take a laptop home and conduct the Iw at 5:00 PM or at midnight, if needed. For Rs far away on a trip, say you will call their hotel if that is the only way to reach them.

TABLE 6.2. *(CONTINUED)*

Respondents' Typical Excuses and Objections	What to Say and Why
Why can't you call someone else?	Take the time to explain, emphasizing the science of sampling.
	In order to get an accurate mix of people, it is necessary that we select people in a scientific manner. Once selected, we can only interview that person.
	People who do not usually participate in surveys do not get their opinions represented, so getting their views is especially important.
	We cannot use substitutes because we do not know that the person we substituted would have the same opinions as you.
	If we remove your telephone number from the call list, it will undermine the scientific legitimacy of this research. You represent hundreds of others like you, but we cannot be sure of finding someone else just like you. Your views are essential to the validity of this survey.
	We need to talk with a wide variety of people. If we just interviewed volunteers, the results of the survey would not represent the population.
I am too busy. I don't have enough time.	For too busy in general, acknowledge R's burden and stress convenience. Know your SRO's hours and offer to make an appointment at any time within those hours that will best suit R's schedule. Suggest an actual day and time; then make sure someone actually calls R at that time.
	I appreciate that you have a busy life. In order for this survey to represent the range of everyone's views accurately, it is very important for us to speak with busy people, like you.
	Because your time is precious, I can schedule an interview at whatever time is convenient for you. We are open from nine in the morning until nine at night. I am sure we can find a time that would fit your schedule. I could call you back at [time].
	I would be happy to call back at a more convenient time. Please tell me when would be a good time.

(continued)

TABLE 6.2. *(CONTINUED)*

Respondents' Typical Excuses and Objections	What to Say and Why
	For too busy right now, apologize and suggest a better time to CB.
	I am sorry I caught you at a bad time. (If a weekday) I can call you back on Saturday morning. (If a weekend) I can call you back on Monday or Tuesday.
	If "too busy" sounds like a polite refusal, try these:
	We could even do the interview while you are [cooking/picking up the house/watching the kids in the backyard] if that would help.
	I can ask the questions as quickly as you can answer them.
	I know what you mean! If we get started right now, we will finish in about _____ minutes.
	Let's do as much as you have time for now and then finish the rest at a convenient time for you.
	If you run out of time now, I can call back tomorrow to finish the rest.
	Perversely, Rs who claim to be too busy to participate in a survey often give the longest interviews.
I am sick now. My health is not good. My sister died yesterday.	For a short illness, express sympathy and offer to CB when R is well.
	I am sorry to hear that. I will call back in a few days to see if you feel well enough to do the interview then. Will this same time of day be the best to reach you again?
	For a lengthy or serious illness, or a family tragedy, express sympathy. If this is a short duration survey, indicate that no one will call again.
	Oh, I am so sorry to hear that. I will remove your telephone number from the call list.

TABLE 6.2. *(CONTINUED)*

Respondents' Typical Excuses and Objections	What to Say and Why
	Unexpectedly, some Rs in these situations will ask you to call back "next week." Others are more amenable to a survey request than they might normally be. Apparently an interview distracts some Rs from their grief or an act of altruism feels especially important at such times. Do not press Rs in such circumstances. Offer only if the survey will be in the field for several more weeks.
	Oh, I am so sorry to hear that. I can call back in a week or two if you would like. [If yes] Would you prefer to be called in the morning, afternoon, or evening?
Quit harassing me! I can tell from my caller ID that you folks have called me ten times in the last week.	Often Rs exaggerate when making this claim, and often they have not yet spoken with an Ir.
	The reason we keep calling is that you are important to this research. We try to reach the people randomly selected for our surveys at the time of day and day of the week that is most convenient to them.
You are invading my privacy.	If an RDD sample:
	This survey is completely anonymous. I do not know who you are or where you live—and I do not need to, or want to, know any identifying information about you. [All I want is your opinions.]
	If a list sample:
	I can certainly understand how you might feel that way. That is why all of our interviews are confidential. Protecting people's privacy is one of our major concerns, and to do it we automatically erase all identifying information from people's answers the moment the interview ends. Also, we release all the results in the form of averages and percentages, so that no single individual can ever be identified. We are much more interested in people's opinions than in who gave them.
How do I know you won't use my telephone number for something else?	Some unethical SROs make money by selling their Rs' TP#s. Such lists are especially valuable if the SRO includes certain HH characteristics, such as known tobacco users or known to have children under age six.

(continued)

TABLE 6.2. *(CONTINUED)*

Respondents' Typical Excuses and Objections	What to Say and Why
	No reputable survey research organization sells telephone numbers, including [organization]. *It would violate our code of ethics.*
	This survey is funded by the federal government, which prohibits anyone from using telephone numbers for any purpose besides this interview.
	Our research must stick to strict ethical standards. Close records are kept about the promises we make to the people who participate in our research. If we violate a promise, we may be subject to civil or criminal liability. For these reasons, we take our promises of [anonymity/confidentiality] *very seriously.*
It is illegal for you to call me because I am on the Do Not Call (DNC) list.	The DNC rules confuse many consumers, and so some may resist when you offer these explanations.
	I am calling to conduct research. Research is exempt under the Do Not Call rules, because we are not selling anything. All we want are your opinions.
	I am not a telemarketer. I am a part of a research organization. The rules for telemarketing do not apply to us, because we protect your privacy, never sell anything, and never ask for donations. We only want to conduct a legitimate interview with you at a convenient time.
	If you look in the front pages of your telephone book, you may find a section called "consumer tips" that describes how telemarketing differs from scientific survey research.
	Please feel free to go to our Web site to examine our privacy and confidentiality policies.
	Even if R hangs up, the second call is likely to be successful. Telemarketers almost never CB, so a second call from your SRO can convince R that you are calling about a real survey.

that they will refuse. Even if they do not give you a final refusal at the moment, your pressure or insufficient answers may cause their soft refusals to harden into defensiveness by the time another interviewer calls back later.

The long list in Table 6.2 is intended to help you identify the issue that is troubling your potential respondent. Know these thoroughly. Pleasantly and patiently attempt to ascertain respondents' concerns, and then fully and directly answer them, but answer only what they ask. Actively listen to the respondent. Incorporate their words and phrases into your answer. Express sincere interest in the respondent. You can persuade most respondents to participate if you address their problem, excuse, or objection convincingly. Active listening also helps you hear the cues that tell you that all the respondent's questions have been answered. When that happens, move quickly to the next CATI screen—COOPERAT:

We appreciate your cooperation. [I would like to begin the survey now.]

The Tough Nuts

Problematically, some potential respondents cannot, or will not, verbalize their true issues. They say they are "too busy." But the real problem may be that they will participate in an interview only with someone of their own sex (or the opposite sex). A husband may deflect a male interviewer asking for his wife because he is suspicious that something else is going on (or vice versa). A family member might repeatedly say that the intended respondent is "not home now" because he or she is embarrassed to reveal that that person is coping with mental health problems. It is impossible for an interviewer to address a respondent's real objection to the interview request if the respondent does not explain it. Just do the best you can by actively listening and then move on.

In trying to determine the underlying issues for these *tough nuts*, take care not to ask questions that can be answered with "no." Allowing "no" answers creates a negative tone, which can reinforce a respondent's lack of enthusiasm. For example, do not ask,

Is there a better time to call back?

Instead, say,

Please tell me a good time to call back.

TABLE 6.3. AVOIDING INTRODUCTORY QUESTIONS THAT RELUCTANT RESPONDENTS CAN ANSWER WITH "NO."

Say This	Do Not Say This
Please tell me a good time to call back.	*Is there a better time to call back?*
(If a weekday) I can call you back on Saturday morning.	*Could you suggest a better day for me to call back when you are not so busy?*
(If a weekend) I can call you back on Monday or Tuesday. What time of day would be best?	
Let's try a few questions.	*Would you like to try a few questions?*
I am sure we can find several reasons why you would be interested in participating.	*Is there any particular reason why you are not interested?*
But we are interested in you, because you represent hundreds of others like you whose opinions need to be heard even if you are not very interested.	*Do you mind if I ask why you are not interested in this topic?*
So that we know whom to ask for when we call back, what is that person's first name?	*May I have that person's first name, so that we know whom to ask for when we call back?*
I would like to begin the interview now.	*Is this a good time to start the interview?*
I will call back in a few days to see if you feel well enough to do the interview then.	*Can I call you back in a few days to see if you feel well enough to do the interview then?*

Table 6.3 provides several examples of how to avoid "no" answers. Notice that each of the preferred questions and statements on the left ("say this") contains the underlying assumption that the respondent will cooperate. For each question on the right ("do not say this"), respondents can too easily answer the questions with "no." The items on the right also require some initiative on the part of the respondent, such as thinking of a better time or day for the interview. Do not give respondents the chance to take over. You are in charge of leading the conversational exchange.

> Do not give respondents the chance to take over. You are in charge of leading the exchange.

If you have addressed all of a potential respondent's issues but you are convinced that he or she will not participate in the interview now, it is time to say,

Thank you for your time. Good-bye.

Make sure to say good-bye before a reluctant respondent refuses outright or says, "never call me again." He or she will think about what you have said, and it may make a world of difference when the next interviewer calls. When your answers do not result in an immediate interview, the most important thing for you to do next is to record the proper call disposition code, leave a thorough message for the next interviewer, and schedule a callback accurately. The next interviewer should have better luck because of the great work you did on the initial call.

Refusals

Most reluctant respondents and tough nuts do, eventually, decide to participate. They might start their interviews suspiciously, uncertainly, or grudgingly, but most will have softened and become quite cooperative by the end. Other reluctant respondents, however, no matter how closely you listen—to them and to yourself—will refuse to participate. Survey researchers understand the necessity of every randomly selected person's participation, but refusers do not. As the number of refusals goes up, the generalizability of the survey results goes down. Therefore, persuading reluctant respondents to complete interviews will be one of your most important and challenging tasks, yet it is also very rewarding.

The purpose of this section is to teach you to recognize the difference between soft and hard refusals, and to give you more strategies for overcoming initial refusals and turning them into completed interviews. Before we get into refusal conversion tactics, however, you should understand two things: (1) do not take refusals personally, and (2) many refusals are not really refusals at all. The following sections explain these two points.

Do Not Take Refusals Personally

Of the many reasons people give for not wanting to participate in a telephone interview, nearly all have nothing to do with you as a person. Most often you have caught someone at a bad time. They might have had a hard day. Perhaps the baby got sick, the car broke down, a coworker quit, or they are coping with a new medication's nauseating side effects. Or it could just be a bad moment. Perhaps Grandma is on the other line, it is time to leave for Junior's basketball game, they are in the middle of an argument with a ruffian teenager, or they are tuning the car. None of these things have anything to do with you! Rarely do you catch people sitting in a comfy chair with their feet up waiting for the telephone to ring.

> Rarely will you catch people sitting in a comfy chair with their feet up hoping you will call.

Sure, some people are sometimes rude, and a very few people are cruel. They reject your interview request, and they want you to feel it as a rejection. We do not know the psychology behind people whose first impulse is to intimidate a polite and sincere telephone interviewer. No matter how rudely or argumentatively someone speaks, you must stay calm, keep your voice low and even, not argue, and not say something sarcastic. No matter how provoked, you still must practice excellent telephone etiquette because you represent your employer and the survey's sponsor.

In the exceptionally rare case, someone may say things that are actually abusive, derisive, insulting, crude, or humiliating. You do not deserve this. Without apology, say,

I am going to hang up the telephone now.

And then do so. Report what happened to your supervisor. Take a short break. If you suspect this person was under the influence of drugs or alcohol and might not even remember his or her behavior, leave an appropriate callback message for an especially thick-skinned interviewer to call again.

To avoid taking refusals and mean people personally, develop a strategy that works for you. One method is to imagine yourself inside a cozy, glass bubble that is mirrored on the outside. Unkind respondents cannot see you (just as they cannot see you as you speak with them on the telephone) and anything they say bounces off the bubble back at them. You can use this technique, or find something similar for yourself.

Not All Refusals Are Really Refusals

Interviewers should not shudder at the prospect of calling back cases that have a callback code showing an initial or final refusal, because a substantial portion of these cases may not be refusals at all. There are four categories of *not really refusals:* (1) the respondent did not mean it, (2) the respondent did not do it, (3) the previous interviewer erred, and (4) the respondent did not know what he or she was refusing. Only by calling back can you verify whether the refusal was genuine.

Most initial refusals result simply from people being called at a bad time ("I am too busy right now"). You can legitimately call them back at a more convenient time. Indeed, you will find that many people are happy to participate when interviewers catch them on a better day of the week or at a better time of day. Maybe they needed time to think about the previous interviewer's answers to their questions, or maybe this time they are more relaxed and can actually hear your answers to their questions and concerns. In any case, many will be convinced that the survey is legitimate and that their contribution will be meaningful.

A subcategory of respondents not meaning a refusal are those who refused under the influence of drugs or alcohol. When people are under the influence, they often say things that they do not intend or remember. Listen for slurred words, overly loud speech, and overly long gaps between utterances. The latter could indicate the person is taking another pull from a bottle, a spliff, or whatever, or it could indicate that the person is lapsing in and out of consciousness. In any case persons under the influence might not remember their refusal a few days hence, or if they do remember, they may be so ashamed of their behavior that they will gladly cooperate now. Leave an appropriate callback message for an impervious colleague.

In some cases the intended respondent did not even speak with an interviewer. Rather, another member of the household (a gatekeeper or a teenager having fun), or even a visitor, refused on behalf of the actual respondent. You cannot identify these cases in advance. Calling them back is not harassment for they have not even spoken with an interviewer yet. Finding them is keenly important to the research. In a list sample survey I directed in 2002, an elderly man's daughter repeatedly refused on his behalf, saying that he was incompetent and hard of hearing. An interviewer finally reached him at a different time of day, when his daughter was gone. She found that he was eager to participate and could hear just fine when the interviewer raised her voice slightly.

Sometimes refusals result from interviewer error: the respondent said, "I can't do this now," and the interviewer mistakenly used the final refusal call disposition code (2.11) instead of the initial refusal code (5.11). In other cases the interviewer may have called when the respondent had the flu or was changing a diaper, preparing to go out for the evening, or mowing the lawn. That person said "no" gruffly at the time without explaining why, but is perfectly willing to participate later. In these cases the first interviewer probably should have used the initial refusal code. Learn to use the call disposition codes correctly every time. If you are uncertain about which code to use for a certain case, ask a supervisor.

Some respondents give the interviewer the brush-off ("take me off your list") without knowing what they are refusing. That is, they cut the interviewer off before hearing the entire introduction. Such respondents typically suspect the call is, for example, a request to buy credit card insurance or donate to their alumni association, or they are confused about DNC lists. Going back to the concept of *informed consent*, a phone slam cannot be considered a legitimate refusal because it is not informed. The respondent has to stay on the telephone line long enough to hear enough survey information to allow an informed decision on whether to participate. You should not hesitate to call back phone slams and to attempt to provide respondents with enough information for them to give informed consent or informed dissent.

The Lucies

Remember Charlie Brown and the football in the classic *Peanuts* cartoon series? Lucy repeatedly invites Charlie to kick the football, then pulls it away just as he kicks, and he falls flat. Trusting the good in everyone, Charlie believes Lucy will not do this to him again. Sometimes he even gets her to promise that she will not pull it away this time. He races to give the football a good hard kick, and she pulls it away yet again, and again, and again. Some respondents act a lot like Lucy.

The Lucies never refuse outright. Rather, they are repeatedly too busy (making dinner, on the way out the door to pick up the kids, and so on). A child picks up the telephone and you can hear Mom's instructions to say, "she is not home now." They repeatedly ask you to call back, sometimes even making interview appointments. But every time an interviewer calls back, the same thing happens.

You will never know what is really going on with the Lucies. Perhaps they are too spineless to give a genuine final refusal. Perhaps something really does come up each time an interviewer calls. Perhaps they think this is the well-mannered way to cover up their reluctance. You should not feel that you are pestering a respondent who repeatedly asks to be called back or who never discourages a callback.

Interviewers groan when a Lucy comes up in the CATI system. They are easily distinguishable, with eight to ten contacts over two to three weeks, all coded "too busy" and with plausible callback messages. Not only are such cases time consuming, they frustrate interviewers who cannot develop callback strategies unless they know what is really going on. In my experience the most fruitful approach is to put a stern tone in your voice, something like a disappointed elementary school teacher speaking to a smart but lazy child. Tell such respondents that data collection ends today, remind them why the survey is important, tell them that their participation is important, and insist on completing the interview right now. Do not accept another appointment. If you do, you are a Charlie Brown.

Final (Hard) Refusals

Before we get to refusal conversion, you need to be able to distinguish what counts as a *hard, final refusal*. These people will never be called back, because the final refusal call disposition code removes them from the call list. First, you must be certain that the person with whom you are speaking is the intended respondent, not another household member or a visitor. Second, make sure that the person is not unduly intoxicated or stoned. Once you are sure you have the right person and that the person is in his or her right mind, the following conditions describe what counts as a hard refusal.

Informed Dissenters These potential respondents know the survey's purpose, sponsor, importance, length of task, and anonymity or confidentiality. They have no questions (or no more questions). They also know that the survey is voluntary, and they do not want to volunteer. Such people are often very polite but immovable, despite refusal conversion attempts. Some informed dissenters are less rational, claiming that they lack the time for an interview yet sending a detailed letter or e-mail that clearly took far longer to compose than the interview would have taken—and often they sign these communications, eliminating their anonymity.

Uninformed Dissenters These people repeatedly cut off interviewers before they get through the entire survey introduction (phone slams). Different interviewers have called at different times of the day on different days of the week to try to inform these people about what they are refusing but have never gotten through. Survey organizations vary in the number of such attempts each will tolerate before considering these cases hard refusals.

Repeated Soft Refusals Some survey research organizations automatically code two or three soft refusals as a hard refusal. This practice avoids fruitless emotional wear and tear on their hardworking interviewers.

Lucies Some survey research organizations automatically code ten or more dial attempts to Lucies as hard refusals, again to avoid fruitless wear and tear on their interviewers.

Victims These potential respondents see themselves as victims of harassment and credibly claim they will call the police, hire a lawyer, file a formal complaint, or sue the interviewer's employer. Such situations are rare, and in my experience those who actually attempt to follow through on such a claim represent roughly

1 out of 10,000 interviewer dial attempts. Even when people do follow through, nothing happens because their claims are often specious or exaggerated.[1] There is nothing illegal about polite, patient, yet persistent interviewers trying to do their work.

Bullies People who threaten you, the interviewer, do not deserve a callback. It is easy for bullies to act in a menacing manner over the telephone, because they do not have to look you in the eye. In fact these cowards never follow through on their threats. These situations are extremely rare. Nonetheless, you do not have to put up with it. Do not apologize. Politely and evenly say,

I am going to hang up the telephone now.

Then do it. Leave a descriptive callback message just in case someone later thinks this person should be called back. Report the event to your supervisor. Take a short break.

The previous list presented the most common forms of final refusals, but every survey organization has its own variations. For example, some organizations tell their interviewers to code people who say, "never call me again," or something similar, as hard refusals. Maybe they do so because their IRB requires it. It is unfortunate to give up on a telephone number without knowing whether an interviewer has reached the right person and without having the intended person hear the entire introduction.

Because cases with final refusals are never called back, some survey research organizations allocate them stingily. Many do not allow interviewers to assign final refusal call disposition codes themselves (as previously mentioned). Rather, a supervisor must do it for them, or they must have a supervisor's permission. The reason for this is that some interviewers feel timid about speaking with the tough nuts, especially more than once. However, it is essential for researchers, to the extent possible, to learn the views, behavior, and knowledge of such respondents. Requiring a supervisor's approval before coding a final refusal is simply a means to ensure that these most difficult potential respondents have had all possible chances to participate before we give up on them.

Refusal Conversion

Refusal conversion is the process of convincing reluctant respondents to participate in a survey by identifying and addressing their concerns, providing the information they need, appealing to their sense of altruism or civic duty, or employing other motivators. Why do we do this? It is imperative to interview as many members as possible from a random sample, because even those who are less than eager to participate represent the opinions and behaviors of others in the population who are like them. Thus you must do everything reasonable in your power to encourage resistant respondents to participate. You need to think about where particular respondents fall in the range of opinions and behaviors and how you will overcome their resistance. This section will help you develop strategies tailored to each reluctant respondent to convince him or her to answer the survey questions.

Calling Back Soft Refusals

Calling back people who have given one or more soft refusals or phone slams can seem daunting, but it need not be. Some interviewers are more successful than others at refusal conversion. Still, all interviewers should know the techniques, if only to demonstrate how prior interviewers' messages about refusals can make all the difference for later interviewers in turning these refusals into completed interviews. It is hard to predict which interviewers will succeed most at refusal conversion, because different interviewers use their vocal qualities and personality characteristics in different ways, depending on how they size up a respondent. For example, assertiveness works well with some respondents, but an attitude of concern works better with others. You will want to develop refusal conversion skills because many employers pay interviewers a premium for those talents.

> Refusal conversion involves developing a strategy tailored to each reluctant respondent to convince him or her to answer the survey questions.

The first step in calling back soft refusals is thoughtful preparation. Review the call record. Who called last? If it was you, do not call back. There may be something about your voice that irritated, upset, or frightened the respondent. A different voice may make a difference in gaining the respondent's cooperation. Was the last interviewer who called male or female? If a male interviewer got the last refusal, try a female interviewer this time (and vice versa). Was the last caller a forceful personality with a strong voice? This time try a more soft-spoken approach, conveying confidence but not insistence.

Carefully read the comments left by prior interviewers. What were the person's specific problems with the interview request? You already know how to respond to survey specifics (Table 6.2). Take note of the emotions or attitudes the person conveyed, as described in the callback record. Although the person might display different feelings when you call, past behavior remains the best predictor of future behavior.

Try to determine the person's understanding of and prior participation in surveys. Some people resist the proposed interview even though they appreciate surveys in general and usually take part in them. Some understand surveys but distrust the claim of confidentiality or how the results will be used. Others may understand surveys and polls only in the vaguest way, fearing that you want them to take some kind of test and listening to you with uncertainty. Some consider surveys a nuisance but complete them out of a sense of civic obligation. Some will participate in surveys but not polls.

Using the information you have gleaned, develop a strategy for approaching the respondent. Plan in advance what you will say. Table 6.4 provides suggestions; with experience you will come to rely on your own instincts. When you reach reluctant respondents, attend particularly to their voices. Note the volume (loud or soft) and the emotion in it. By actively listening, you can identify the manner in which they feel about the survey and then respond with information and in a voice that will heighten their willingness to participate.

Strategies for Refusal Conversion

Once you have done your homework on the reluctant respondent, you have three basic strategies for refusal conversion: (1) varying the opening sentences, (2) calling with concern, and (3) treating the callback as a cold call. No matter which one you choose, you will find it useful to write down on a piece of scratch paper what you plan to say. Writing your own script helps you tailor your opening sentences to a particular person, rather than falling back on the standard, unvarying language that training has ingrained in your interviewing. It might take you a few minutes to decide on the best approach and the best words to use for a particular respondent; that's OK. If you are uncertain, ask a supervisor for input on your ideas and what you have written.

For refusal conversions, most survey research organizations allow interviewers to vary the survey introduction on the basis of actively listening to respondents in order to get around those respondents' preconceived notions of your call and, if they understand why you are calling, their objections to participating. When you vary the introduction, you still must convey all the essential words and phrases required for protection of human subjects (identifying the survey sponsor, survey topic, task length, confidentiality or anonymity, and voluntariness).

TABLE 6.4. SUGGESTED STRATEGIES FOR HANDLING
RESPONDENTS' REFUSAL-RELATED MANNERS.

Respondent Manner	Suggested Strategies for Obtaining an Interview
Quiet, uncertain, cautious	Project confidence. Be definite in what you say.
	Assure Rs of their ability to complete the task.
	I am sure you will not have any problems with the interview. The questions apply to everyone and they are easy to answer.
	Suggest trying out a few Qs, but also offer an escape route.
	Let's try a few questions. You'll see that they are interesting and easy. You can skip any question that makes you uncomfortable.
	Say you would like to begin the Iw now.
Congenially stubborn	Keep your voice equally congenial, but assertive, serious, and professional.
	Reexplain the survey's purpose.
	Clarify how the survey will benefit others, inform the public, contribute to scientific research, or influence public policy.
	Stress that R's opinions represent those of many others.
	Appeal to R's sense of civic duty.
	It is like voting, but everyone can vote and only a few are selected to give their detailed opinions.
Edgy, hassled, hurried	Pick up the pace of your speech slightly, but do not sacrifice words.
	Do not allow R to push or upset you. Keep your tone calm and even.
	Start the Iw. Now is better than later.
	In that case, let's start right now. I can speak as quickly as you can answer.
	For Rs who insist that now is not a good time, say,
	Please tell me a good time to call back.
Mistrustful, wary	Keep your voice serious, deliberate, slow, and professional.
	Emphasize the legitimacy of your employer, the survey, and the sponsor.

(continued)

TABLE 6.4. *(CONTINUED)*

Respondent Manner	Suggested Strategies for Obtaining an Interview
	Offer telephone numbers, e-mail addresses, and Web sites of your supervisor, project director, organization, and client.
	Explain confidentiality or anonymity, if relevant:
	This survey is completely confidential. That means that no one will ever be able to connect you to your answers.
	This survey is completely anonymous. I have no idea who you are or where you live, and I do not need to know. All I need are your opinions.
Inappropriate	Inappropriate Rs try to interest you in them: for example, they ask for a date or ask for help, or they try to get you to buy, join, or do something irrelevant to the survey task. Most Rs ask innocuous Qs, such as wanting to know if you are a student if you call from a university-related survey center. Say that you can only answer such Qs at the Iw's end. By then, Rs have usually forgotten these questions.
	I can only answer questions like that after we finish the interview.
	If R is pushy, explain that you are calling for one purpose only.
	I am calling to ask you to conduct a survey interview only. I am not allowed to answer personal questions or carry on a personal conversation. [I could get fired.]
	Repeat the survey topic, goals, and so forth. Attempt to begin the Iw.
	If R persists, say you that you have to hang up now. Do so. Record comments in the call record. Report the incident to a supervisor.
Antagonistic, indignant	R is angry, offended, resentful, hostile, or trying to pick a fight. Try to determine if R is under the influence.
	Retreat. Say,
	Now does not seem like a good time. Someone will call you back in a few days.
Impolite, abrupt, rude	Ignore R's affect.
	Project professionalism.
	Keep your voice even and calm. Speak politely. Do not rise to the bait or argue.

TABLE 6.4. *(CONTINUED)*

Respondent Manner	Suggested Strategies for Obtaining an Interview
	Identify R's specific issues and respond to them with information.
	Address R's Qs in an unemotional, down-to-earth way.
Abusive	Abusive Rs speak vulgarly or in a demeaning or offensive manner.
	Inform R that you are going to hang up, then hang up at once. Record detailed comments in the call record. Report the incident to a supervisor. Take a short break. You do not deserve this.

If you need to call a potential respondent who repeatedly has refused or done a phone slam after the first sentence of the introduction, do not use those same introductory words. Try starting with:

I am not selling anything or asking for money. All I need is your opinions.

When reluctant respondents hear the same phrases repeatedly, we inadvertently train them on how to evade us, and then we cannot give the full introduction or explain further. Break it up a little. For example, instead of this:

Hello. The Oregon Department of Transportation has asked the Survey Research Laboratory at [organization] *to conduct a 16 to 20 minute survey with adults [age 18 or over] about transportation issues in your area.*

try starting with one of these introductions:

Hi. I am calling from [organization]. *Are you the woman who asked us to call back, to get your opinions about Oregon's highways, roads, and bridges?*

Hello. This is [name], *calling from* [organization]. *I am not sure if I have spoken with you before. Have you heard about the research we are doing for the Oregon Department of Transportation?*

Is now a good time to do the statewide survey on transportation issues in your area?

In using the second approach, *calling with concern*, determine in advance to whom or what you will direct your concern—the respondent or the survey task. Directing concern to the respondent suggests that an interviewer or the survey request wronged the person in some way. Your call essentially expresses regret, allowing the person to graciously accept your contrition and decide to participate. For example:

Is this telephone number 123-456-7890? (If yes) I am just calling back from [organization] *one last time to make sure we didn't upset you or rub you the wrong way the last time we called. We really appreciate what you have to say, and we would still like you to share your opinions with us. Many people who were reluctant at first to take part in the survey later said that they were glad they did because they had the opportunity to voice their ideas and opinions. I hope now is a convenient time to finish the interview.*

Note that the first sentence establishes distance and implies anonymity. Thus, it is useful even for a named list sample. The second sentence suggests regret for a prior caller's mistake. Inviting the respondent to forgive and forget is an approach that may work with some potential respondents. But it could backfire if the person decides to chew you out for the prior callers' (purported) bad behavior.

I prefer directing concern to the survey, as in the next example, for it places the responsibility for the problem on the respondent (biased survey results, wrong public policy decisions). Your call essentially allows respondents to assume guilt and to rectify their potential wrongs by participating. For example:

Is this telephone number 123-456-7890? (If yes) I am just calling back from [organization] *one last time to make sure you understand the importance of your participation in the survey. If we do not interview people like you, who are reluctant to participate, the survey results will not accurately represent* [the target population]. *The entire survey's results could end up biased, and public policymakers could draw the wrong conclusions. You represent thousands of people similar to you. They need you to voice their ideas and opinions. I hope now is a convenient time to finish the interview.*

Note the final clauses. "... thousands of people similar to you ... need you ..." Guilt, guilt, guilt. If the respondent does not talk now, thousands of others will never have a voice. And note the phrase "... to finish the interview." This deliberately implies that the interview was previously started and that the end is near. Although the calling-with-concern approach may seem heavy-handed, this is your last chance to get this person to participate, so pull out all the stops.

In the third approach, the cold-call, you act as if this is a brand-new survey and no one from your organization has ever called before. It takes courage to pull off this polite fiction. However, it also gives respondents who have changed their mind a chance to participate without hand wringing. Indeed, you will find many formerly reluctant respondents happy to cooperate.

EXHIBIT 6.2. INTERVIEWERS' COMMENTS ABOUT SUCCESSFUL REFUSAL CONVERSIONS.

- EF refused to do it and was going to hang up many times. I tried real hard to keep her on the line and explained how important it was, encouraged her to try some questions. Finally, she said, "Read me some questions," and then she answered all the way. She did it!!! She was very kind actually.

- MR was very skeptical about the survey. However, after encouraging him, he participated. He gave lots of comments on many questions and laughed at the questions. . . . He said he has never participated in a telephone survey [before]. The question on race: He said human race. He was, however, very cooperative. At the end he asked for the sponsors; I gave all the names and tel. #s of the sponsors.

- EF refused to do the survey. After I explained it to her, then she wanted to try. She answered with sounds of interest . . .

- MR refused and was going to hang up. After explaining how important the survey was, he tried it. Cooperative.

- FR refused firmly and tried to hang up. Luckily, I persuaded her successfully. She did the survey. Very cooperative.

- At first, she thought it was too long and only wanted to do five minutes at a time [with callbacks] but she ended up doing the whole thing!

- Did not want to take survey, had "attitude," but it's done.

- EF didn't want to participate. After long conversion techniques, she agreed to try. She did it! She was nice.

- I had to use almost every refusal conversion technique—egads.

Source: Oregon Annual Social Indicators Survey, 2000; Oregon Annual Social Indicators Survey, 2001; Oregon Transportation Needs and Issues Survey 2001. Retrieved January 2, 2007, from http://hdl.handle.net/1794/1051 and http://hdl.handle.net/1794/1052.

These variations have all resulted in successful refusal conversions. You can make up others that work well for you or for a particular type of respondent. Of course, you still must always convey the informed consent language. You will just follow a slightly different path.

Refusal conversion is hard work emotionally. If you succeed, pat yourself on the back heartily. Note which strategies tend to work best for you and remember to reuse them. See Exhibit 6.2 for examples of what some interviewers have had to say about their successful refusal conversions.

Once you convert a refusal, do not slack off! When interviewers know they are working with a reluctant respondent, they often probe an open-ended answer less fully and tend to accept a "don't know" answer more readily than they would with an eager respondent. Do not let the glory of your success in landing the respondent undermine the quality of the data obtained for that person.

Of course you must always remember in the back of your mind that every adult has a right to refuse an interview. If all your strategies fail and the respondent refuses persistently, thank the person politely and hang up.

If you seem to be getting many initial refusals and phone slams on a certain day or for a certain survey, take a hard look at yourself in your mental mirror. You owe it to your employer and your fellow interviewers to work in top form. Is there something in your voice, your attitude, or the way you are delivering questions that could be affecting your calls? If so, rectify it or explain to your supervisor that you are having a bad day and ask to go home early. Did you miss something in the interviewer training for a particular survey: for example, by arriving late or running outside for a bathroom break at a crucial moment? If your refusals seem higher than normal for a particular survey, be honest about it with your supervisor. Ask for assistance so as not to make things harder for your coworkers.

Unusual Situations

Occasionally, you will encounter unusual situations before you can start an interview. For example, you may discover that an intended respondent cannot speak or hear or does not speak English, or you may be pretty sure that the respondent was your high school English teacher many years ago. This section explains what to do in such circumstances.

Speech or Hearing Impaired

What should you do if your randomly selected adult seems to have extreme difficulty speaking or hearing? For hard-of-hearing respondents, try cupping your hands around your microphone to enhance your voice. You need to determine whether that person's disability is temporary. For respondents who are half asleep, sick, emotionally upset, or under the influence of drugs or alcohol, you may be able to conduct the interview at a later date. If so, arrange a callback, using call disposition code 5.21, or if appropriate within study guidelines, ask to speak with another household member.

If the speech or hearing impairment seems chronic or permanent, ask to speak with someone else in the household in order to confirm the problem. If no one else is available, thank the respondent and assign call disposition code 2.32 or 5.21, as appropriate. In exceptionally rare situations, an able-bodied adult may be allowed to translate for the respondent who cannot speak or hear. But you must receive permission from an interviewer supervisor for such a decision. Translators, no matter how well meaning, can inadvertently edit the intended respondent's answers. Using a TTY (teletypewriter) service is preferable.

Many survey organizations encourage accommodating respondents who have difficulty communicating. Determine whether a severely hearing-disabled respondent has TTY service. If so, follow these steps. (1) When you get off the telephone with the respondent, do not assign a call disposition code yet. (2) Find the telephone number for your state or local TTY service and call it. (3) Give the TTY operator your respondent's telephone number, after briefly explaining that the person will be participating in an interview. (4) Wait while the operator connects with your respondent. (5) Once connected, you will read the questions, the operator will transcribe them and transmit them to the respondent, the respondent will then reply to the operator, and the operator will read you his or her answers. Although time consuming, this procedure enables an important subgroup of the population to be represented in the survey.

Does Not Speak English

What should you do with respondents who cannot speak English or whose English is so heavily accented that you cannot understand what they mean to say? Ask to speak with someone who speaks English (or better English). Ask that person the basic questions to determine the appropriate respondent. If the person you need is the one who does not speak sufficient English, find out the language your respondent prefers. If your employer has interviewers available who can conduct interviews in that language, use an appropriate call disposition code or procedure to transfer that respondent to the bilingual interviewer. If all you need is basic information in order to determine the appropriate respondent in the household, ask whether there is someone else available for you to talk with. If no one else is available, thank the respondent for his or her time, record the call as a language barrier (disposition code 5.32), and note in the message box the language spoken or your best guess of what it is.

You Know the Respondent

What should you do if you realize that you are about to interview someone you know personally or by reputation? Under no circumstances should you conduct the interview. This will occur very rarely; many interviewers never experience it. You are not likely to recognize a friend's or relative's telephone number because you will usually press a computer key and the telephone will be dialed automatically. Instead, you are likely to recognize the person's voice in the first few introductory exchanges or questions. I have had interviewers who recognized the voices of a neighbor from their childhood, a well-known athlete, and a former high school teacher. Once an interviewer I employed even reached our state governor, on an unlisted line at the governor's mansion. Because this interviewer did not follow politics or vote, he did not realize with whom he was speaking until the governor identified himself.

If you recognize a respondent's voice, follow these steps quickly. Raise your hand to catch the attention of an interviewer supervisor, tell your respondent that you have a "computer problem," press the mute button so that the respondent cannot hear you, and quickly tell your supervisor that you know (or know of) this person. Your supervisor will take your seat and complete the interview on your behalf, explaining to the respondent that you were called away for a moment.

Interviewing someone you know may cause biases in how you ask questions (that is, the inflection of voice) or how you record answers. It can also put you in a difficult position for maintaining confidentiality. Knowing a famous person's opinions on an issue can be difficult to keep to yourself. Ultimately, the state governor my interviewer contacted refused to participate in the survey, arguing that because it was a state-sponsored research project he was essentially the client. He might also have had confidentiality concerns.

Summing Up

Remember, you are the link between the researchers who need data to solve social problems and the respondents whose answers to questions will help solve these problems. The statistical validity of the survey results depends on many of your interviewing qualities, including tone of voice, impartiality, pace, timing, awareness, and professionalism. Each survey introduction and each interview demands and exercises these skills. In order to increase survey response rates and accuracy, you should always do what you can to persuade each respondent to complete the interview. You must try to gain the confidence of skeptical persons, and you must try to interview busy and less cooperative people as well as the people who eagerly and cooperatively complete the interview.

> Now is always better than later to conduct an interview.

In fact most respondents readily agree to participate in a survey immediately or after a token question or two. Learn to control your voice's inflection, volume, timbre, and pace—and learn how to adapt your voice appropriately as needed. Do not read statements as questions (remember *Clueless*). Know each survey thoroughly in order to be able to answer respondents' questions without hesitation. Memorize answers to common questions for each survey. Actively listen to respondents' questions or objections. Answer only the questions respondents ask; nothing more or less. Never ask reluctant respondents a question that they can answer with "no." Understand the difference between a soft refusal and a hard refusal, and use the appropriate call disposition code. When respondents refuse to participate, do not take it personally. Always write clear, detailed messages for the next interviewer. In calling back refusals, develop a strategy in advance for approaching the person. Remember that now is always better than later to conduct an interview.

This chapter's focus on respondents' questions, objections, and refusals makes it easy to forget that a survey interview is usually an enjoyable experience for respondents (and for you). The standardized interview is designed to enhance respondents' experience of the survey. Throughout the question and answer process, interviewers employ various forms of feedback to encourage and guide respondents. These both build respondents' confidence and give them a feeling of accomplishment. Anonymous telephone interviews, in particular, allow respondents to feel safe about expressing beliefs, behavior, and opinions that persons in the general populace may consider deviant. The attentive listening and subtle, personal consideration that respondents receive from interviewers is rare in everyday conversation. Some respondents say that they enjoy the intellectual stimulation of an interview. Some say that participating gives them insights into a topic they had not thought much about before. Like voting or donating blood, completing a telephone interview appeals to most people's sense of altruism and civic duty. All in all, a ten- to fifteen-minute telephone interviewing experience can prove very satisfying to most people. The next chapter discusses the interview process itself.

CHAPTER SEVEN

ASKING QUESTIONS IN THE STANDARDIZED INTERVIEW

Finally, a respondent agrees to participate in the interview! The actual time between placing the telephone call and reaching this point is generally less than two minutes. Think of the interview as a guided conversation and yourself as the navigator. You steer respondents through the survey questions with your voice and with well-placed feedback.

This chapter focuses on guidelines for asking questions in the standardized interview. It includes information on the psychology of survey response, as well as detailed suggestions on how to ask questions, use feedback effectively, probe respondents' answers, recognize and avoid bias, and record the data accurately.

About Survey Questions

Before you begin asking questions, you will find it helpful to learn about different types of survey questions and different question-and-answer formats.

Question Types

Up to this point, this book has talked about survey questions as if they were mainly about people's opinions. In fact, opinion questions are just one of several types of questions that survey researchers ask. The six basic types of survey questions ask people what they do, what they think, what they believe, what they know, who they are, and where they live. Not every survey includes every type of question, but most surveys contain three or more different types. Table 7.1 displays examples of the different types of questions.

Behavior Behavioral questions ask people what they do, such as how they get to work and how often they exercise. These questions concern people's actions or activities, including what they are doing now, what they have done in the past, and what they plan to do in the future. For example, for the present a survey might ask a woman if she is pregnant or trying to get pregnant. For the past it might ask if she has ever been pregnant. For the future it might ask if she plans to become pregnant.

Table 7.1 shows two behavior-related questions, one for the past and one for the present. In the question labeled YRSRES the behavior is living in a place:

How many years have you lived in Oregon [altogether]?

The optional word "altogether" is included to capture the experience of people who resided in the state in multiple spells, for example, were born and raised there, went away for college and a career, and then returned for retirement. "Altogether" tells respondents that this question is asking for the total number of years, across all intervals. Because the question asks the respondent to think retrospectively, it is a behavioral question about the past. In the question MILES the behavior is driving:

How many miles did you drive a personal vehicle yesterday [altogether]?

Although the question asks about yesterday, not today, it is considered a question related to the present. Surveys do not ask respondents about how many miles they drove on the day of the interview because the time of day that the interview takes place could systematically bias respondents' answers.

Print Conventions

- Interviewers read aloud only the words and sentences printed in lowercase.
- Interviewers never read aloud anything typed in UPPERCASE, such as instructions, answer categories, notes, and the word PROBE.
- Most questions allow the answers "refused," "don't know," "no answer," and—less frequently—"if volunteered." Do not read these answer categories aloud to respondents.

TABLE 7.1. EXAMPLES OF QUESTION TYPES.

Question Type	Example
Behavior (past)	**Q:YRSRES** How many years have you lived in Oregon [altogether]? PROBE FOR "MY WHOLE LIFE": How many years is that? RECORD EXACT NUMBER OF YEARS, NO DECIMALS, ZERO TO 96 OR MORE YEARS 0 = LESS THAN 1 YEAR 96 = 96 OR MORE YEARS 97 REFUSED 98 DON'T KNOW 99 NO ANSWER
Behavior (present)	**Q:MILES** How many miles did you drive a personal vehicle yesterday [altogether]? PROBE: If you drive a vehicle as part of your job, exclude those miles from your answer to this question. PROBE: Apart from the driving you did for your job, how many miles did you drive a personal vehicle yesterday? PROBE FOR "DON'T KNOW": To the best of your knowledge [how many miles did you drive by personal vehicle yesterday]? PROBE FOR "DON'T KNOW": Please give your best estimate. ENTER EXACT NUMBER OF MILES, 0 TO 996 OR MORE 0 = LESS THAN ONE MILE 996 = 996 OR MORE 997 REFUSED 998 DON'T KNOW 999 NO ANSWER
Attitude	**Q:MAINTAIN** I will begin by asking you some questions about how satisfied you are with how the Oregon Department of Transportation does its job on major Oregon highways. For each one, please tell me if you are very satisfied, somewhat satisfied, not very satisfied, or not at all satisfied. First, how satisfied are you with how (ODOT/Oregon Department of Transportation) maintains Oregon's major highways, roads, and bridges?

TABLE 7.1. *(CONTINUED)*

Question Type	Example
	PROBE: Are you very satisfied, somewhat satisfied, not very satisfied, or not at all satisfied?
	1 VERY SATISFIED 2 SOMEWHAT SATISFIED 3 NOT VERY SATISFIED 4 NOT AT ALL SATISFIED 5 IF VOLUNTEERED: IT VARIES/IT DEPENDS
	7 REFUSED 8 DON'T KNOW 9 NO ANSWER
Belief	**Q:GOODJOB** Overall, how good a job do you think the Oregon Department of Transportation is doing—excellent, good, fair, or poor? PROBE: Would you say excellent, good, fair, or poor?
	1 EXCELLENT 2 GOOD 3 FAIR 4 POOR
	7 REFUSED 8 DON'T KNOW 9 NO ANSWER
Knowledge	**Q:EMPOPT1** Some employers offer employees options and incentives that are meant to reduce travel and traffic congestion. As I read a list of these, please tell me if any are available to you where you work. Can you work at home one or more days a week?
	1 YES 2 NO
	7 REFUSED 8 DON'T KNOW 9 NO ANSWER
Demographic	**Q:EDUC** What is the highest level of education you have completed? PROBE FROM LIST
	1 0–8 YEARS, NO GED 2 9–12 YEARS, NO HIGH SCHOOL DIPLOMA OR GED 3 HIGH SCHOOL DIPLOMA OR GED

(continued)

TABLE 7.1. *(CONTINUED)*

Question Type	Example
	4 SOME COLLEGE, NO DEGREE
	5 ASSOCIATE'S DEGREE (AA, AS)
	6 BACHELOR'S DEGREE (BA, BS, AB)
	7 MASTER'S DEGREE (MA, MS, MBA)
	8 DOCTORATE OR PROFESSIONAL DEGREE (PHD, JD, EDD, MD, DDS)
	9 OTHER
	97 REFUSED
	98 DON'T KNOW
	99 NO ANSWER

Attitude Opinion and attitude questions ask people how they think or feel about particular topics, such as local schools, a presidential candidate, or a product. These questions capture respondents' opinions, expectations, moods, and feelings and other psychological states about something or someone. Table 7.1 offers one example of an attitude question in MAINTAIN:

. . . how satisfied are you with how (ODOT/Oregon Department of Transportation) maintains Oregon's major highways, roads, and bridges?

People's satisfaction with something is one dimension of an attitude. This question was the first in a series of five satisfaction questions about how the state maintains its road network.

Belief Questions about beliefs ask people what they think is true. The topics of belief questions might include religious convictions, a public figure's trustworthiness, or perceptions of confidence in something. Several years ago I conducted a large, representative, sample survey of college students asking, in part, how much alcohol they believed other students consumed (a belief question). The survey also asked respondents how much alcohol they consumed (behavioral question). In the data analysis stage of the survey, my colleagues and I compared how much alcohol students actually consumed to their beliefs about how much students in general consumed. We found that students believe that students in general drink a lot more than they actually do. Why is this important? It turns out the more students believe their peers drink, the greater their own alcohol consumption and binge drinking. In other words, their beliefs about student culture appear to validate their own behavior.

The example of a belief question in Table 7.1, GOODJOB, concerns respondents' beliefs about how well a state agency does its job:

Overall, how good a job do you think the Oregon Department of Transportation is doing—excellent, good, fair, or poor?

In this context the word *think* is synonymous with *believe,* because very few people have the information or experience to know with certainty the extent to which a state agency fulfills its mission within the context of its resources. Instead, they answer with what they believe is accurate, based on their experience, what they have heard from others, and the way their culture regards state agencies.

Knowledge Questions asking people about factual items are knowledge questions. Some examples of what knowledge questions might ask include the name of respondents' congressional representative, the number of the congressional district in which respondents reside, or the legal blood alcohol limit in their state. Survey researchers ask knowledge questions carefully, because respondents do not like questions that sound as though they belong on a test. In addition, knowledge often gets mixed up with belief. For example, in a survey I once asked respondents what they knew about "life imprisonment without parole" for convicted murderers. Most did not know that it means convicted murderers with this sentence will stay in prison for the rest of their lives. Rather, they believed that murderers who received that sentence could be paroled some day. (Respondents who did not know the real meaning also more often supported the death penalty.) The point is this: When respondents do not know something, they often answer with what they believe is correct.

The knowledge question in Table 7.1, EMPOPT1, asks employed respondents if they know whether their employer offers policies to reduce employees' commuting hassles:

Some employers offer employees options and incentives that are meant to reduce travel and traffic congestion. As I read a list of these, please tell me if any are available to you where you work. Can you work at home one or more days a week?

Subsequent questions asked respondents if their employers offered bus passes, carpool incentives, and flexible scheduling. As is typical of knowledge questions, many respondents answered "don't know."

Demographic Questions asking people about who they are, that is, their ascribed and achieved characteristics, are demographic questions. Ascribed characteristics are the ones people cannot do anything about, such as age, sex, race, ethnicity, nationality, and first language. Achieved characteristics are those people acquire as they mature, such as education, marital status, parental status, occupation, and income. Surveys almost always include some demographic questions. Survey researchers use these data to describe the sample, to compare the sample to the larger population to assess its representativeness, and to compare the results for people in one group to results for other groups. EDUC in Table 7.1 is a demographic question:

What is the highest level of education you have completed?

Some respondents perceive some demographic questions to be sensitive, such as those about household income. Even in anonymous surveys, typically 10 to 20 percent of respondents refuse to answer income questions. Every so often you will get a respondent who asks, "Why do you need to know my (age/sex/race/income)?" I suspect that such respondents think we intend to examine their individual answers. They do not understand that researchers analyze people's answers in groups and statistical categories. Here are some possible responses, using a firm, businesslike tone of voice:

We need this information to compare groups of people to each other.
We also need it to make sure our sample matches all of the people in [the target population].
This is the best way to examine the data anonymously.

Most demographic questions are positioned at the end of the interview, because they are not the main topic of the survey. (The opening groups of questions should be about the survey topic, because that topic is part of the reason respondents agree to participate.) Placing potentially sensitive questions at the end is also strategic. By then almost all respondents have fully committed to the task of completing the interview, have trusted you this far, and are likely to continue trusting you through to the end.

Question Formats

Survey questions come in three basic formats, defined by the type of answer they seek: closed-ended, open-ended, and combination, as described in the following sections.

Closed-Ended Questions For closed-ended questions the survey supplies all possible answer categories, such as yes or no, male or female, agree-disagree scales (strongly agree, somewhat agree, somewhat disagree, or strongly disagree), and frequencies (always, often, sometimes, rarely, or never). The respondent's task is

EXHIBIT 7.1. EXAMPLES OF CLOSED-ENDED QUESTIONS.

Q:CONGEST

How serious a problem is traffic congestion in your community—[is it] very serious, somewhat serious, a minor problem, or no problem at all?

1 VERY SERIOUS
2 SOMEWHAT SERIOUS
3 MINOR PROBLEM
4 NO PROBLEM AT ALL

7 REFUSED
8 DON'T KNOW
9 NO ANSWER

Q:EMPOPT2

Can you work four ten-hour days instead of the usual five eight-hour days?
PROBE: All I need is a yes or no answer.

1 YES
2 NO
3 IF VOLUNTEERED: R WORKS PART-TIME

7 REFUSED
8 DON'T KNOW
9 NO ANSWER

to choose the answer category that best suits him or her. Your task is to record that person's choice accurately.

Closed-ended questions should be phrased so that respondents need little probing from you to understand their answer options. Usually this means that the answer choices from which the respondent must choose are embedded in the question. Alternatively, when a series of questions all use the same answer categories, the first one stresses the answer categories, and subsequent questions repeat them only in probes (as shown in the question MAINTAIN in Table 7.1).

Exhibit 7.1 shows two examples of closed-ended questions. For CONGEST the answer categories are embedded in the question:

How serious a problem is traffic congestion in your community—[is it] very serious, somewhat serious, a minor problem, or no problem at all?

You must read the entire question exactly as written, all the way to the end, in order for respondents to hear all the answer categories. Answer categories that are optional or repetitive will appear in probes or as text in brackets.

In the second example, EMPOPT2, the answer categories—yes or no—are implicit in the question:

Can you work four ten-hour days instead of the usual five eight-hour days?

EMPOPT2 is actually what survey researchers call a partially closed-ended question, because it has an "if volunteered" answer category. Skip logic directed only employed respondents to this question, but it did not distinguish between full-time and part-time workers. The wording of EMPOPT2 assumes all respondents are employed full-time. For respondents who volunteer that they work part-time, interviewers use code 3. Sometimes chatty respondents feel obligated to explain their employment options, not realizing that survey answer categories are limited. You can use the probe below the question to guide respondents and keep them on track:

All I need is a yes or no answer.

As with the survey questions, interviewers must read probes exactly as written.

Open-Ended Questions   When questions allow respondents to give free, or open, responses—that is, responses in a respondent's own words, without using precoded answer categories—they are called *open-ended questions*. Answers to open-ended questions can be *numeric* (numbers) or *alpha* (words), depending on the question.

Numeric answers include responses to questions about counts of miles, years, inches, pounds, dollars, days, events, and people. TRIP1 (Exhibit 7.2) offers an example of an open-ended question that elicits a numeric answer:

How many one-way trips did you make by any means of transportation [yesterday]?

The several probes in TRIP1 help respondents understand what is meant by a one-way trip. The interviewer records the number the respondent gives: 0, 1, 2, and so on up to 30, which signifies 30 or more one-way trips per day.

> Never paraphrase respondents or interpret what you thought they were trying to say when you record answers to open-ended questions.

Alpha answers consist of respondents' narratives, their answers in their own words. ENDING1 (Exhibit 7.2) offers an example of an open-ended question that elicits an alpha answer:

Is there anything you would like to add?

EXHIBIT 7.2. EXAMPLES OF OPEN-ENDED QUESTIONS.

Example of a Numeric Question

Q:TRIP1

Now I need you to think about your own travel yesterday. How many one-way trips did you make by any means of transportation [yesterday]?
PROBE FOR "ONE-WAY": A trip is defined as one-way travel to a place that is three or more blocks away, or more than a five-minute walk away.
PROBE: Travel to and from work would be considered two trips.
PROBE: Even if yesterday was not a typical day for you.

ENTER EXACT NUMBER OF TRIPS, 0 TO 30 OR MORE

0 = NO TRIPS YESTERDAY
30 = 30 OR MORE

97 REFUSED
98 DON'T KNOW
99 NO ANSWER

Example of an Alpha Question

Q:ENDING1

That is the end of the survey. On behalf of the Oregon Department of Transportation, we thank you sincerely for your time and opinions on these questions. Is there anything you would like to add?

OPEN-ENDED
TYPE EXACT RESPONSE BELOW

When respondents answer open-ended questions, interviewers must type exactly what they say, verbatim (word for word). You should include even "uh," "um," "oh, I don't know," partial sentences, ungrammatical phrases, and profanity. Never, ever paraphrase a respondent or interpret what you thought someone was trying to say when you record answers to open-ended questions. Some researchers look for patterns in these narratives, and any changes you introduce could ruin their studies. If you type, "She said . . ." your supervisor will know you interpreted or paraphrased.

Combination Questions When questions mix open-ended and closed-ended formats, they are called *combination questions*. They appear in two basic forms: (1) partially closed-ended questions, that is, questions offering mostly closed-ended, precoded answer categories plus an "other → specify" option, and (2) questions that sound open-ended to respondents even though interviewers will assign their answers to precoded answer categories. Some combination questions contain elements of both forms. Exhibit 7.3 shows examples.

EXHIBIT 7.3. EXAMPLES OF COMBINATION QUESTIONS.

Q:RACE

What is your race [or ethnicity]?
PROBE FROM LIST: Are you:

1 WHITE/CAUCASIAN
2 BLACK/AFRICAN AMERICAN
3 ASIAN AMERICAN/PACIFIC ISLANDER
4 LATINO, HISPANIC
5 AMERICAN INDIAN/NATIVE AMERICAN/ALASKA NATIVE
6 IF VOLUNTEERED: BIRACIAL/MIXED RACE
7 IF VOLUNTEERED: OTHER → SPECIFY

97 REFUSED
98 DON'T KNOW
99 NO ANSWER

Q:NEWSERVA

ODOT is thinking about a number of new ways to deliver travel information to road users. When you need information about traffic conditions, weather conditions, road construction, and road closures, what source of travel information do you use first?
PROBE FROM LIST—ROTATING

1 ELECTRONIC SIGNS OR READER BOARDS ALONG THE HIGHWAY
2 RADIO BROADCASTS
3 INFORMATION CENTERS AT PARKS AND REST AREAS
4 INTERNET FOR LIVE VIDEO CONDITIONS (*WWW.TRIPCHECK.COM*)
5 FREE (1–800) TELEPHONE NUMBER
6 A CABLE TV CHANNEL
7 OTHER (CB RADIO, NON-CABLE TV, AND SO FORTH)

97 REFUSED
98 DON'T KNOW
99 NO ANSWER

Partially closed-ended questions offer an "other → specify" for respondents who volunteer an answer different from the categories provided. Questions are designed this way when the researchers want to know what each respondent said. The question RACE (Exhibit 7.3)—*What is your race [or ethnicity]?*—contains an "other → specify" option. When you type the code number for "other → specify" (code 7 in RACE), the computer-assisted telephone interviewing (CATI) system jumps automatically to a pop-up screen in which you type exactly what this respondent said. In this case, you might record "the human race," "Middle Eastern," or whatever else the respondent said that did not fit another category. Use the "other → specify" option prudently, only when respondents' answers cannot fit into a closed-ended category or when respondents refuse to place their answer into such a category, as discussed in the section on probing below. (When an "other" answer category lacks the "specify" aspect, it is considered closed-ended. See, for example, code 7 for NEWSERVA in Exhibit 7.3 and code 9 for EDUC in Table 7.1.)

Both NEWSERVA and RACE (Exhibit 7.3) exemplify the second type of combination question. That is, they both sound like open-ended questions when read aloud because the questions lack answer categories. However, the answer categories that interviewers use are closed-ended (except for the "other → specify" option in RACE). Most respondents will answer these questions quickly and spontaneously. Your task is to fit what each respondent says into the existing answer categories.

With this type of question you must be very familiar with the answer categories in advance. You cannot take the time to read all the answer categories to yourself in trying to find the correct one for a respondent's answer. Both RACE and NEWSERVA show unordered answer categories, meaning that the code numbers beside the answers could be reversed or randomized without consequences. Unordered answer categories are more challenging for interviewers to memorize than ordered answer categories are.

Both questions contain an interviewer probing instruction. In RACE, interviewers are told to "probe from list." This means that if a respondent fumbles or pauses, you should not hesitate to read a few categories aloud until the respondent chooses one. The goal is to help respondents bring their own words to mind. (Note that this RACE question does not meet federal guidelines for asking people's race and ethnicity. This subject is discussed in more detail later in this chapter.)

NEWSERVA further instructs interviewers to "probe from list—rotating," meaning that you should rotate the probe you offer first. So the first time you need to probe, start with answer category 1 and work your way down until the respondent chooses the answer he or she was searching for. The second time you need to probe this question, start with category 2, work your way down and then to back to the top, ending by reading category 1. The third time, start with category 3, work your way down, go back to the top, and end with category 2. Because you will not be using this technique very often, you will need to keep track of which probe to start with next. Most interviewers keep track by making notes on a scratch pad. Why rotate? Respondents have a tendency to choose the first or last answer category offered, especially if they are lazy or were reluctant from the start. Rotating the probe you offer first helps the survey to avoid this bias for one code category over another, but rotating accurately takes special interviewer care and concentration.

Answer Formats

As you have undoubtedly noticed by now, each answer to a closed-ended question has a number code attached to it. For example, in Exhibit 7.3, code 1 for RACE corresponds with the answer category "white/Caucasian" and code 2 corresponds with "black/African American."

The way in which the numbers are assigned to answer categories often makes no difference to researchers. By custom, researchers generally assign code 1 to yes and code 2 to no. But it would make no difference if yes and no were assigned the opposite numbers. Similarly, it does not matter if the answer categories "strongly agree," "somewhat agree," "somewhat disagree," and "strongly disagree" are numbered 1 through 4 or 4 through 1. When the numbering scheme and the numbers themselves have no intrinsic meaning, the answer categories are called *unordered*.

Sometimes the numbers assigned to answer categories have some significance. For example, it makes more sense to number a frequency question's answer categories of "never," "rarely," "sometimes," "often," and "always" as 0, 1, 2, 3, and 4, rather than vice versa, because "none" corresponds to 0. Similarly, it makes sense to number age categories from low to high. These are called *ordered* answer categories.

Also notice that some answers require you to record more than one digit. Codes for most lists of closed-ended answer categories range from 1 to 9. They are one digit wide. In contrast, numeric answers to open-ended questions are often two or three digits wide. Exhibit 7.4 shows, for example, the question YRSRES—"*How many years have you lived in Oregon [altogether]?*" Answers to this question are allowed two digits. Answers to MILES—"*How many miles did you drive a personal vehicle yesterday [altogether]?*"—are allowed three digits. A question asking for respondents' ZIP codes would require five-digit answers (for example, for the ZIP code 97403). *Answer width* refers to the number of digits you record.

Take a close look at the numbered code categories and notes to interviewers for YRSRES and MILES. Zero signifies less than one year (or mile). For YRSRES, code 96 indicates that the respondent lived in Oregon for 96 or more years. For MILES, code 996 indicates that the respondent drove a personal vehicle for 996 or more miles on the preceding day. For numbers between 0 and 96 (or between 0 and 996), you should type exactly what the respondent says, for example, "25" if the respondent says "twenty-five years," or, "9," for "nine miles." The interviewer notes instruct you to record the "exact number" of years and miles, using no decimals. "No decimals" means that if a respondent says he drove "eight and one-half miles," you must probe by saying,

EXHIBIT 7.4. EXAMPLES OF ANSWER CATEGORIES.

Q:YRSRES

How many years have you lived in Oregon [altogether]?
PROBE FOR "MY WHOLE LIFE": How many years is that?
RECORD EXACT NUMBER OF YEARS, NO DECIMALS, 0 TO 96 OR MORE YEARS

0 = LESS THAN 1 YEAR
96 = 96 OR MORE YEARS

97 REFUSED
98 DON'T KNOW
99 NO ANSWER

Q:MILES

How many miles did you drive a personal vehicle yesterday [altogether]?
PROBE: If you drive a vehicle as part of your job, exclude those miles from your answer to this question.
PROBE: Apart from driving you did for your job, how many miles did you drive a personal vehicle yesterday?
PROBE FOR "DON'T KNOW": To the best of your knowledge [how many miles did you drive by personal vehicle yesterday]?
PROBE FOR "DON'T KNOW": Please give your best estimate.
RECORD EXACT NUMBER OF MILES, NO DECIMALS, 0 TO 996 OR MORE

0 = LESS THAN ONE MILE
996 = 996 OR MORE

997 REFUSED
998 DON'T KNOW
999 NO ANSWER

Was that closer to eight or closer to nine miles?

You will learn more about probing later in this chapter.

In these examples, codes 7, 97, and 997 are reserved for refusals; that is, when a respondent refuses to answer the question. The codes 8, 98, and 998 are reserved for "don't know" (or "not sure") answers. The codes 9, 99, and 999 are reserved for questions that the respondent did not answer at all. Interviewers should use the "no answer" codes only rarely. For example, if a respondent says, "I am going to hang up if you keep asking me questions about how far I drive," you can press 9 as many times as you need to get to the next question group (all the while saying cooing things to keep the respondent on the line, a concern we will get to later).

Not all survey organizations use the same codes for "refused," "don't know," and "no answer." Some, for example, combine "don't know" and "refused" answers into a single category (even though they mean very different things). Others do not allow interviewer-initiated "no answer" coding. Most survey organizations, however, use something similar to the codes shown here.

For alpha open-ended questions, there are no codes 7, 8, or 9. When respondents answer these questions, you should always type in exactly what they say.

Now that you know the basics of question and answer structures, we turn to what respondents experience in the process of answering survey questions.

How Respondents Answer Survey Questions

When respondents hear a survey question, how do they go about answering it? What mental processes underlie how respondents choose their answers? The most current psychological model of survey response says that respondents experience four basic cognitive processes when answering survey questions: comprehension, retrieval, judgment, and response.[1] This means, basically, that respondents decide what a question means, search their memories for related information, combine that information into decisions, and fit their decisions onto the answer categories offered. Each step is described in more detail in the following sections, with special attention to problems that can affect answer accuracy and to your role as an interviewer in the process.

Comprehension

Comprehension refers to how respondents come to understand a survey question. Respondents listen to a question and any instructions that go with it. They figure out what the question means and the type of information the question seeks. Even this first step can be fraught with potential problems, such as not completely understanding a word or term, mishearing part of the question, or getting distracted in the process of listening so that they miss certain words or clauses altogether. The question itself should not interfere with respondents' understanding by being, for example, too long, too complicated, or double-barreled.

Retrieval

In the retrieval step, respondents search their memories for relevant experience or information. The quality of their memories is influenced by the salience of the event, feeling, attribute, knowledge, or belief they attempt to recall, that is, how much it stands out in their memories. When salience is high, the memory is easier to find, more complete once it is found, and more accurately reported. Salience is determined by whether respondents have direct, personal experience with the question topic, how long ago that experience occurred, and the meanings they attach to the experience, such as how distinctive it was and whether it had an emotional impact. When salience is not high, respondents cobble together an answer based on whatever generic memories related to the question topic they can summon. The task is more difficult and the accuracy of their report may be lower.

Judgment

The ability to retrieve memories relevant to the question does not automatically create an answer. In the judgment step, respondents integrate their memories into an answer. Judgment depends in part on the type of question, that is, whether it concerns behavior, demographic characteristics, attitude, belief, or knowledge. Factual answers (for example, about whether, where, when, or how something occurred) to the first two types of questions can depend on how much difficulty respondents experienced retrieving the memory, how much information respondents can remember, and how they repair gaps in what they remember. Attitude answers depend on how well respondents' thoughts on the matter cohere and on how well reasoned their thoughts are—and whether they have thought about the issue at all—as well as the context in which the questions are presented.

Response

Once respondents have sifted through and integrated their memories about the question topic, they must decide how to plot or map their judgments onto the answer categories provided. How they do this will depend on whether the answer categories are closed-ended or open-ended and, if open, whether they are alpha or numeric. For numeric answers, such as an answer to MILES—*"How many miles did you drive a personal vehicle yesterday [altogether]?"*—a common respondent error is rounding to the nearest zero or five. That is, respondents are more likely to remember driving fifty miles than the actual forty-eight miles that they drove that day. On rating scales that range from "positive" to "negative" or from "strongly agree" to "strongly disagree," respondents who lack strong feelings on the topic tend to give the positive and agree answers. This is called *positivity bias*.

Most of the literature on the psychology of survey response is intended for professional survey researchers, not interviewers. The studies on this topic guide researchers in creating the best possible questions and in understanding the patterns of responses that they find when analyzing the survey data. However, it is also important for interviewers such as you to understand how respondents experience the question and answer process, so that you can help them become the best possible respondents. The next sections are intended to integrate your new knowledge with best practices for interviewers. We start with the guidelines for asking questions and then turn to handling problems in the question and answer process.

Guidelines for Asking Questions in the Standardized Interview

A survey instrument is a scientific instrument. Your job is to administer that instrument to a few randomly chosen people who represent an entire population. To do that, you will read the survey script systematically, in the ways described here. The manner in which you give the survey should not influence respondents' replies. That is, respondents should give the same answers to you that they would give to any interviewer trained as you are trained. You should be able to get in and out of respondents' lives so smoothly that next week they barely recall participating in a survey. In order to do all this, follow these essential rules of the standardized survey interview.

Read All Questions Exactly as Written

Each question has a certain purpose behind it. The people who designed the instrument chose each word and phrase with care so that respondents from different places and different backgrounds would understand them. Pretesters tested each question to make sure that respondents understood it, that their answers fit the answer categories, and that the question caused no bias. If any problems arose, the question was revised and pretested again. Your job is to deliver the question to respondents exactly as written so that they will give comparable results across all interviewers.

> The manner in which you read the survey instrument should not influence a respondent's replies. Another interviewer should obtain the same answers from a respondent that you did.

Be very careful not to add, remove, or change words or phrases in questions. Never reword questions to match your perceptions of a respondent. For example, never substitute simpler words for a respondent with a foreign accent or upgrade language for a respondent who seems highly educated. It is a mistake to stereotype respondents. The one with a foreign accent may be a brilliant chemist, and the one who seems cultured and knowledgeable may have just finished a long sentence in prison (where there is lots of time to read). No matter who respondents seem to be, you must expose them to the survey instrument in a standard manner, varying language only with scripted probes, fill, and optional language.

Shortening questions can be tempting when you have rushed or impatient respondents, when the interview is taking more time than it should, or when respondents' prior answers suggest how they will answer the current question. Dropping words can happen easily if a respondent interrupts you. Sometimes you will get tired, and then you may inadvertently forget words or substitute words that you use in everyday conversation for the scripted words. Do not do it! Table 7.2 offers some examples of the damage that can occur when the words in a question are altered.

Always avoid going off script. Never, ever change the way in which a question is worded. If a respondent interrupts you, start over and read the question again. If a respondent asks you to explain a word, term, or phrase, use only scripted answers. If no scripted reply is offered to guide you, say, in a friendly tone,

Whatever it means to you.

Never assume that a respondent's prior answers will predict a subsequent answer. Listen to yourself. If you find yourself getting sloppy with how you are reading questions, take a break. You may be overtired.

It is your responsibility to ensure that every respondent is fully exposed to every appropriate question. Remember, another interviewer should be able to obtain the exact same answers from the respondent that you did. Follow-up verification calls by your supervisors will check this.

Read All Questions in the Order Presented

Always ask all questions in their proper sequence in the interview. Survey interviews are constructed so that a series of questions develops an idea, or a series of linked ideas, in a specific manner. The interview should flow smoothly and naturally from one topic to the next, as in ordinary conversation, to maximize respondents' attention. Asking questions out of order will disrupt this development. With telephone interviews programmed in CATI, the opportunity for interviewers to jump around in the instrument is minimized. If you find a way to read questions out of order, the interview will probably last longer and you might get confounded by preprogrammed question skips.

TABLE 7.2. ERRORS CAUSED BY ALTERED WORDS IN QUESTIONS.

	Question Asked	Comments
Example 1		
Question as written	*How many minutes does it usually take you to get to work?*	As written, the question asks for the usual number of minutes. The word "usually" suggests that respondents ignore temporary, abnormal conditions, such as traffic associated with road repair.
Question reworded	*How long does it usually take you to get to work?*	Asking "how long" instead of "how many minutes" may elicit responses in hours rather than in minutes, making answers less precise than the researcher intended. For example, a respondent might answer "a quarter hour" instead of the actual time of 16 minutes. In addition, the interviewer must quickly translate "an hour and 5 minutes" into 65 minutes, which takes extra moments and is error prone. Worse, the interviewer might accidentally record a 1 (for 1 hour) instead of 65 (the actual number of minutes).
Word in question dropped	*How many minutes does it take you to get to work?*	Leaving out "usually" could cause respondents to think of their recent commute time rather than their usual commute time. But their recent commute may be temporarily abnormal due to a month of road repair.
Example 2		
Question as written	*What is the highest level of education you have completed?*	As written, this question elicits degrees, grade level, years, or some combination of the two, such as "a high school diploma," "2 years of college past high school," or "eighth grade." The respondents who most often answer with grade levels are the elderly and certain immigrants.

TABLE 7.2. *(CONTINUED)*

	Question Asked	Comments
Question reworded	*How many years of education you have completed?*	Changing "level of education" to "years of education" elicits answers in years. A high school diploma, for example, is typically 12 years. When respondents answer "20 years," does it mean that they achieved an advanced graduate degree or that they just took a long time to achieve a bachelor's degree? The original question captures more, and clearer, information.

Most surveys include skip logic that keep you from asking certain respondents inappropriate questions. Skip logic branches from contingency questions, such as, "*Last week, did you work for pay, either full- or part-time?*" and, "*Do any children age eighteen or under live in your home?*" The CATI system is programmed so that those who answer yes to such questions flow automatically into related questions appropriate to them and those who answer no are automatically skipped past those follow-up questions. With skip logic, interviewers will not belabor unemployed persons with questions about their jobs or childless households with questions about children. Skip logic keeps interviews to the point. Some surveys have extensive skip logic; others have little. Because of skip logic, each interview you conduct for a particular survey may differ somewhat from all the others.

Never Skip a Question

Read all questions in the instrument as CATI presents them to you, no matter what the circumstances. Sometimes in answering one question, respondents provide information that answers (or appears to answer) a later question. For example, when asked, "*How many years have you lived in Oregon [altogether]?*", a respondent might answer, "My whole life," to which you would reply with the scripted probe: "*How many years is that?*" Then near the end of the interview, you will find yourself asking the question, "*How old are you?*" Do not try to remember what the respondent told you previously. If you do remember, do not answer the second question on the respondent's behalf. If you notice an inconsistency between a respondent's reply to the current question and that person's reply to an earlier question, even on factual items like age, do not say anything about it (except in the rare surveys that specifically train you to do so). Pointing out inconsistencies can make respondents feel stupid and resentful, which is not a good tactic for completing an interview. If the respondent complains, "I already told you that!" offer one of these replies, as appropriate:

I have to ask every question in the order it is presented (apologetic tone).
Please repeat your answer. I don't recall what you said (polite tone).

In this situation, do not ask yes or no questions, such as, "*Would you mind repeating your answer?*" Respondents can too easily answer such questions negatively or refuse, saying, for example, "Yes, as a matter of fact, I do mind."

Sometimes a respondent thinks two questions are the same when they really are not; the respondent has not listened carefully. If a respondent complains about perceived repetition, say,

I have to ask every question in turn (apologetic tone).

Understand too that researchers sometimes deliberately build redundant questions into a survey instrument to check respondents' consistency. As a matter of fact, respondents do answer inconsistently at times. Inconsistency can be a normal outcome of participating in an interview. That is, in the process of taking the interview, respondents think about a topic more than they would have on their own. In thinking about it more, their views change. Such changes occur most often in respondents whose views were weakly held or not well considered at the start. Survey researchers study such inconsistencies for clues to respondent behavior. If you try to make the data consistent on the respondent's behalf, you will undermine that research.

Sometimes respondents will ask you to skip questions. For example, when you are in the process of asking a topical series of questions with identical answer categories, a respondent may say something like this: "Just put me down as a 'somewhat agree' on all of them." Do not do so. You must ask every respondent every appropriate question. Instead, say,

I have to ask every question in the order it is listed (apologetic tone).
We are almost done (cheery tone).

How to Use Fill and Optional Language in Survey Questions

At times interviewers must choose appropriate, standardized words or phrases in a question; this material is called *fill*. Fill is obligatory—that is, interviewers must choose one of the words or phrases offered, selecting the one that best fits each respondent. *Optional* language is discretionary; interviewers use their best judgment to determine whether each respondent needs to hear it. To distinguish obligatory language from discretionary fill, I present obligatory words in parentheses and optional words in brackets. However, some survey research organizations use parentheses for both, not distinguishing between obligatory and optional language.

> Obligatory fill appears in parentheses. Interviewers *must* choose a word or phrase that best suits the respondent. Optional words appear in brackets. Interviewers *may* use a word or phrase, as they see fit.

Optional survey language also appears in standardized probes. Often probes are developed to address issues that appear in pretesting. Other probes emerge when groups of survey questions have identical answer categories or identical lead-in language. It can be tedious and time consuming to repeat the exact same lead-in for ten parallel questions ten times. When the interviewer asks a group of questions with identical answer categories, most respondents do not need to hear these categories repeated more than two or three times. Probes for identical lead-ins and answer categories allow interviewers to repeat them at their discretion, based on actively listening to respondents.

Exhibit 7.5 presents examples of fill and optional language. OPIN1 introduces a series of twelve questions, of which this exhibit displays three, with this transitional sentence:

Now, I need your opinions on where Oregon resources and money should be spent.

This is followed with a sentence instructing respondents on how to answer the upcoming questions:

For each item I read, please tell me if you think it is very important, somewhat important, or not important [for spending state resources and money].

Note that the last clause in that sentence is in brackets, meaning that it is optional. It repeats a clause from the first sentence that you can read when, in your judgment, a particular respondent needs to hear it again.

The third sentence of the OPIN1 question is a statement, implicitly asking respondents to apply the answer categories that they have already heard. The question itself is in the probe. Because OPIN1 is the first question in the series, most interviewers go directly from the statement into the probe, to make sure respondents learn the answer categories:

EXHIBIT 7.5. EXAMPLES OF FILL, OPTIONAL LANGUAGE, AND PROBES.

Q:OPIN1

Now, I need your opinions on where Oregon resources and money should be spent. For each item I read, please tell me if you think it is very important, somewhat important, or not important *[for spending state resources and money]*. The first item is local public transportation service in cities.
PROBE: Do you think this issue is very important, somewhat important, or not important *[for spending state resources and money]*?

1 VERY IMPORTANT
2 SOMEWHAT IMPORTANT
3 NOT IMPORTANT

7 REFUSED
8 DON'T KNOW
9 NO ANSWER

Q:OPIN2

(What about/The next item is) bus services between cities?
PROBE: Do you think this issue is very important, somewhat important, or not important [for spending state resources and money]?

1 VERY IMPORTANT
2 SOMEWHAT IMPORTANT
3 NOT IMPORTANT

7 REFUSED
8 DON'T KNOW
9 NO ANSWER

Q:OPIN3

(What about/The next item is) adding sidewalks and bike paths to existing streets?
PROBE: Do you think this issue is very important, somewhat important, or not important [for spending state resources and money]?

1 VERY IMPORTANT
2 SOMEWHAT IMPORTANT
3 NOT IMPORTANT

7 REFUSED
8 DON'T KNOW
9 NO ANSWER

The first item is local public transportation service in cities. Do you think this issue is very important, somewhat important, or not important [for spending state resources and money]?

OPIN2 and OPIN3 begin with obligatory fill. That is, you must choose to say either,

What about bus services between cities?

or,

The next item is bus services between cities.

basing your choice on your judgment of the respondent. You should repeat the probe containing the answer categories until you are sure the respondent remembers them. Once you reach OPIN7 or OPIN8, it is a good idea to repeat the entire probe, including the optional language, to make sure the respondent stays focused on the issue's importance "for spending state resources and money."

You choose fill and optional language based on actively listening to your respondents. Active listening allows you to vary certain questions in standardized ways, based on your assessment of the respondent's comprehension, memory retrieval, judgment, and answers to the questions. For words and phrases in parentheses, or fill, you must choose one item. Words and phrases in brackets, and also probes, are optional; read these at your discretion.

Read Questions in a Deliberate Manner

Although Chapter Six advised you to get through the survey introduction at a brisk pace, slow down when you get to the interview itself. Read questions in an intentional, methodical, yet pleasant manner in order to give respondents time to comprehend the entire question, search their memories, make a judgment, map their thoughts to the answer categories, and then put their answers into words.

Interviewers' speaking pace tends to accelerate after they become very familiar with the interview script. Interviewers sometimes race each other to see who can complete the most interviews in a work shift. But speaking overly quickly runs the risk that respondents will miss a key word or phrase or feel rushed to answer before they have time to formulate their true answer. Give respondents the full opportunity they need to respond to each question, but at the same time do not treat them like morons. In other words, pace yourself, but do not speak too slowly. Remember to listen to your voice. Speak politely, firmly, and professionally. Convey confidence.

Remain Neutral

Also convey utter neutrality. Make sure that nothing in your voice or your words suggests or implies disapproval, displeasure, or shock at respondents' answers or support for those answers either. Your opinions, no matter how subtly expressed, could influence—indeed bias—respondents' answers. Certain respondents will want to please you or impress you. You represent authority. If you express your opinions or ideas, such respondents may adopt them as their own, especially if their thoughts on the topic are vague or uncertain.

> Never express shock, approval, disapproval, displeasure, fear, or endorsement regarding respondents' answers, either in your words or in tone of voice.

Others may respond in the opposite way. They will consider you inappropriate and unprofessional if you express your judgments or views, which in turn could undermine their perception of the legitimacy of the survey, diminish their respect for you, and cause them to take the survey task less seriously—diminishing the accuracy of their answers and the care they taking in answering.

Similarly, do not confirm a respondent's opinion or offer your opinion about a survey question in words or tone of voice. If a respondent says, "That was sure a stupid question!" offer one of these replies, as appropriate:

The next one is . . . (normal tone).
I have to ask every question that is listed (apologetic tone).
We are almost done (cheery tone).

Keep Respondents on Task

During the question-and-answer process, discourage respondents from rambling or talking about things unrelated to the interview. Even interested, cooperative people may not fully understand how we want them to act as respondents. Do not hesitate to interrupt in order to bring them back on task. Remember, most are trying to help, and you are trying to teach them how to be helpful.

Inappropriate chattiness tends to occur more with questions having implicit answer categories than for those with answer categories embedded in the question. For example, in asking a question like EMPOPT2 (Exhibit 7.1)—"*Can you work four ten-hour days instead of the usual five eight-hour days?*"—the yes or no answer categories are implicit. Talkative respondents, wanting to be helpful, may happily embark on an explanation of their employer's policies for you. Interrupt and guide such respondents using one of these phrases:

All I need is a yes or no answer (firm tone).
Um-hmm. Here's the next question (firm, polite tone).

I don't want to keep you too long. Here's the next question (brisk, polite tone).
I don't have any room to write that down here (apologetic tone).

If there is space at the survey's end for respondents' comments, add:

After we have finished the interview, I have space to record your comments, if you have time.

That last comment about time hints to respondents that their comments are lengthening the interview unnecessarily. If, in the middle of an inappropriate tangent, a respondent says something associated with a future question, use it as a handle to bring the person back to the task. Interrupt, saying,

Wait a moment—I have a question about that coming up soon (brisk tone).

> Remember, very few people have participated in scientific survey interviews before. Even motivated respondents need you to teach them how to behave as good respondents. Teach them by modeling good behavior in your conversational interactions.

If you seem to get more verbose respondents than your coworkers do or tend to have longer interviews, listen to yourself. Are you saying things that contribute to the frequency and duration of respondent chattiness? Make sure that you are not overprobing. Make sure that you never make substantive comments on what respondents say during an interview. You should never answer a respondent's question about yourself or about how you feel. Likewise, never volunteer information about yourself or how you feel about something in the interview.[2] And, of course, never deviate from the script by asking respondents something unrelated to the interview.

Again, chatty respondents are usually just trying to be helpful, so most will not mind if you interrupt them and bring them back to the task at hand. Some respondents will inevitably be more voluble than others, ignoring your guidance. Some have a disproportionate sense of their own importance. Others are just "think aloud" types of people. Some have few others who listen to them as intently as you do. Active listening is also a form of caring.

No matter the reason, be patient. If you let impatience creep into your voice, your businesslike tone can become brittle, which could alienate or antagonize your respondents. Keep your voice firm yet polite and professional. Be sure to vary the ways that you interrupt and steer respondents.

Keeping respondents on task is a form of corrective feedback. That is, you gently interrupt respondents to steer them to better response behaviors. But most feedback you will use is positive, subtle, and nonsubstantive in content, as the next section describes.

Use Positive Feedback to Guide and Reward Respondents

Positive feedback refers to the words and short phrases interviewers use to let respondents know when they are performing well as respondents. When you use such feedback well, it helps you to establish rapport with respondents and enhances the overall value of the interview experience.

TABLE 7.3. EXAMPLES OF POSITIVE FEEDBACK: SHORT, LONG, GOOD, AND BAD.

Good Short Feedback	Good Long Feedback
Thank you.	For any question
Thanks.	
Uh-huh.	*That's helpful to know.*
Um-hmm.	*It is useful to have your answers on that.*
That's helpful.	*Thanks. What you think about that is useful.*
That's useful.	*It is important to get your opinion.*
I see.	*Thank you. That's important to know.*
	It is important to get your opinion on that.
	Scripted PROBEs.
Repeat answer, for example,	For open-ended questions
	Thank you for those comments.
	Let me get that down.
yes, often, or, 33 miles.	*I am typing exactly what you are saying.*
	I want to make sure I have that right. (Repeat answer.)

Bad Short Feedback	Bad Long Feedback
Okay.	For any question
Good.	
Yes.	*Oh, a lot of people say that.*
Sure.	*Gee, I have never heard of that before.*
All right.	*I feel exactly the same way.*
Oh really.	*I know what you mean!*
How strange.	
No kidding!	For open-ended questions
Is that it?	
	You are talking too fast for me to type in what you are saying.
	Are you finished now?
	Giving respondents advice or counseling.

Examples of good and bad feedback appear in Table 7.3. When respondents answer a question appropriately, saying *"thanks"* or *"thank you"* as you record their answer reinforces their good behavior. Before saying the feedback phrase, wait for a second or two. That brief pause underscores the reward, thereby enhancing the feedback's effectiveness in guiding respondent behavior.

Give more feedback early in the interview than later. Provide feedback for roughly one-half of respondents' satisfactory answers in the first third of the interview. In the rest of the interview offer feedback to roughly one-third of respondents' acceptable answers. Of course, give positive feedback only to suitable answers, that is, those that fit an answer category or fully address an open-ended question. Keep in mind that there are no good, correct, right, or wrong answers in a survey. A survey is not a test. Rather, your feedback rewards respondents' good behavior in answering questions.

Good feedback is neutral and task related. Use short feedback phrases (two or three syllables) when the questions and answers are short. It is very effective simply to repeat what a respondent just said—for example, *"33 miles"* or *"often."* A simple *"thank you"* is also very effective.

> Wait for a second or two before saying a feedback phrase.
> Give more feedback at the beginning of the interview.
> Use short feedback phrases for short answers.
> Use longer feedback phrases for longer and more thoughtful answers.
> Use a polite, encouraging tone of voice.

Use longer feedback phrases after answers to complex, difficult questions or after thoughtful answers to open-ended questions. Notice that the long feedback phrases in Table 7.3 are all simple statements (about five to ten syllables) on the usefulness, helpfulness, and importance of respondents' answers: for example, *"That's helpful to know,"* or, *"Thank you. That's important to know."* Scripted probes can act as feedback too, lightly guiding respondents by repeating key words or answer categories.

Interviewers' task-related comments also act as feedback: for example, *"I want to make sure I have that right."* It motivates respondents to know that you are recording exactly what they are saying. Vary the feedback phrases that you use.

Avoid feedback that might sound approving or disapproving. Also avoid feedback that could make respondents feel that they are not special and unique. Feedback words and phrases such as *"yes,"* *"good,"* *"OK,"* and *"all right"* may sound to respondents as if you are congratulating them for giving a correct answer. No, no, no! There is no such thing as a *good* or a *correct* answer in survey interviews. You want to reward only good respondent behavior, such as efficiently choosing an answer category.

It is not just words that can impart a sense of approval or disapproval to a respondent. Be careful not to use a tone of voice that implies support or censure. The feedback phrase "*I see*" can be short and neutral, or it can sound like the words of an angry mother, "*I seeeee . . .*" Use only a polite, encouraging tone of voice. Listen to your voice, especially if you have a frustrating respondent or you are nearing the end of your work shift.

"*OK*" is often used as a conversational transition by interviewers in certain parts of the United States, as in "*OK. The next question is. . .*" People in your region might regard the word "*OK*" as neutral, but people in other areas might regard it as sounding judgmental. You cannot alter your interviewing habits for each region of the country in which you conduct interviews, so develop good habits now. To remind yourself, put a sticker like the one shown in Figure 7.1 next to your computer screen.

Avoid feedback that can sound as though you are scolding the respondent: for example, "*You are talking too fast for me to type all that you are saying.*" Even though this comment is task related, it can alienate respondents. Avoid feedback that can make respondents feel as if they are just like everyone else, such as, "*Oh, a lot of people say that*." Similarly, avoid feedback can make them feel like weirdos, such as, "*How strange!* " or, "*Gee, I have never heard of that before.*" Many people have in-group and out-group sensitivities, and you cannot predict which ones feel which way, so dodge the issue altogether. Of course, never, ever reveal your own opinions, observations, or ideas—and never, ever offer counsel to respondents.

FIGURE 7.1. A REMINDER TO STOP SAYING "OK" BETWEEN QUESTIONS.

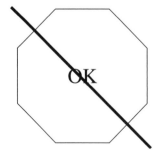

Asking Sensitive Questions

People's ideas of what counts as a sensitive question vary widely. Some respondents will be happy to answer questions about their sex lives but balk at revealing their age or religion. You cannot predict the questions that will upset any given respondent or make that person feel vulnerable. The question topics most often labeled sensitive are those that concern sexuality, drug use, alcohol consumption, illegal acts, suicide, religion, wealth, culturally deviant behavior, and unpopular opinions.

Researchers must receive special human subjects permission to ask questions on these topics. Many survey research organizations send precontact letters when their surveys address these topics, explaining the survey's purpose and importance, providing contact information for respondents who want a personal explanation, and informing respondents that they can skip any question they wish or halt the interview at any time (although we would prefer they not do that). Respondents generally appreciate knowing in advance that they will be contacted to participate in a survey, especially when sensitive topics are involved.

Rarely are sensitive topics the subject of an entire survey. Rather, they are likely to be the focus of a short group of questions surrounded by questions on more mundane topics.

Moreover, instrument designers place sensitive questions strategically. One tactic is to surround the most sensitive questions with easy questions on ordinary topics—not to surprise respondents but to lessen the burden of answering the sensitive questions. Another tactic is to start with the least sensitive questions in a series and build to the most sensitive ones. For example, when researchers need to know about respondents' participation in illegal behaviors, the questions often build from shoplifting to theft to burglary to assault to kidnapping to murder. After respondents agree to answer the first couple of questions in such a series, they rarely object to the more extreme questions.

> **Ask sensitive questions in a normal voice, at a normal question pace, with no pauses.**

When you encounter a potentially sensitive question while conducting an interview, proceed in a normal tone of voice and at a normal pace, as if it were a perfectly normal question. Most respondents will not blink at all. Following your tone and pace, they just proceed. When respondents object, say,

Please remember that this interview is completely (anonymous/confidential). No one will ever connect your answers to your name.

Then—without allowing a pause—repeat the question or the answer categories. Avoiding the pause helps you to get the respondent back on task and to avoid starting an exchange about question propriety. If a respondent still flinches, record a refusal and move on to the next question as if nothing untoward has happened. Never enter into a debate with a respondent about the necessity or importance of such questions.

With some sensitive survey topics, such as crime victimization and suicide, the process of retrieving memories and formulating answers stirs unhappy thoughts or memories in some respondents. A very few of them may mention it to you. Realize that respondents can reveal unhappy memories or events to you on any topic in an interview.

Years ago, as I finished a customer satisfaction interview, my respondent began weeping and told me that she had been raped at a party the night before. Since then I have recommended that interviewers keep the telephone number of this nationwide crisis line posted nearby: 1-800-448-3000. Counselors are available there twenty-four hours per day, seven days a week. They will speak with any person of any age about any topic. They will also give callers contact information to obtain assistance from sources near to them. When conducting surveys on sensitive subjects in particular localities, get the local numbers of appropriate crisis lines too. Say to respondents who need help,

I have the telephone number of someone you can call for help right here. Please get a pencil to write this down.

> 1-800-448-3000
> Offer this 24/7 nationwide crisis line to respondents who are in distress. Never counsel a respondent yourself.

Note that you are not asking respondents like this whether they want the telephone number or if they have a pencil handy. Rather, you are acting in a directive manner, consistent with your being in charge of the interview. Again, do not attempt under any circumstances to counsel the respondent.

You may find your respondents' frank answers to sensitive questions disturbing or disgusting. Do not gasp or reveal anything judgmental in your words or tone of voice. Continue with the interview script as if nothing has occurred. Very rarely, respondents might, in the natural process of answering questions, reveal that they have committed a crime. Indeed, once in a series of questions about crimes committed in the previous year, at the ultimate question, about murder, a respondent asked one of my interviewers if he should answer affirmatively even though he had not been caught. In that way he revealed that he had committed murder in the previous year. Even in these extreme circumstances, our obligations to maintain our respondents' anonymity or confidentiality outweigh everything else. When a respondent's answers disturb you, take a break or talk it over with a supervisor.

Summary Guidelines for Asking Questions

- Read all Qs, in the order presented, exactly as written.
- Choose the appropriate fill and optional language based on what you have learned about an R.
- Read the entire Q before accepting an answer.
- Probe to clarify or expand Rs' answers.
- Do not try to make Rs' answers consistent across questions.
- Use a pleasant, deliberate tone of voice that conveys confidence, interest, and professionalism.
- Keep Rs on task using corrective feedback.
- Use positive feedback to guide and reward Rs.

Probing

Probing refers to a set of techniques used by interviewers to clarify respondents' answers to questions or to obtain more information when respondents give incomplete, irrelevant, imprecise, or evasive answers. A probe stimulates additional responses that explain or complete respondents' answers. A probe should not, however, stimulate a discussion between you and a respondent.

Probing is an ever-present part of interviewing. You will need to probe at least once in almost every interview. This section teaches you when to probe, how to probe in ways that do not affect respondents' answers, and when to stop probing. Special sections are devoted to probing race, ethnicity, industry, and occupation questions.

When to Probe

In order to identify unsuitable or inadequate answers, you must understand each question's purpose and meaning. You will learn these details in project-specific training. If you are unsure about a particular question, ask your trainer or supervisor. Only by knowing a question's objective can you recognize a partial or imprecise answer.

Other conditions in which you should probe respondents' replies include nonanswers, nonsense answers, answers that do not use response categories, and answers that give a range rather than a single answer. Using active listening skills, you also should probe when you hear evasiveness or uncertainty behind respondents' answers.

Some instruments contain scripted probes for you, printed below the question. For example, take another look at the questions YRSRES and MILES in Table 7.1. Their scripted probes emerged from instrument pretesting. Several pretest respondents answered the question about how many years they had lived in Oregon by saying, "My whole life." Thus, this scripted probe appears below the question:

PROBE FOR "MY WHOLE LIFE": *How many years is that?*

Similarly, when asked how many miles they drove a personal vehicle on the preceding day, several pretest respondents had questions about driving as part of their job and many answered "don't know." To assist interviewers, four scripted probes were included that address these predictable issues:

PROBE: *If you drive a vehicle as part of your job, exclude those miles from your answer to this question.*
PROBE: *Apart from driving you did for your job, how many miles did you drive a personal vehicle yesterday?*
PROBE FOR "DON'T KNOW": *To the best of your knowledge [how many miles did you drive by personal vehicle yesterday]?*
PROBE FOR "DON'T KNOW": *Please give your best estimate.*

Scripted probes are easy for interviewers to implement. Often, however, you will encounter situations in which no scripted probe is offered. You must learn the conditions under which to probe and know how to do it.

Table 7.4 offers an example for the survey question URB_RUR: "*Do you currently live in a rural or urban area?*" In a real survey, you would learn in project-specific training that respondents' lived experiences affect how they understand the words "urban" and "rural" and that their understandings do not necessarily match those of social scientists. For example, people who live most of their lives on a remote ranch or farm often regard a place with 10,000 people as a big city. In contrast those who have lived mostly in dense metropolitan areas may regard an area with 300,000 people as a small town. The survey question does not define the terms for respondents. Rather, respondents choose the answer category that best fits their meaning. Your job is to know what answers count.

TABLE 7.4. EXAMPLES OF ANSWERS THAT SHOULD BE PROBED.

Question	Answers	Comments	Suggested Probes
Do you currently live in a rural or urban area?	I lived in a city when I went to college.	So what? Is the answer intended to imply that college was the only time R lived in a city?	Repeat the Q, a little more slowly the second time, emphasizing the word "currently."
	I live in Elmtown.	This answer is immaterial to the question. Irs cannot assume that Elmtown is urban because "town" is part of the name; it could be a rural crossroads.	Repeat the entire Q, a little more slowly the second time. Or you can shorten it to: *Would that be urban or rural?* You can drop "currently" from the Q because R has specified "I live in," and you can drop "area" because R has specified an area, namely Elmtown.
	I live on a farm.	This answer is unclear. It suggests that R currently lives in a rural area, but urban farms exist.	Because R has specified "I live on," you can drop "currently" from the Q. But you cannot drop "area" because R's answer has not specified one. Ask: *Would that be an urban or rural area?* When in doubt, repeat the entire Q.

Table 7.4 shows three respondent replies that did not directly answer the question. It explains why each answer is inadequate and suggests probes you can use to get a full answer.

Probes are clearly needed when respondents do not use the answer categories provided in the question, as Table 7.4 illustrates. You also should probe respondents who cannot make up their minds about an answer category, who wander from the topic, who volunteer that they do not understand, and whose answers could be interpreted in multiple ways.

Keep in mind that sometimes the manner in which respondents answer is a better indicator that you need to probe than their actual words are. Use active listening to comprehend what each respondent is saying or trying to say. When respondents' oral behavior is hesitant, timid, unsure, or seems to contradict their words, probe them out.

Respondents who start their answers by saying, "Oh, I don't know," or, "it depends," do not always mean it. Some say it as a way to stall while searching their memories for an appropriate answer. Others are embarrassed to admit that they did not hear the question fully. Lazy respondents who do not want to exert much mental effort rely on "don't know" answers to sidestep questions. Cautious or uncertain respondents may say they "don't know" while seeking clues from you on how to answer. Probe "don't know" answers for a complete answer. Every so often you will encounter respondents who truly have no experience with the question topic or have never heard of the issue. They are rare, however, for most surveys ask relatively general questions. The point is that you should probe "don't know" answers as far as you reasonably can.

Then there are the "it depends" respondents. Often these are the thoughtful respondents who want to give the best possible reply. They mentally weigh all facets of a possible answer, attempting to compensate for their own perceived biases, editing their answer, and generally working harder than needed. Their exactitude can be a nuisance when a broad-sweeping question about a general topic, such as their perception of the economy's health these days, needs only a general, broad-sweeping answer. Probe those who hem and haw in order to bring them back to the question's requirements.

> Remember, your voice is as important as your words in motivating respondents to answer fully and accurately.

Ultimately, you will learn to identify quickly the situations in which respondents' answers require probing. You will learn to recognize immediately when respondents' answers do not meet a question's purpose. In respondents' oral behaviors, you will hear clues that something more is under the surface of their answers. You will be able to choose instantly a probe suitable to the problem at hand. Then you will casually initiate a neutral probing technique, using a tone that conveys natural curiosity (not that the respondent has failed in some way). With practice these probing techniques will become second nature for you.

How to Probe

After identifying respondents' answers that require probing, choose the best approach for the particular problem at hand. Use neutral techniques, that is, those that clarify or enhance respondents' answers but do not influence the answers' direction or nature. Remember that your voice is as important as your words in motivating respondents to answer fully and accurately. This section offers both generic and specific probing suggestions to help you probe wisely.

Generic Probes Some probes are useful in numerous interviewing situations and for many types of questions. Perhaps the best neutral probe is silence. In western culture, long gaps between conversational exchanges make people feel uncomfortable. When I conduct new interviewer training sessions, at this point I fall silent for longer than the group anticipates. Inevitably, several people start nervously giggling. Then everyone starts laughing, realizing that the point was made. That is, a silence of fifteen to twenty seconds makes people uneasy.

When people engage in a back-and-forth conversation, even in a structured interview, it can be unnerving when one person falls silent for several seconds longer than the other person internally expects. Typically, the person who last spoke will rush to fill the empty conversational "space." You, as the person in charge of the interview, can use silence to pull your respondent into saying more. Silence is certainly neutral; you do not need to worry about uttering a potentially leading word or phrase. This *expectant pause* technique is especially useful for open-ended questions, as it suggests to respondents that they have just begun to answer the question.

Another very effective neutral technique for probing is simply to repeat the original question, the answer categories, or both. Repeat the entire question or the entire set of answer categories unless the respondent has clearly eliminated some elements. The second time around, speak more slowly, emphasizing key words. This type of probe indicates that you recognize the respondent has started an answer but has additional things to say. This approach gives respondents more time to search their memories, make a judgment, and map their response to the answer categories. Repeating the question is an exceptionally safe method of ensuring reliable and comparable responses from all respondents.

> A moment of silence is an excellent, neutral probe.

Similarly, repeating respondents' answers to open-ended questions, in exactly the words they used, almost always precipitates a fuller answer. Hearing back what they just said helps respondents to refine and clarify what they intend to express. This technique is neutral as long as you do not interject your own words. Of course, keep your tone of voice neutral as well. Repeating respondents' answers in a sarcastic, incredulous, bored, or impatient tone of voice is neither neutral nor helpful to your respondent relationships.

Here are some useful, neutral generic probes:

What do you mean exactly?
Please be more specific about that.
What else can you think of?
I don't quite understand what you mean.

These questions and comments, said in a neutral tone, demonstrate your interest. They encourage respondents to answer more fully and clearly. Using a somewhat bewildered tone of voice can be effective, for it suggests that the inadequacy is in you rather than in the respondent's answer. Acting as if you need help with understanding a respondent's answer stimulates a desire to help you and, in the process, results in a fuller answer. Do not use this technique more than once or twice with the same respondent, however, as it can convey the notion that you do not recognize when a question is completely answered.

Respondents who give timid, hesitant, or half-hearted answers generally do so for all questions, not just for one or two. It is patterned behavior. Use positive feedback to boost their confidence in their question-answering skills. When generally confident respondents give a timid, hesitant, or half-hearted answer to a particular question, it may mean that they did not hear the entire question, did not understand the question (or part of it), or that they are unfamiliar with the topic. Start by repeating the question, slowly. If that does not work, gently confront the respondent with his or her answer, saying,

You sound a little unsure. What did you mean to answer?

Specific Probes Certain particular probes best resolve common respondent problems, such as not using the required answer categories, not understanding a word, or giving a range when a single number is needed.

When respondents reply without using the answer categories provided in the question, as in Table 7.4, the best thing to do is to repeat the question a little more slowly the second time, emphasizing words that the answer suggests respondents need to focus on.

When respondents say that they do not understand a word, term, or phrase in a question, the first thing to do is to check whether an explanation is offered in a probe for that question. If no probe is provided, use one of these statements:

Whatever it means to you.
Whatever you think it means.

> Never suggest an answer to a respondent, and never supply your own definition of a word or term.

Under no circumstances should you try to explain a word or term. If all interviewers offered their own meanings in their own words, it could bias the results.

Sometimes, respondents express their uncertainty by giving a range. For example, in response to the question, *"How many miles did you drive a personal vehicle yesterday [altogether]?"* a respondent might answer, "Oh, I'd say sixty or seventy miles." Probe by asking,

Was it closer to sixty miles or to seventy miles?

If the respondent still stalls in narrowing it down, blame CATI, saying,

The software we use will only let me type in one number. Which number is closest to what you actually drove yesterday?

Under no circumstances should you suggest an answer to the respondent, such as, *"How about if I type in sixty-five miles?"*

Listen carefully for those instances when respondents do not use the exact answer categories but narrow the range in their replies. For the question, *"How satisfied are you with how (ODOT / Oregon Department of Transportation) maintains Oregon's major highways, roads, and bridges?"* the answer categories are very satisfied, somewhat satisfied, not very satisfied, and not at all satisfied. A respondent who answers, "I am satisfied," has removed half of the answer categories from consideration. So appropriate probes now would be these:

Are you very satisfied or somewhat satisfied?
Which would be closer to how you feel, very satisfied or somewhat satisfied?

Sometimes it may seem that respondents are deliberately replying without using the intended answer categories in order to use a question as a venue for expressing another idea. If you ask, *"How many one-way trips did you make by any means of transportation [yesterday]?"* and a respondent answers, "I don't believe in driving cars," there is no way for you to know if this answer is purposeful, the respondent is not listening to you, or the respondent misunderstands the question. Clearly, you cannot record a belief answer for a frequency question. In such cases, no matter the cause of the problem, the best thing to do is to repeat the question a little more slowly, this time emphasizing *"by any means of transportation."*

Respondents who are unable to make up their minds about an answer category might not have heard all the categories the first time. Repeat all the answer categories, unless a respondent has explicitly removed one or more from consideration. Do not hesitate to repeat the entire question, speaking more slowly this time, emphasizing the answer categories. Respondents who stumble over answer categories might have misheard the question the first time or missed the question's emphasis. You can also prompt and assure such respondents by saying,

This is just about what you (think/feel/believe/prefer). There is no right or wrong answer.

When respondents reply "I don't know" to a question, they might just need more time to think, so count to ten. Remember, silence can be a powerful motivator. After a pause, if no answer is yet forthcoming, repeat the question, speaking more slowly and emphasizing key words and phrases. For open-ended questions, once respondents say something, you can stimulate them to enlarge their answers by repeating their words. When respondents claim that they really do not know, try asking one of these questions:

What do you expect?
What do you think?

Of course if a respondent really does not know, that is, if he or she has no basis on which to answer the question, accept it and go on.

In some surveys the principal investigators may prefer that you not probe out the "don't know" answers. Project-specific training should explain this point. If you are unsure, ask a trainer or supervisor.

When respondents say "it depends" in response to a question, they may see two sides to the issue, they may be thinking of a contingency that the question does not take into account, or they may have in mind an answer that does not match the question. Help respondents let go of their perceived contingencies and what-if issues. Try pulling these respondents back to the surface by repeating the question and emphasizing its key words, such as *"generally speaking," "these days," "usually," "on average,"* and *"in the past four weeks."*

Open-ended questions may need special probing. Some surveys require getting as much information as possible about respondents' thinking about a certain question. In such cases use the following neutral probes, as appropriate, to get your respondents to elaborate:

Is there anything else?
Tell me more.
Please be more specific.
What are your reasons for (thinking/feeling/saying/doing/believing) that?
I am not sure what you mean by that. Tell me a little more, please.
Tell me why you (think/feel/believe) that way.

Avoid three common mistakes in probing open-ended questions. First, take care not to probe with a "yes" or "no" question, such as: "*Could you be more specific?*" It is too easy for a recalcitrant respondent to say, "No, I could not." Second, do not let respondents stray from the topic. Some tend to ramble on. Keep them on task by, for example, repeating the question. Finally, do not probe open-ended questions just because they are open-ended. Probe them only if you are instructed to do so and to the extent you are instructed. Probing without cause lengthens the interview unnecessarily. Moreover, if you have not been instructed to probe, probably no one will analyze those additional words you worked to extract from respondents.

Never Use Directive Probes When respondents dither about their answers, you may be tempted to urge them to a decision by rephrasing their answers in the way you think they intend. For example:

Does that mean you think that adding sidewalks and bike paths to existing streets is very important?
Are you saying you drove a personal vehicle about ten miles yesterday?
You sound a little unsure. Did you mean to answer (yes or no/strongly agree or somewhat agree/always or often)?

Why should you avoid directive probes? Because respondents tend to comply with interviewers' suggestions, saying "yes" more often than resisting or saying "no." Many respondents take the path of least resistance, especially those who lack firm ideas or feelings on a subject. It is easier for them to go along with the interviewer's suggestions than to negotiate a different answer.

Directive probes are nonstandard, nonneutral probes that interviewers create by rewording respondents' answers in the ways interviewers think respondents meant to say. Directive probes are not standard, because interviewers make them up as they go. Directive probes are also not neutral, because the interviewers do the cognitive work of mapping respondents' answers onto answer categories. Once that work is done, respondents are reluctant to say it is wrong. Directive probes have the potential to cause patterns of bias.

Listen to Your Voice The manner in which you convey a neutral probe can affect respondents' replies. Use your voice to convey interest and patience. In so doing, you communicate to respondents your desire to ensure that they are represented fully, fairly, and accurately. Never use a shrill or challenging tone of voice, no matter how much a respondent tests your nerves. Not only will it damage your exchange relationship with respondents, it is also impolite.

Probing Race and Ethnicity Questions

Many, if not most, surveys in the United States ask respondents to identify their race and ethnicity. Therefore you need to understand the concepts underlying those terms, usual practices for asking about them, issues you may confront when asking the questions, and how to handle these issues.

Background Race refers to human groups who share biologically transmitted traits that society sees as socially significant, such as skin color, hair texture, facial features, and body types. Ethnicity, in contrast, refers to human groups who share a cultural heritage, including language, religion, food preferences, migration patterns, customs, and intermarriage.

The U.S. government identifies five racial groups: American Indian or Alaska Native, Asian, black or African American, Native Hawaiian or other Pacific Islander, and white. Two categories exist for ethnicity: Hispanic or Latino and not Hispanic or Latino.[3] Consistent with Office of Management and Budget (OMB) policy, sponsored surveys ask race and ethnicity separately. Usually, they ask ethnicity first: *"Are you Spanish, Hispanic, or Latino?"* Then they ask, *"What is your race?"*

Race Categories

American Indian or Alaska Native

Asian

Black or African American

Native Hawaiian or other Pacific Islander

White

Ethnicity Categories

> Hispanic or Latino
>
> Not Hispanic or Latino

Census 2000 was the first national census to allow people to check more than one race. However, just 2.6 percent of the population did so. Some surveys also allow respondents to choose multiple races. Many, if not most, nongovernmental surveys still require respondents to choose one race, or they lump biracial and multiracial respondents into a single "if volunteered" category (such as code 6 in Exhibit 7.3).

Social scientists understand the crudeness of racial and ethnic categories. Indeed, they generally agree that the diversity within racial groups exceeds the diversity between them. However, so long as these groups' life chances (such as educational attainment, poverty, and years expected to live) differ significantly, researchers must capture racial and ethnic differences in surveys.

Problems in Asking About Race and Ethnicity Interviewers experience certain predictable difficulties when asking race and ethnicity questions, which in turn will require them to probe. For example, some Americans, mainly whites, refuse to answer race and ethnicity questions because they believe that "race does not matter anymore." Some even believe that asking such questions creates or perpetuates group differences. However, if surveys did not ask race, no one would know, for example, that 62 percent of blacks report experiencing unfair treatment in any given month, compared to 21 percent of whites, or that 78 percent of blacks prefer to live in mixed-race neighborhoods, compared to 57 percent of whites.[4]

Biracial and multiracial persons often experience exasperation in answering race questions when surveys require them to choose one answer category. Choosing just one category can be especially difficult for those who self-identify with one race because of their upbringing, but who also know that externally they appear to be a different race. Asking about race and ethnicity can be even more problematic because OMB-defined categories have been highly politicized, with various groups lobbying to be labeled and counted separately. In addition, cultural values about race and ethnicity have changed. In recent decades young Americans have developed a tendency to exaggerate their minority heritage (for example, claiming a great-great-grandmother who was Navajo). Before the 1970s, in contrast, many people attempted to hide their racial backgrounds.

Probing Suggestions What all this means is that race and ethnicity questions can trigger emotions that may affect certain respondents' answers. This subsection describes the most common issues and how interviewers should handle them.

The best general strategy for avoiding problems is to read these questions in a matter-of-fact manner. Usually, instrument designers place race and ethnicity questions with other demographic items near the interview's end, where respondents tend to be most compliant.

Do not engage in a debate with respondents about the value of these questions. It is not your job to decide which questions to include or exclude. For those few respondents who hassle you, use the same probes you would use for other demographic questions:

We need this information to compare groups of people to each other.
We also need it to make sure the people we interview match all of the people in [the target population].

When respondents refuse to choose a race category, record what they say appropriately (as "refused" or "other → specify," for example). Then mention what happened in your interviewer observations at the end.

The most frequent issue that arises is actually mild. Many Hispanics do not hear the ethnicity question (*"Are you Spanish, Hispanic, or Latino?"*) as a "yes" or "no" question. Instead, they often answer it by saying, "I'm Mexican American," "I'm Guatemalan," "My grandmother came from Cuba," or something similar. This is a small issue, because you have enough information from such an answer to record it simply as "yes."

A larger problem arises when asking Hispanics the question about race. A 2002 survey of Hispanic Americans found that 56 percent regard their ethnicity as their race.[5] Thus, when you ask the race question, you can expect many Hispanics to pause and perplexedly say something like this: "I just told you—I'm Mexican American." When you encounter this type of response, probe by saying,

Yes, thank you. But do you consider yourself to be white or black, or something else?

About 2 percent of Hispanics say that they are black, usually of Caribbean origin. About 20 percent say that they are white. The remaining generally choose "don't know" or "other → specify" categories.

To ease and simplify Hispanic respondents' difficulties with the OMB-required race and ethnicity questions, many nongovernmental surveys combine race and ethnicity into one question, as the question RACE does (Exhibit 7.3). In addition, many nongovernmental surveys combine Native Hawaiians and other Pacific Islanders with Asians, as federal surveys did prior to 2000. The combined race and ethnicity question is easier for both respondents and interviewers.

Some respondents do not have problems with the race question at all. Nor do they argue. Some show pride in their heritage by offering very specific answers, such as, "My mother is half white and half Korean American, and my father's family came from Germany a long time ago"; "My family has been in California for six generations; I am a Californian"; or simply "Italian" or "Irish." But these respondents' answers do not match the response categories.

> Whenever you are not sure about a respondent's race from that person's answer, probe by reading the entire list.

Your job is to help respondents select the closed-ended answer category that best matches their notion of their race. Probe from the answer categories using the information you hear using active listening. When respondents narrow the categories, it makes your probe easier. For example, you can probe the person of white-Korean-German ancestry, by saying,

Thank you. That is helpful information. Do you consider yourself to be mainly white, Asian, or something else?

If your instrument includes a multiracial category, expand your probe by saying,

Thank you. That is helpful information. Do you consider yourself to be mainly white, Asian, multiracial, or something else?

For the Californian, say,

Thank you. That's interesting. Do you consider yourself to be mainly white, black, Asian, Hispanic or Latino, American Indian, multiracial, or something else?

California is second only to Hawaii in racial diversity, so it is appropriate to read the entire list. Whenever in doubt, probe by reading the entire list.

Note that the United States contains many groups of *white ethnics,* that is, people of European descent who maintain a cultural affinity with their mother country, thinking of themselves as, for example, Irish or Italian. Some will want you to classify them separately, but surveys group them with other whites. For persons who self-identify as Irish or Italian, probe by saying,

Thank you for that information. Do you consider yourself to be mainly white or something else?

One term particular to the United States is often misunderstood, and you should avoid using it as a probe, namely "Native American." In probing for the indigenous peoples of the United States, use only the terms "American Indian" or "Alaska Native," or both. The label "Indian" came about hundreds of years ago, when European explorers believed they would land in India when sailing west from Europe. They called the indigenous peoples of the Americas Indians, and the appellation stuck.

> Never use the term "Native American" as a race probe, because many native-born people with no American Indian ancestry will incorrectly choose it.

In the late twentieth century some people began calling American Indians "Native Americans," thinking that it was less racist or more proper. The problem is that millions of non-Indian Americans also can call themselves Native Americans, because they were born in the United States. (Native-born Canadians, Brazilians, Nicaraguans, and others born in North, Central, and South America also can call themselves Native Americans.) The point is this: any time you probe using the term "Native American," many people will take it literally and say "yes" because they were born in the United States or the Americas. But they lack even a drop of indigenous ancestry. Thus, when probing this aspect of race, stick to using American Indian or Alaska Native.

In recording answers to the race question, put only the oddest cases in the "other → specify" category. This includes the respondent who will answer only "the human race" and Hispanics who cannot choose a race. Respondents who say they are Irish, Italian, or another white ethnic name should be probed, because most can logically go into the white category. Use "other → specify" for them only if they refuse to choose. The "other → specify" answers create a lot of coding work later, so do your best to convince respondents to choose the answer category that best fits them.

Probing Industry and Occupation Questions

Industry and occupation questions determine an employed person's employer, the type of business that employer is in, and what the person does on the job. As concepts, industry and occupation differ from each other. *Industry* refers to what the respondent's employer (a business or company) makes or does. *Occupation* refers to what respondents make or do within the organization that employs them.

These questions do not appear in all surveys. For this reason your trainers might skip this section during your general interviewer training. When these questions do appear, they produce answers that are important indicators of respondents' socioeconomic status, especially for various federally sponsored surveys. Take care to learn and understand the concepts fully. You are likely to receive extra project-specific training when they appear in surveys you conduct.

Examine the industry and occupation questions in Exhibit 7.6. Note that they are open-ended. You must be careful to use any probes provided to get complete and appropriate answers. Type everything respondents say. Do not paraphrase. After the survey is complete, specially trained coders will map the answers you record to a complex industry and occupation classification system, such as that used by the U.S. Census Bureau or the Bureau of Labor Statistics.

Industry When we ask for respondents' industry of employment ("*What kind of business or industry is this?*"), we want to know the type of economic activity engaged in by their employers. An extractive industry, for example, takes things out of the ground; it might be a mine, a fishery, or a farm. Companies

EXHIBIT 7.6. EXAMPLES OF INDUSTRY AND OCCUPATION SURVEY QUESTIONS.

Industry

Q:IND
What kind of business or industry is this?
PROBE: What do they make or do there?
PROBE: What is the name of the (business/organization/government agency)?
PROBE: Is this (business/organization) mainly manufacturing, retail trade, wholesale trade, or something else?
PROBE SCHOOL, COLLEGE, OR HOSPITAL: Is that public or private?

OPEN-ENDED
TYPE EXACT RESPONSE BELOW

Occupation

Q:OCC
What is your current occupation?
PROBE: What kind of work do you do?
PROBE: What is your job title?
PROBE: What are your usual activities or duties at this job?

OPEN-ENDED
TYPE EXACT RESPONSE BELOW

in manufacturing industries make things, like refrigerators and automobiles (durable goods manufacturing), or potato chips and boxes (nondurable goods manufacturing). Many businesses provide services, such as health care (hospitals or doctors' or dentists' offices), personal care (haircutting, housekeeping, or manicuring), or repair services. Many companies sell goods or services (retail or wholesale) or real estate. Banks and insurance companies provide financial services.

You need to get a clear and specific description of the industry in which each employed respondent works. Ask respondents to clarify acronyms they use. Employers' names are especially valuable in assigning accurate industry codes. For respondents who balk at naming their employers, remind them that the interview is anonymous or confidential. For respondents who are unsure, ask for the company name on their paycheck.

A very short answer rarely suffices. Here are three examples of insufficient answers: "I am a farmer," "I work at a school," and "I work with computers." Use as many probes as needed, such as these:

What do you make or do there?
What is the name of the business?
Is that public or private?

Here are three clear and specific industry answers: "I own and operate a dairy farm," "I work at Fox Hollow School, a public elementary school," and "I work for Hewlett-Packard. We design, manufacture, and sell personal computers."

For respondents who do not understand the question, the standard probe is,

Is this business or organization mainly manufacturing, retail trade, wholesale trade, or something else?

A manufacturer makes things and sells them in big lots to other manufacturers, wholesalers, or retailers. A wholesaler buys things from manufacturers in big lots to sell to retailers or other wholesalers. A retailer sells mainly to consumers. Under the "something else" category are banks, restaurants, beauty shops, repair shops, motels, dry cleaners, utility companies, dentists' offices, ranches, farms, advertising agencies, insurance firms, and so on.

Some businesses and industries are tricky for coders to place accurately in the industry classification scheme. Table 7.5 lists these businesses and industries, explains how they need greater explication, and recommends probes for you to use. Read it over carefully.

TABLE 7.5. EXPLANATIONS AND PROBES FOR HARD-TO-CODE INDUSTRIES.

Industry Type	Explanations and Probes
Armed forces	Determine whether this person is a current member of the military or a civilian employee. *Are you enlisted, a civilian employee, or something else?*
Child-care facilities	Be sure to get the location where the child care is provided. *Where is this child care located? (In your home, someone else's home, a church, a business or agency, or a child-care center that is its own business?)*
Government	Find out what level of government it is (federal, state, local, regional, or tribal). Ask for the specific governmental agency's name. Use only commonly known agency abbreviations (such as IRS, CIA, or FBI); otherwise, spell the name out fully. Make certain that you describe the activity of the person's place or department within the agency. For example, a job with a state department of transportation could involve road repair, road building, contracting for road repair or building, or basic research. *What level of government is that? [PROBE: Federal, state, county, city, regional, tribal, or something else?]* *What is the name of the government agency for which you work?* *What does your department actually do for that agency?*
Multiple business activities in one place	Some businesses engage in multiple activities. For example, an electronics firm may do research, manufacturing, sales, and repair at the same location. Respondents should describe the *main* activities where they work. For example, if a firm mainly bottles milk but makes yogurt on the side, employees will be counted as working for a milk bottler, even if they work mainly with yogurt.
Odd jobs, household workers	Record "various employers" for housekeepers, gardeners, babysitters, and others who receive pay from several sources.
School, college, or hospital	Be sure to determine whether a school, college, or hospital is public or private. *Is that public or private?*
Self-employed	For self-employed persons, enter "self-employed" and other descriptors, such as "in-home child care" or "family farm." Try to get the name of the respondent's business.

Occupation When asking for employed respondents' occupations (*"What is your current occupation?"*), we want to know the actual work they do in a usual workday. Whenever you get a very short answer (two to five words), probe it out:

What kind of work do you do?
What is your job title?
What are your usual activities or duties at this job?

Avoid, however, settling for descriptions that only name the department or work area, such as "I work in the shipping department," "I'm with the warehouse crew," or "I'm in inventory." Also, stop respondents who launch into descriptions of the places where they work. Their portrayal of the shipping department does not help in assigning an occupation code. Interrupt with probes asking what they do in the shipping department.

A job title is helpful, such as accountant, inventory clerk, cashier, laborer, shipping department supervisor, plumber, dental assistant, or firefighter. But it does not suffice as a complete answer. For example, for respondents who say they are teachers, scientists, assemblers, managers, supervisors, clerks, or engineers, you must probe it out to determine with whom or what they work. A teacher of physics at the college level differs substantially in training and socioeconomic status from a preschool teacher (even though both occupations are valuable to society). Ask respondents to explain any acronyms.

As with industries, some occupations require greater explication for coders to use the information you record. The first section of Table 7.6 describes distinctions within each of six difficult-to-code occupational groups. The second section shows eleven difficult-to-code occupations and the probes you should use to get complete answers.

Table 7.7 shows examples of good and bad probing, taken from actual survey interviews. Only interviewers' spelling and punctuation have been corrected. Interviewers indicated when they probed by typing "(p)." This survey experimented with asking the industry and occupation questions in a combined form, using the same questions and probes as in Exhibit 7.6. Thus, you will see occupation and industry in the same narrative answer. The first section of the table shows satisfactory answers to the combined question, that is, industry and occupation codes can be derived from these answers. The second section shows examples of insufficient answers, with comments explaining how interviewers should have probed.

Again, you have to know the objectives of the questions in order to know when to probe and how to probe. The industry and occupation questions are

TABLE 7.6. EXPLANATIONS AND PROBES FOR DIFFICULT-TO-CODE OCCUPATIONS.

Distinctions Within Occupational Groups	Explanations and Probes
Apprentices and trainees	Apprentices are under a contract for their training period (for example, apprentice electrician). Trainees are not under contract (for example, trainee bank teller). Write in exactly what Rs say, making sure to get the occupation name after "apprentice" or "trainee."
Consultants	Rs who say they do not have a business but who contract themselves out as consultants or provide other services for a fee are considered self-employed. However, consultants in a consulting firm work for a private company.
Machinists, machine operators, and mechanics	Machinists are skilled in the craft of making metal tools, parts, and machines using precise measuring instruments, blueprints, small machines, and hand tools. Machine operators run big machines in a factory, such as drill presses. Mechanics inspect, service, and repair machinery. For machinists, ask: *Do you do both setup and operation [of the machines]?* For machine operators, ask: *"What type of machine do you operate [the most]? How many machines do you operate?"* For mechanics, ask: *"What type of mechanic are you? Auto body, auto engine, appliance, line, truck, or valve?"*
Official and regular secretaries	Regular secretaries perform typing, filing, and telephone work in an office. Official secretaries are elected or appointed officers of an association, union, volunteer organization, or business.
Persons working for temp agencies or employment contractors	Rs who work through a temporary agency or employment contractor are employees of that agency or contractor, not of the place where they actually work. A union hiring list is not an employment contractor. The employer of these union workers is the business or person writing the paycheck.
Self-employed	For self-employed Rs who spend most of their time in an actual trade or craft, enter their generic title as the occupation, such as "doctor," "carpenter," "barber," "shoe repairer," and so on. Type "manager" only if R actually mainly manages the business.

(continued)

TABLE 7.6. *(CONTINUED)*

Occupational Group	Probes
Assembler	*What do you assemble? Automobiles, electric motors, farm equipment, boxes?*
Clerk	*What type of clerk are you? Accounting, filing, shipping, statistical, or sales?*
Craftsman	*What type of craftsman? Cabinetmaker, electrician, or plumber?*
Engineer	*What kind of engineer? Civil, electrical, mechanical, nuclear, chemical, train, stationary, or building?*
Inspector	*What do you inspect? Autos, restaurants, elevators, buildings, or meats?*
Manager	*What do you manage? A bakery, garage, hotel, office, property, or store?* (For a large firm) *What department do you manage?*
Nurse	*What type of nurse are you? Registered, licensed, practical, vocational, or an aide?*
Sales worker	*What do you sell? Advertising, insurance, refrigerators, real estate, shoes, or tickets? Is that wholesale or retail?*
Scientist or researcher	*What type of (science/research) do you do? Neurobiology, astrophysics, organic chemistry, history, linguistics, or internal medicine?*
Supervisor	*Whom do you supervise? Clerical workers, counselors, laborers, or field representatives?*
Teacher	*Do you teach at the preschool, elementary, high school, or college level? What subject do you teach?*

among the most difficult open-ended questions you will ever need to probe, but they are also very interesting. Imagine talking with a herdsman, a group life coordinator, a greenskeeper, a logger, a catering coordinator, and an income tax accountant all on the same day! Probe the inadequate responses using the probes printed on the instrument as well as the in-depth probes displayed in Tables 7.5 and 7.6. Do not accept vague answers that do not fully answer the question.

When to Stop Probing

Knowing when to stop probing is just as important as knowing when you need to probe. Stop probing when you have obtained the necessary information to answer the question. Stop probing if respondents become irritated or annoyed.

TABLE 7.7. EXAMPLES OF SUFFICIENT AND INSUFFICIENT OCCUPATION AND INDUSTRY ANSWERS, WITH COMMENTS AND SUGGESTED PROBES.

Sufficient Answers, No Further Probes Needed

Administrative assistant for, it's hard to explain, I work with apprentices. (p) I guess you would say construction.

Greenskeeper at a golf course. (p) Public, nonprofit.

Group life coordinator. (p) At a youth correctional facility. (p) State.

Head dental hygienist for a dentist office. (p) Private.

Health and safety specialist. (p) For the American Red Cross. (p) Health and safety marketing, and I teach CPR, first aid, and all of our classes.

Health and social services. (p) I am an outreach and education coordinator for the Oregon Health Plan. (p) A health insurance program for the poor. (p) State.

Herdsman. (p) They're a registered Angus ranch. (p) Feeding and breeding, showing and then marketing cattle.

I work for Oregon State University. (p) I am a catering coordinator.

I work for the military. (p) Civilian. (p) I am an education and training program manager.

I work in public relations in the biotechnology industry. (p) Assistant account executive.

I am a high school agriculture teacher. (p) Public.

Marketing assistant. (p) New home construction.

Minority community liaison in a school district for parents and students of color.

Insufficient Answers	Comments and Suggested Probes
2nd grade teacher.	Public or private school?
Logging.	What does R do with regard to logging? Operate heavy machinery? Own the company?
Medical assistant.	Doing what? For whom? What does the employer do or make?
GTA at college and a part-time job.	Is a GTA an acronym for *graduate teaching assistant*? Private or public college? In what field? What duties? What is that part-time job R also mentioned?
I work for a small biotech company.	What does R do there? Guard the front door? Arrange employee travel? Practice biology?
I work for the courts. (p) In the probate department.	Which court? What does R do or make there? R could be a judge, transcriptionist, bailiff, or attorney.
I work for the federal government. (p) I am an engineering technician.	What agency of the federal government? What type of engineering—civil, electrical, railroad, or what?
I work for the Oregon Department of Fisheries and Wildlife. (p) I am a research assistant on a salmon and trout enhancement project.	What does R do on the job? Is this lab work, like biochemistry, or is it fieldwork, like counting or tagging fish in a river?
I work in a sawmill.	What does R do in the sawmill? Payroll? Green chain? Cleaning?
Income tax accountant.	Is R self-employed, working for H&R Block (a large private company), or for some branch of government?

TABLE 7.8. SUMMARY OF PROBING DO'S AND DON'TS.

Do	Don't
Know when answers need probing, given each question's objectives.	Suggest answers.
Listen to Rs' oral behaviors as well as their actual answers.	Say anything that will influence Rs' answers.
Tailor your probes to each R based on active listening.	Initiate a debate or discussion.
Memorize an arsenal of appropriate probes.	Use probes that can be answered yes or no.
Pause slightly before offering a probe.	Lengthen an interview by probing unnecessarily.
Record a "(p)" when probing open-ended questions.	Use a sharp or demanding tone of voice.
Know when to stop probing.	Convey annoyance.
Speak in a neutral manner, using a casual tone of voice.	
Convey patience and interest.	

Although this is rare, you do not want to encourage a telephone break-off. Stop probing when the respondent has nothing more to say. Do not increase respondents' burden or prolong the interview unnecessarily by probing beyond respondents' ability to answer.

Probing Wrap-Up

Your goal is to represent each respondent accurately on each survey question. Probes are techniques to help you do so. Know when respondents' answers are insufficient by knowing the objectives behind each question. Choose the best probe for each question and each particular respondent based on active listening. Neither your words nor your tone of voice should influence or affect respondents' final answers after probing. Table 7.8 summarizes the do's and don'ts of probing.

Recording Respondents' Answers

After respondents fully answer a question, your next task is to record their answers accurately. Recording the data from an interview requires careful typing and attention. Accuracy is far more important than speed in recording respondents' answers. Watch your screen to make sure that you have recorded each answer category correctly for each question. The techniques of recording answers to closed-ended and to open-ended questions differ substantially.

Answers to Closed-Ended Questions

Most survey questions are closed-ended. All you need to do for each question is depress the number key that corresponds to the answer category the respondent has chosen. Most CATI systems then automatically jump to the next appropriate question (you do not also need to press the Enter key). If you realize that you mistakenly pressed the wrong key, follow your CATI system's procedures for backing up (for example, press the Esc key). Most CATI systems allow you to go back as many questions as you need to. When you get there, depress the correct number key.

Properly programmed CATI systems will not allow you to record numbers that are out of range. For example, with a "yes" or "no" question, you can register a 1 for "yes," a 2 for "no," a 7 for "refused," an 8 for "don't know," and a 9 for "no answer." The codes 3, 4, 5, and 6 are out of range. If your finger slips to one of these keys, the computer will beep at you, indicating that you must record a different answer. You will be unable to advance to the next question until you register a number that is within range. But the computer cannot read your mind; if you intended to register a 2 and accidentally hit the 1 key, it cannot tell.

CATI programmers also embed logical limits on the numbers you can record. For example, I once had a survey with a series of questions about racial profiling. It included questions that asked how many times a respondent was stopped by a police officer while in a vehicle in the preceding twelve months, how many times an officer searched the vehicle, and how many times the respondent was ticketed, cited, or arrested. The answers to the second two questions could not exceed the answer to the first. Logically, the respondent's vehicle could not have been searched on five occasions if he had been stopped only three times. Thus, if you recorded a 3 in answer to the first question, indicating that a respondent said he had been stopped three times, the numbers that you then recorded in answer to the next two questions must be 3 or fewer. If you accidentally typed a number that exceeded the logical limits of your preceding answers, the computer would beep at you and not allow you to proceed until you entered a within-range number.

Responses to the "Other → Specify" Answer Category The combination questions, presented earlier in this chapter, allow "other → specify" answers. When you depress the key for these answers, a pop-up box will automatically appear in most CATI systems, allowing you to type in a word or a short phrase that the respondent uttered. The space is limited.

Remember to use the "other → specify" answer only when a respondent's answer truly does not fit extant answer categories. After data collection is complete, there is nothing more frustrating for those preparing data files to encounter an "other → specify" that could have fit into an existing answer category. For example, "Irish" in response to RACE should be probed to see if the respondent will choose the "white" answer category.

What to Do If You Make a Mistake If you realize that you made a mistake in recording a respondent's answer, almost all CATI systems allow you to back up one question at a time (for example, by using the escape key, Esc). As soon as you realize your error, go back and correct it. The answers you have recorded since then should remain intact, except in the rare situation in which the changed answer affects skip logic.

If you make a mistake that you cannot correct on the CATI system for some reason, follow your employer's instructions on how to correct it. Some organizations use a data correction form, like the one shown in Exhibit B.4 in Appendix B. Be sure to record all relevant information, such as the respondent number, record number, telephone number, question name, and nature of the correction. Give the form to your supervisor or put it in another designated place (for example, a manila envelope placed on the bulletin board for that purpose).

Do not try to hide the fact that you made an error you could not correct. An incorrect answer left uncorrected can contribute to survey bias. Correcting the error demonstrates that your primary concern is data quality and will enhance your value on the survey team.

What to Do If a Respondent Asks You to Change an Answer Sometimes respondents will ask you to alter their response to a previous question. Your procedure is the same whether the question was the last one you asked or ten questions back. If the question was objective, asking for a fact such as age or number of miles driven, most survey organizations will allow you to back up and make the change. If the question concerned an attitude, opinion, value, knowledge, or something similarly nonfactual, most survey organizations will instruct you to leave the answer as is. The reasoning is that respondents' thinking about survey issues can change naturally during the interview process, as they think further about these issues. Also, some respondents may believe that they have answered two questions inconsistently and may want to alter their answers to appear more coherent. But a certain amount of inconsistency is natural in humans. Most survey researchers want to hear respondents' initial, unedited feelings about something, even if those feelings seem contradictory over the course of the interview.

You are responsible for learning your employer's policies on changing respondents' answers. When in doubt, jot down notes on exactly what the respondent said. Using a form such as a data correction form is helpful because it will prompt you to include all the necessary information (such as question name, respondent number, what you originally recorded, and what the respondent would like it changed to). With the information you provide, the interviewer supervisor or the project director can decide whether the change is warranted.

Answers to Open-Ended Questions

Recording answers to open-ended questions requires skill because you should record them verbatim, but respondents tend to speak faster than the average interviewer can type. Luckily, most answers to open-ended questions are short.

As you read an open-ended question, your hands should hover over the keyboard. Respondents' answers usually occur quickly, so be prepared. Begin typing immediately when respondents utter something, even if they say something like "hum," "ah," or "jeez—I'm not sure." Always record answers to open-ended questions verbatim. Do not summarize. In addition to words, record respondents' speech behaviors, such as sighs and giggles, in parentheses. Use the entire array of abbreviations, acronyms, and shorthand shown in Table 1.2 to speed your recording of respondents' exact answers. Do not worry too much about spelling and punctuation, but make sure your typing is accurate and clear.

> You are the navigator for the interview. You are in charge of gathering data that accurately represent all respondents.

Do not hesitate to ask respondents to slow down as they answer. Often interviewers are disinclined to ask impatient respondents to speak a bit more slowly, to repeat what they just said, or to pause a moment until you catch up. But never sacrifice accuracy worrying that you will annoy respondents. In fact, most will be pleased that you *"want to get this all down"* or you *"do not want to miss anything."* Speak with confidence, and remember that you are the navigator for the interview. You are in charge of gathering data that accurately represent all respondents.

To ensure the accuracy of open-ended answers, repeat aloud what respondents have said as you type it, or read back to them what you have typed. If you speak slowly yourself, respondents will mimic your behavior. If you miss the second part of what a respondent said, read aloud the first part and ask the respondent to complete the sentence. In those rare instances in which a respondent's answer gets away from you and the respondent will not or cannot repeat it, you must summarize. Indicate that these are your words by putting them all in parentheses.

Indicate when you have used a standard probe (such as "*Whatever it means to you*") by typing "(p)." If you use a nonstandard probe, write out exactly what you said and put it in parentheses.

Respondents tend to use incomplete thoughts and phrases when answering open-ended questions. This is fine; researchers expect it. Do not clean up respondents' language. Do not correct bad grammar. Do not omit profane language.

If you run out of space, tell the respondent that you have run out of space, say thank you, and move to the next question (usually by pressing the Enter key or by clicking the Next button on your screen). The narrative you have typed is saved by the computer when you move to the next question. If you realize midway through filling in a screen that you need to change a respondent's prior answer, be sure to save what you have typed by moving forward before you go backward; otherwise all the data you typed on that screen will be lost.

Exhibit 7.7 shows a collection of real respondents' answers to an open-ended question. Nothing has been changed in how the interviewers recorded the answers. Note that most answers are short. Note the partial sentences and incorrect grammar. Notice interviewers' use of the scripted probes, as indicated by (p).

Unusual Circumstances While Conducting Interviews

Most interviews progress smoothly. Even though each one may not be thrilling, most display a unique facet of human diversity. If something goes wrong in a respondent's home during an interview, such as a pot boiling over or a child falling off a bike, it is an easy matter to schedule a callback for an hour or a day later. Most CATI systems will automatically pick up where the interview left off. Every so often, however, you will get a clunker. This section aims to help you handle these situations.

Problem Respondents

As an interview progresses, you may start noticing respondent characteristics that were not clear at the start. Only rarely will these characteristics disrupt the interview or cause you to halt it. For example, if a respondent starts giggling and sounding very young, you may suspect that you have landed a teenager

EXHIBIT 7.7. EXAMPLES OF ANSWERS TO AN OPEN-ENDED QUESTION.

The Question

Q:STOP4
What reasons did the officer[s] give you for the stop[s]?
PROBE FOR 'SPEEDING': How far over the speed limit did the officer say you were driving?
PROBE: Is there anything else?

OPEN-ENDED
PLEASE ENTER EXACT RESPONSE

Selected Actual Answers as Recorded by Interviewers

ran a red light

told me I had a tail light out

once I was not using a blinker. The second time . . . let me think . . . I don't remember

too much exhaust

um, what did he tell me? he pulled me over cause he said what the heck was, he pulled me over, asked me some questions, and let me go.

oh, okay, let's see, um, (sigh) let's see, there were two of them. I never was given a straight answer, let's see, the vague license plate light being out, but when I went to the rear of the car the light was on; um, let's see, there was the non-use of blinker, in a turn only lane. sort like this conversation, there wasn't much point to it, I have to turn or hit a brick wall, what's the point, everyone knows where I'm going

Speeding (p) twenty miles an hour over the speed limit (p)

I was not wearing my seat belt. that was true.

five mph over speed limit. (p) once for license plate. (p) I had michigan plates on the car and an oregon plate in the window. (p) tires going over white line

I dropped a little old lady off at the doctors office and I did a half U turn out of the drs office over the double line median, it was in the morning, no traffic, but technically it was a wrong turn. because I said I local, and the little old lady was bleeding, so he understood that it was circumstances that made it innocuous. so he let me off

One was I wasn't wearing a seat belt and the other was that I was going over the speed limit. (p) I think it was 8 or 10 miles per hour over the speed limit. It was a 35 mph zone.

going too fast, not using my turn signal, and rolling through a stop sign. (p) 10 mph

having some fun. If a respondent pauses with long silences after your questions, no matter how much you probe, you may wonder if that person is falling asleep, under the influence, or otherwise incompetent to complete the interview. If a respondent's answers seem wild or inconsistent but otherwise the person sounds knowledgeable and competent, you can reasonably speculate that the person is deliberately pulling your leg. Very infrequently, a respondent will become combative, aggressive, angry, or overly personal.

> No single, correct path is available for handling problem respondents. Choose the approach that best preserves data quality without comprising your sanity.

No single, correct path is available for you to follow in handling such atypical problems, but you have some choices. You can confront the person. For the respondent who seems to be nodding off, you can offer to call back at a more convenient time:

You seem awfully tired right now. How about if I call back (in two hours / tomorrow evening)?

For the person you suspect is underage, ask, as if it were part of the interview,

In what year were you born?

You never have to put up with an abusive respondent. Say firmly and without hesitation,

I am going to hang up now.

Choose the approach or combination of approaches that in your judgment best preserves the quality of the data without compromising your sanity.

If you are uncertain what to do, you can always claim that a problem just came up in your computer system and you need to call back tomorrow. Most jokesters are not interested in keeping up a charade through a second call. Many seemingly abusive people behave in a civilized manner when called at a different time of day or on a different day of the week. Take a few minutes to discuss problem cases with your supervisor. Together, you and the supervisor can develop a strategy for determining whether the data you collect from such a respondent are legitimate; if they are not, let them go.

Break-Offs

Once respondents get into an interview's conversational rhythm, it is rare for them to threaten to break off the call or actually do so. Those who threaten to hang up midway through the interview are often frustrated by the survey questions, saying that they are "silly," "too personal," or "do not apply" to them. Often it seems that every third person and his dog believe they can design better survey questions than the experts. They cannot, but they do not know it, so there is not much you can say.

An elderly woman once complained to an interviewer I employed that the racial profiling questions were both too personal and not applicable to her. These questions concerned car color, car maintenance (noise, exhaust, scratches, chips, working lights, and signals), and aftermarket improvements (tinted windows, special wheels, custom paint, and special stereo systems). To her personally they were indeed irrelevant. She did not understand that researchers can understand the full extent of racial profiling only if they have a picture of the persons who are not singled out, like her, to compare to those who are. Her answers, combined with answers from others like her, were extremely important to the researchers trying to understand this social problem.

In such situations, depend on your skills in working with reluctant respondents (discussed in Chapter Six). In the case of the woman who disliked the racial profiling questions, her interviewer wrote this observation at the end: "She was going to terminate the survey, but once I talked to her about the fact she could pass on any questions she felt were too personal, she continued and finished it." Try doing what this interviewer did, that is, remind respondents that they can refuse any question—even though we prefer that they do not.

Also stress the very practical importance of the survey to society and the respondent's importance to the research. For example, you may know from project-specific training that a survey's results will influence the state's decisions about repairing bridges and maintaining roads. People care about things as basic as bridges and roads. A single respondent's answers are unlikely to influence state policy, just as a single voter's vote rarely determines a candidate's election. But respondents' voices, like voters' votes, may sway such decision making when they are numerous and combined together. Be careful not to overpromise, however. Do not let your respondent start thinking that the state will repair a particular bridge.

If a respondent actually hangs up, do not take it personally. If you can do so credibly, try calling back immediately, saying that something strange happened with the telephone lines. If this tactic will not be credible, code a break-off and let a refusal conversion expert handle the case the next time.

Ending the Interview

Often the interview script signals that the interview is nearly over. For example, the demographic questions at the end might start by saying,

The last few questions are about you.

The words "last few" tell respondents that the end is close. Some surveys' final questions ask respondents for their opinions of surveys in general or of the one they are completing. Such a question might ask,

Finally, do you believe that participating in telephone surveys, like the one you are about to complete, is very important, somewhat important, or not important?

Often interviews end with an open-ended question, such as this:

That's the end of the interview! Is there anything else you would like to add?

Most respondents will say no. Some will thank you and compliment your interviewing skills. A few will ask how the survey results will be used. A handful of respondents will ask you to record something particular. These respondents understand that the survey results will be used by authorities, and they want those people to hear their specific thoughts about an issue. Again, record these comments verbatim. Noting such messages builds goodwill for public opinion research generally.

Occasionally, a respondent will take the opportunity to ask a question about you. A benign question is okay, such as, "Do you live in [*city*]?" or, "How do you like your job?" Respondents have just given you ten to twenty minutes of careful thought in answering the survey questions, and thus some mutual exchange may feel appropriate, but keep it businesslike. Answer in less than five words; do not dawdle.

Never answer a political question, such as what you think about the president. Never answer a personal question, such as your marital status, or give out personal contact information. Some respondents will interpret your friendly tone of voice as flirting, even though you do not intend it that way. Say to them,

I'm not allowed to answer that. But I would like to thank you for participating in this survey.

By sidestepping the question and transitioning to a good-bye, you signal that now is the time to hang up. Within these guidelines, use your judgment. You do not want to alienate cooperative respondents at this point. Nor, however, do you want to promise an ongoing relationship.

The good-bye at the interview's ultimate conclusion is often unscripted. Just about anything you say sincerely will work. Always thank respondents. For example, you might say,

Thank you for your time and answers to these questions.

After you hang up, some surveys will ask you to answer a few short questions about the respondent, such as your estimation of the respondent's ability to understand the questions. Often the instrument offers interviewers a section to note their observations or provide a thumbnail sketch of the interview and respondent. Use it to comment on the issues in which you were instructed and to record pertinent information that you think will be useful for that study's researchers. You can also use it to blow off steam after an interview. Here are some real examples:

Man. did this dude like to talk. yak, yak, yak.
Oh wow. um. MR, there's a warrant out for his arrest, sad story. is extremely concerned that his story be told . . .
Really, what a nice lady!!!! I'd call her again if I could.
This was an old codger type who would not shut up and pick a category easily.

Such end-of-interview options serve as an important closure device for some interviewers. However, because few researchers will actually analyze what you write, you should allocate no more than two minutes to recording your remarks.

Summing Up

The standardized interviewing techniques described in this chapter, combined with the information on the psychology of survey response, are your tools for gathering high-quality, unbiased data. Every part of this chapter concerns tools for avoiding interviewer-related error and bias in the data collection process. The easy parts are reading all questions in their entirety, in the order presented, and exactly as written, and knowing when and how to offer scripted definitions and probes. Learning to use a consistently confident, congenial, neutral tone of voice takes practice—sometimes diligent practice for certain types of voices. Memorizing the standard probes and feedback phrases, ascertaining when to use them, and becoming effective at using them also will take practice. Interviewers who focus on what to do rather than what not to do will be most successful.

CHAPTER EIGHT

WHAT TO EXPECT IN THE SURVEY WORKPLACE

This chapter covers the survey workplace, including the physical environment, the equipment, workplace policies, and interviewer supervision. Of course, not every organization is the same, but this discussion will give new interviewers an idea of what to expect.

Workplace Settings

The setting in which telephone interviewers work can significantly affect the quality of their employment experience as well as the quantity and quality of work they produce. The workplace setting comprises all aspects of the interviewer's surroundings, from environmental concerns, such as sound, temperature, and room layout, to equipment and ergonomics. This section presents what call center settings should be like ideally, although not all survey organizations match the ideal.

Workplace Environment

Telephone interviewers should work in a sound-reduced environment, that is, space with a carpeted floor, sound-minimizing ceiling tiles, and interviewing carrels with high, padded dividers. No survey respondent should ever be able to hear the hum of other interviews underway. (When they do, they think of telemarketers and fundraisers.) Likewise, no interviewer should be distracted by other interviewers' voices nearby.

The interviewing carrels should be designed to help interviewers focus. The carrel dividers should extend behind interviewers' shoulders, directing their voices inward. The dividers should also stretch at least one or two feet above the average interviewer's head when the interviewer is seated, to prevent the sound of voices from traveling over them. Interviewing stations should be configured to impede interviewers' ability to see distracting things or movement and to minimize their opportunity to interact with other interviewers within this workspace.

Interviewing rooms should be maintained at a constant temperature, without annoying breezes across interviewers' ankles or shoulders. Workstations should be located away from a building's uninsulated outer walls and noisy fans, heaters, and air-conditioning units. Uninsulated outer walls get very cold in winter and very hot in summer, no matter how constant the entire room's temperature may be. For workers who sit in one place for several hours at a time, the discomfort of such temperature extremes is distracting. Interviewers should be able to concentrate on their work, without the physical interruption of feeling too hot or too cold. Employers who lack a choice of the space provided for interviewers should, at a minimum, invest in space heaters during the winter and fans in the summer. However, these devices must be quiet, for the mechanical sounds of a fan, heater, or air-conditioning unit also can interfere with interviews, especially if respondents can hear them too.

> Interviewing stations should be configured to help interviewers focus, impeding sight and sound distractions and minimizing the chance to interact with others.

Interviewing carrels should be arranged so that a supervisor can scan the entire room from one place. A supervisor should easily be able to see interviewers' hands pop up whenever they get into situations in which they need help. The aisles between carrels should be wide enough for wheelchair-using interviewers to cruise and turn around readily.

It is helpful to have a small separate space for hanging up coats. Because few survey organizations have enough workstations for all interviewers to have their own, a wall of cubbies or large mailboxes is also useful, so that interviewers have a place to store a few personal belongings from day to day, such as their interviewing microphone, a water bottle, some snacks, a sweater, and interviewer training materials and notes. Such cubbies also benefit employers, who may use them to place interviewer messages and documents, for example, statements of total hours worked in the pay period, notification that the probationary period is over, and announcements of upcoming project-specific training sessions.

Because of call centers' long hours, many are equipped with a kitchenette containing such things as a hot water spigot, refrigerator, microwave oven, and coffee machine, as well as miscellaneous communal dishware. A separate area for taking breaks is also useful, with comfortable couches, reading materials, and views of the outdoors. Such features enhance interviewers' and other employees' comfort and collegiality during their work lives.

Work Equipment and Ergonomics

Every interviewer's workstation should be equipped with a telephone, a telephone headset, a networked computer with computer-assisted telephone interviewing (CATI) software, and a keyboard. Often CATI is the only software accessible on interviewers' computers. This is deliberate, to prevent people from using the computers for other purposes during interviewing hours. The computer's hardware or network configuration should allow interviewers to move swiftly from question to question when conducting interviews. Computers with mismatched software, hardware, and network configurations, as well as computers with insufficient memory, can add several seconds to each question. This, in turn, artificially lengthens interviews and makes it difficult for interviewers to keep their conversations with respondents going at a proper pace.

> Interviewers' microphones are like toothbrushes—all interviewers should have their own.

Interviewers' computer monitors should have at least fourteen-inch screens. An even larger one will be easier on interviewers' eyes. The screens should also have reflection-reduction devices installed, if needed.

Interviewers' equipment should sit atop a desk that can be adapted to different-sized interviewers. The desktop should move up and down several inches so that it is comfortable for both a five-foot-one interviewer and a six-foot-three interviewer. The keyboard should rest on a separate surface or tray that interviewers can both adjust up and down and rotate forward or backward several degrees to accommodate interviewers' varying girths. Interviewing work is unlikely to cause any repetitive stress injuries, such as carpal tunnel, because it involves just a little typing. However, interviewers' wrists should be able to rest in a manner that is comfortable to them. Wrist rests should be available to all interviewers who need them.

The walls of each workstation should have surfaces that allow interviewers to post notes for themselves and others. These might include a calendar for figuring out callback dates, different surveys' long-distance billing codes, and the answers to common questions for each survey. Each workstation also should have a pen and a pencil, scrap paper for taking notes, and a pad of data correction slips, similar to the example in Exhibit B.4 in Appendix B.

The telephone headsets for interviewers should be light and unnoticeable when in use. The microphone that attaches to the headset is as personal as a toothbrush, carrying each interviewer's scents and germs; all interviewers should have their own. Microphones of excellent quality are essential. Because good microphones are costly, some survey organizations have supervisors collect them at the end of each work shift and put them in a safe place. Others require interviewers to make a nominal cash deposit to encourage safekeeping. Interviewers should never remove their microphones from the workplace. Keep them in a safe place, such as a personal cubby or mailbox.

Good chairs are essential. Interviewers' chairs should be wheeled and should have armrests, a high, padded, adjustable back, and a padded, adjustable seat. Footrests should be available for interviewers who need them. Some terrific interviewers are extra wide, and their employers should have chairs with extra-large seats available for their use. Most employers prefer to invest in a supersized chair rather than deal with an on-the-job-injury claim.

A good-quality chair is useful only for those who know how to sit on it properly. Interviewers should never sit in a C-shaped slump, which can strain the lower back and neck. Instead, try out the three neutral sitting body postures suggested by the Occupational Safety & Health Administration of the U.S. Department of Labor (shown in Figure 8.1). Interviewers should train themselves to use consistently the posture they find most comfortable.

In the upright posture, the interviewer's seat should be flat, with thighs flat, torso and neck straight up, and lower legs vertical. For the declined posture, the interviewer's seat should slope slightly downhill, so that the buttocks are higher than the knees with thighs tilting downward, feet slightly forward, and the torso upright or slightly reclined. For the reclined posture, the interviewer's seat tilts slightly backward, with knees above the buttocks, lower legs vertical, and the torso and neck straight but leaning slightly backward. In all positions interviewers' feet should be flat. In all positions interviewers' eyes should naturally rest in the middle of the computer monitor. An interviewer's head consistently tilting up or down may result in strained neck muscles or cervical (neck) vertebrae. Interviewers should alter their seated posture to prevent such strain.

New interviewers should experiment with the three postures. Try putting a little pillow behind the small of your back or putting your feet on a small footrest.

FIGURE 8.1. THREE NEUTRAL BODY POSTURES FOR SITTING AT AN INTERVIEWER WORKSTATION.

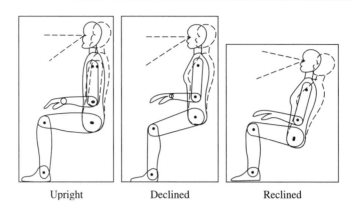

Upright   Declined   Reclined

Source: U.S. Department of Labor, Occupational Safety & Health Administration, n.d., *Good working positions,* retrieved July 22, 2006, from http://www.osha.gov/SLTC/etools/computerwork-stations/positions.html.

After finding the combination that suits you best, use it consistently. Each day when you start working, adjust the chair on which you will be sitting to your best neutral posture.

Workplace Routines

This section presents the most important workplace routines in survey research organizations' call centers. Knowing these in advance will help new interviewers adapt to a new workplace smoothly. Some of the issues raised may seem like common courtesy, too obvious to discuss, but they each take on new dimensions in a telephone interviewing work environment. Of course, your employer's work patterns may differ somewhat from those presented here, and you will need to adapt accordingly.

Work Hours

Survey organizations' call centers tend to be open very long hours, often seventy to ninety hours per week over six or seven days. The work shifts they offer to interviewers are variously structured, depending on the nature of the surveys in the field in any given week and the season of the year.

For random-digit-dial (RDD) surveys, some survey research organizations have interviewers call only on evenings and weekends, when most people are home. Although cost effective, this risks underrepresenting those who typically work during those hours. Most organizations run a small crew during the day and bring in more interviewers in the evenings and on weekends. From May through August, however, it is often hard to find people home on fine weekend afternoons. In order to use interviewers' time wisely then, a call center may offer a morning shift and an evening shift, with nothing in between. To my knowledge, no call centers schedule interviewing work on Sunday mornings. Indeed, for many years most did no calling on Sundays at all. Presently, however, it is common to have calling hours from Sunday midafternoon to 9:00 PM. Interviewers also may be asked to work certain nonreligious holidays, such as Presidents' Day, Martin Luther King Day, Memorial Day, the Fourth of July, Labor Day, and the day after Thanksgiving. These are excellent days for finding hard-to-reach respondents.

Only surveys of special populations, such as schools, businesses, governmental agencies, or the elderly, focus on daytime calling hours. For all surveys interviewers generally want to reach people between 9:00 AM and 9:00 PM, unless a respondent specifically requests an interview appointment outside those hours. However, interviewing hours will vary by the region of the country in which you live, the region that you are calling, and the interviewing hours that are most productive for a particular survey.

> Only surveys of special populations, such as schools, businesses, governmental agencies, or the elderly, focus on daytime calling hours. Most household surveys focus on evening and weekend calling hours.

For telephone surveys in your own time zone, interviewing usually takes place between 9:00 AM and 9:00 PM Monday through Saturday. But most interviewers will work between 4:00 PM and 9:00 PM, when interviewing is most productive. For interviewers calling from the Pacific time zone for a nationwide survey, the best hours to reach those in the Eastern time zone are from 1:00 PM to 6:00 PM local time, which is 4:00 PM to 9:00 PM respondents' time. If calling from the Eastern time zone to the Pacific time zone, the best hours to reach respondents are 7:00 PM to midnight local time, which is 4:00 PM to 9:00 PM their time. Because almost fifty million Americans live in the Pacific time zone (about one-sixth of the U.S. population), many interviewers in the Eastern states work late nights. Reaching respondents in Hawaii and Alaska can be quite punishing for interviewers located in the East, requiring calling in the wee morning hours. Because Hawaiians and

Alaskans represent less than 1 percent of the U.S. population, some national surveys exclude those states altogether.

The hours available for interviewers to work vary substantially by how many surveys are in the field. In large, busy survey organizations, several surveys may be in progress at any given time and interviewer work opportunities are numerous. However, many smaller organizations conduct just twenty to thirty surveys per year. This means that interviewers may have lots of work one month but almost no work in another. Moreover, when a survey is winding down, interviewers may receive a call saying that they are not needed for a planned work shift because no telephone numbers are left to call that day or only four interviewers are needed instead of the scheduled ten. Call centers have leeway in deciding which interviewers to continue as a survey winds down and which to schedule down in hours. The most productive and helpful interviewers will be favored. Sometimes a survey employer will have other work for down scheduled interviewers to fill in with, but do not count on it.

What this means is that interviewers generally work odd, varying, and sometimes unpredictable hours. For example, one week an interviewer might work on a new survey in the 4:00 PM to 9:00 PM shift Tuesday through Friday, plus the 9:00 AM to noon shift on Saturday. The next week, as the survey winds down, the same interviewer might be scheduled to work noon to 4:00 PM Monday and 4:00 PM to 9:00 PM Tuesday through Thursday. If the survey finishes Thursday evening at 7:30 PM, that person will be sent home early. As this example illustrates, interviewers' work hours can be erratic, especially when the employer has only one survey in the field at a time.

Many survey organizations also set minimum or maximum numbers of hours that interviewers can work. Some call centers require their interviewers to sign up for at least three four-hour work shifts each week, that is, a minimum of twelve hours per week. Yet others, in order to prevent burnout, will not allow interviewers to work more than six shifts per week, that is, no more than eighteen to twenty-four hours per week. Some also restrict interviewers to six or fewer hours per day. The Council for Marketing and Opinion Research (CMOR) conducted a study of telephone interviewing practices in market research organizations in 2000 and found that fully three-quarters of interviewers work part-time.[1]

Interviewers typically tell their employers the hours that they are available to work by completing a schedule request form (see the example in Exhibit B.1 in Appendix B). Interviewers should request a work schedule that makes the best use of their skill set. For example, those who enjoy the very start of RDD surveys, when dial attempts vastly outnumber interviews, should request more work shifts in the first few days of the survey than later. Likewise, interviewers who get bored silly by so much dialing and so little talking should request more work shifts in the middle of the anticipated data collection period. Those who enjoy the challenge of refusal conversion should request more shifts at the end of the survey than at the beginning and middle.

> Some survey organizations require interviewers to work a minimum of ten to twelve hours per week, to keep their skills honed. Some do not allow interviewers to work more than twenty or twenty-five hours per week, to prevent burnout.

The persons responsible for scheduling interviewers will map interviewers' available hours to their best estimates of how many interviewing hours are needed by the surveys in the field over the next few weeks. Schedulers will then post interviewers' hours on a bulletin board or a secure Web site, and perhaps call or e-mail you. The hours you have been assigned may not match the work hours you requested. It is your responsibility to find out the hours for which you are actually scheduled.

Interviewers who are available to work more hours than they are assigned should let the schedulers know. Some call centers create *standby* lists for surveys on which more interviewers want to work than there are shifts available. Standby lists are used to find people to fill in for interviewers who get sick or fail to show up. If you put yourself on a standby list, you must be both reachable and available to come to work on short notice.

Another way to get more hours is to check the posted interviewers' work schedule. Most call centers post the daily schedule for a week or more in a central place. If you see gaps in the schedule that fit you, check with a scheduler or supervisor to see if your name can be added. But never alter the posted work schedule yourself. Only a scheduler or supervisor may add or remove a name to the interviewers' work schedule.[2]

Be aware that schedulers' prospective estimates of how many hours each survey needs are just estimates. They are not always accurate. Some surveys finish more quickly than anticipated, and some take longer. Your employer should have a reliable method of communicating with interviewers about the progress of surveys in the field and how it affects the scheduled shifts. (Communication between interviewers and their employer is discussed more later in this chapter.)

Arrival at Work

Interviewers should arrive five minutes before their scheduled interviewing shift. Punch the time clock or sign in. Those who forget to do this might not get paid for that interviewing shift or for all the time they were present. Never ask a coworker to sign you in or out, and never do so for someone else. Be considerate of others by arriving on time, ready to work. Arriving late disrupts other interviewers' work.

Interviewers should use these few minutes before their shift starts to accomplish small tasks that will enable them to begin work promptly. For example, put away personal items (including cell phones, which must be turned off and placed out of reach). Check your mailbox for messages and announcements. Typically, daily updates for the surveys in progress will be posted in a central area. Reviewing these carefully helps interviewers contribute to continuity in the surveys. Because most interviewers share a workstation with others, you should adjust the chair and desk where you will sit to your proper height and position. During the flu and cold season, you may want to spray a cleanser on a rag and wipe off any viruses or germs lurking on the keyboard and desktop where you will be working. (Actually, periodically sanitizing shared workspaces is a good idea in any season.)

A supervisor typically will meet the interviewers working that shift and explain each survey's status. Some survey organizations set aside three or four minutes for a mini-training session before interviewers start calling. Such training is especially useful when surveys have challenging features. It is also a good warm-up if for interviewers who have not worked in several days. When multiple surveys are in the field, a supervisor will assign one for each interviewer to work on, or interviewers can negotiate with the supervisor for the survey they prefer. In most places a supervisor also assigns each interviewer to a particular or customary workstation for that shift.

While Working

As soon as the usual shift-starting protocol is complete, interviewers should sit down at their stations, sign onto CATI with their interviewer ID numbers, and start calling.

While working, most call centers will allow interviewers to refer to their project-specific training materials and this *Handbook*. For example, interviewers who encounter an unusual situation may need to refresh their memories on a particular call disposition code or interviewing technique by consulting their training materials. Similarly, interviewers who notice that they are getting more refusals than usual should restore their skills by consulting those documents. For particularly difficult or reluctant respondents, interviewers should not hesitate to take a few moments to consult their training materials and to script what they intend to say.

Whenever interviewers encounter problems or difficulties that they cannot resolve quickly on their own, they should ask a supervisor for assistance. Do not be shy about it. If one interviewer is having a problem, other interviewers are probably going to have the same problem. Be sure to hold conversations with a supervisor outside the interviewing area to avoid interrupting other interviewers' attentiveness to their work.

> Interviewers should stay hydrated by sipping from a sealed, spill-proof container kept nearby on the floor. Interviewers should never sip, snack, chew gum, gnaw fingernails, or put anything in their mouth while on the telephone. All cell phones should be turned off and put away.

Similarly, interviewers should not whisper comments or jokes or otherwise interact with others in neighboring workstations while working or leaving for a break. Even if that coworker is not conducting an interview at the moment, another interviewer might be and hearing or seeing others can disrupt their focus. In addition, it is unprofessional for respondents to hear interviewers' chat or laughter buzzing in the background. Passing notes is just as bad; it can disrupt interviewers' routines as much as voices.

Interviewers should never make outgoing personal telephone calls from their workstations. Most call centers automatically record the telephone numbers of all outgoing calls, and they know the numbers each interviewer should be calling, so people who do this will hear about it and may be disciplined. Also, interviewers should never give their workstation telephone number to a family member or friend. Most call centers have a special telephone number for family members to call in case of an emergency.

On days that involve a lot of talking interviewers should be sure to stay hydrated. Nearly all employers allow interviewers to keep beverages in sealed, spill-proof containers, either on the floor or some other surface away from the computer. Sip liquids only between interviews, not during them. Interviewers should never eat, chew gum, gnaw their fingernails, and otherwise put things in their mouths while calling. Similarly they should never blow their nose, clear their throat, or cough. Most people regard the sounds of chewing, crunching, slurping, snuffling, and hacking as rude on the other end of the telephone. Interviewers should avoid behavior that might alienate respondents.

Interviewers who work on the same survey for an entire shift or work on the same survey for weeks on end with no other surveys in the field must guard against a sense of boredom creeping into their voice. Reading the same interview script over and over can, frankly, get tedious. But interviewers who convey monotony will undermine their respondents' efforts. Even when the interview script varies little, interviewers can find interesting variations in their respondents to keep them alert.

Working on multiple surveys in one shift minimizes the chance of getting bored with one. However, interviewers should take a few minutes to reorient when shifting. A quick read through the new script should suffice for those who have already worked on it for a few shifts. Switching back and forth across surveys multiple times in one work shift is not recommended. It is too easy for interviewers to lose focus and subtly damage data quality.

Down scheduling is the practice of giving fewer and less desirable work hours to less productive and less motivated interviewers, often as an indirect method of discipline.

Under no circumstances should interviewers try to knit or read a book or magazine while dialing from their workstation. Such activities undermine concentration and productivity. Interviewers who attempt these sidebar activities make fewer dial attempts per hour, which some employers track as a productivity measure. Less productive interviewers are the first to get down scheduled and the last to get the more favorable work assignments.

Breaks

Interviewers are expected to remain at their workstations, working, for their entire shift, except for breaks. The paid work breaks allowed vary somewhat from state to state. A typical rule is one ten-minute rest break for every four hours of work. For those who work five or more hours, some states give the option of taking a paid fifteen-minute break or an unpaid thirty-minute break. Your employer will explain what laws apply in your state. However, call centers have to be somewhat relaxed about exactly when interviewers' breaks occur, for they cannot halt an interview in progress in order to take a break at a specific time.

In addition to state-required breaks, some call centers allow interviewers a few minutes each hour to stretch, use the restroom, and get a drink of water. Interviewers who have this privilege should not drag it out to six or eight minutes, for example, to smoke a cigarette or grab a snack at a nearby eatery. An employer can easily take away this special allowance. Also, interviewers cannot save up those minutes hour to hour to add onto their ten-minute break. The point of the mini-breaks is to help interviewers perform their jobs better hour by hour.

Interviewers should take breaks away from their workstations. Get up and move around to get your blood flowing. Take a few deep breaths. Go for a short walk. Interviewers should always let a supervisor know when they leave on a break and when they plan to return. Returning on time is crucial, because a late return can be considered a *tardy*, and too many tardies can blotch an employment record.

Breaks are also the time when interviewers can place personal telephone calls. Many call centers designate a telephone line for that purpose for interviewers. But this is not the time to resolve a disagreement with a spouse or have a conference call with your child's teacher, because another interviewer is likely to need the telephone too. Most call centers will not allow interviewers to place personal calls for which a fee is charged. If yours does, you will need advance approval to make such a call and you must reimburse your employer for that cost. Using a project's long-distance billing code for personal long-distance calls can result in disciplinary action or getting fired.

People who use their employer's kitchenette on breaks should of course do their share to keep the area clean, sanitary, and quiet. Wash your dishes and clean up after yourself. Take a turn in volunteering to clean the appliances.

Departure

Interviewers are expected to keep calling up to the last minute of their shifts. An interviewer whose shift ends at 9:00 PM should dial their last telephone number at 8:59 PM. If that call results in an interview, the interviewer must be prepared to see it through to the end. This means that an interviewer's actual departure times may vary from 9:01 PM to 9:30 PM. Interviewers must be prepared for these variations.

Interviewers are also expected to leave their workstations clean and neat for the next interviewers. This involves properly disposing of all personal materials and gathering personal belongings. While leaving, interviewers should check again for survey-related announcements, recheck the posted interviewers' schedule for the next several days, say good-bye to their supervisor, and then clock out. Forgetting to sign out may affect an interviewer's paycheck, especially if that person stayed to complete a late interview.

Miscellaneous Issues

Some survey organizations give interviewers the opportunity to express their ideas to their supervisors and others on the research team about the surveys in progress and their jobs in general. This may be accomplished with an *interviewer logbook,* for example, a three-ring binder where interviewers can make constructive comments about how data collection could be conducted more efficiently, easily, or effectively. A logbook also gives interviewers a chance to describe their poignant experiences with respondents or unload their frustrations. Entries can be signed or anonymous. At times I have photocopied comments in an interviewer logbook for survey sponsors or clients to help them better understand their survey or the respondents. I have also seen employers place sheets of butcher paper on a wall and ask interviewers to make their comments about surveys in progress there.

Finally, interviewers should not solicit coworkers to buy a daughter's Girl Scout cookies, contribute to a fundraiser, or purchase any other products without receiving advance permission from their employer. Even with permission, interviewers should not of course solicit their coworkers during work hours or in the main work areas, and they should never press unwilling or uninterested coworkers to purchase anything.

Communication with Your Employer

Because of the fluid nature of interviewing work, survey organizations typically maintain various ways of communicating with interviewers. They may use a telephone hotline with a recorded message, send group e-mails, or set up a secure Web site for interviewers only. These sources contain information on the status of surveys in progress, which surveys are finished, and the dates of upcoming project-specific training sessions, as well as updates on pay periods and various human resource matters. On the days interviewers do not work, they can access these information sources in order to stay up-to-date on the interviewing work that their employer has available. In this way, for example, an interviewer will know when a survey has finished earlier than expected and will not show up for a scheduled work shift unnecessarily.

In order for interviewers to receive regular communication from their employer, they must have the proper equipment in their homes. Interviewers whose employer posts information on a Web site will need a computer and Internet access. Interviewers whose employer relies on e-mail must also have an e-mail account that they can access easily. Interviewers whose employer relies on telephone communication will be required to have a telephone number with voice mail or an answering machine. A good interviewer has the tools to receive regular communications from their survey employer and checks messages and updates daily. Note that the flow of information is from the survey employer to interviewers. Interviewers should not call in or send e-mails on every day that they do not work.

> Interviewers should have Internet access, e-mail, or a telephone answering machine to receive regular communication from their employer about the progress of surveys in the field.

Employment Status, Pay, and Benefits

During general interviewer training, interviewers will find out the particulars of their employment status, such as starting pay, opportunities for raises, and the employment benefits for which they are eligible. Interviewers will also learn whether their pay period will be weekly, biweekly, or monthly and when they can expect to receive their first paycheck. Remember, you should be paid for your many hours spent in training. Training is your employer's investment in you.

Benefits and Wages

Telephone interviewers' employment status, pay, and benefits vary substantially by their type of employer. Only about one-fourth of telephone interviewers employed by private, for-profit firms work full-time, and only half of them receive employment benefits. Among part-time interviewers working for private, for-profit employers, roughly one-third receive benefits. The employment benefits most often reported are paid vacation time, paid holidays, health insurance, and a 401(k) savings plan. Among interviewers who work for public and private, non-profit organizations, fewer than one-fifth receive benefits.[3] Those who do receive benefits most often get paid sick leave and vacations.

No current data exist on hourly wage rates for telephone interviewers. CMOR's 2000 study of telephone interviewing practices in market research organizations found that interviewers' median starting pay in these firms was $6.90 per hour.

The median top hourly rate was $10.00 per hour. A 1998 survey of nonprofit survey organizations showed that starting pay ranged from $5.25 to $10.25 per hour, with over half starting at $5.25 to $7.00. Survey organizations in large metropolitan areas, high cost-of-living areas, and states with high minimum wages tend to pay telephone interviewers more on average. Given the continuous and ongoing training interviewers receive, their ability to understand the details of a wide array of projects, the importance of their work to society, and the odd and inconsistent hours they typically work, I recommend that interviewers' starting hourly wage should be 15 to 20 percent above minimum wage.

Many survey employers offer regular pay raises and some type of bonus, or incentive pay. But the criteria vary widely. Raises may be granted after interviewers have completed a certain number of interviews, interviewing hours, work shifts, weeks worked, or months worked—and the thresholds within those criteria vary too. Interviewers most often receive bonuses when they perform exceptionally, such as exceeding a certain quota of interviews completed or dial attempts, conducting interviews in a foreign language, or having perfect attendance. Some organizations give incentive pay for working on holidays and on Friday and Saturday evenings (the most difficult work shifts to fill), for long or difficult interviews, and for performing difficult refusal conversions.

Not all bonuses involve cash payments. Some organizations celebrate the end of particularly long or onerous survey projects with pizza parties. Some celebrate particular interviewers with custom T-shirts, gift certificates, and *interviewer of the month* awards. These employee recognition mechanisms properly reward interviewers for ongoing excellence in their work and help to maintain a group of motivated interviewers. In addition, some interviewer supervisors take it upon themselves to bring cookies, banana bread, or candy for their interviewing teams.

The bottom line is that the quality of employment varies a great deal for telephone interviewers. Despite the scientific importance of your work, the detailed training you receive, the odd hours you typically work, and the perspicacity and quickness you need to perform well on a wide range of projects with a diverse assortment of respondents, most interviewers will be part-time, temporary employees with no benefits. Frankly, many employers do not fully appreciate or understand interviewers' work. Almost all telephone interviewer employment is *at will,* meaning that employers can terminate interviewers with or without cause, and with or without notice, at any time, except as otherwise provided by law. Few interviewing positions are protected by union contracts. However, these rather gloomy features are offset by the chance to work on wide-ranging survey topics, with a flexible schedule, and the knowledge that the results of your work can improve people's lives—or at least make them more interesting.

Inactive Status

Interviewers who miss a certain number of project-specific interviewer training sessions (four to six, depending on how far apart they occur) or conduct no interviews in a certain time period (three months is typical) are likely to be placed on their employer's list of inactive interviewers. This means that the organization will stop regularly sending them information about upcoming project-specific training sessions. Interviewers should receive formal notification of this status change. Those who wish to remain active or decide to reactivate later must take the initiative to let their employer know.

Those who decide to reactivate as an interviewer after a separation of more than six months will probably be required to repeat their employer's general interviewer training and testing before starting to interview again. Interviewers who attend the initial general interviewer training but do not work on any surveys for six weeks subsequently are also likely to be required to repeat general interviewer training.

Possible Work Between Surveys

In between telephone survey projects many survey research organizations rely on their best interviewers to assist in other parts of the survey process. For example, interviewers can learn how to pretest new survey instruments and conduct open-ended coding. They might also be asked to help with other types of surveys, for example, by signing, stuffing, and stamping precontact letters or mail questionnaires, scanning returned mail questionnaires, or doing direct data entry. Survey employers are most likely to ask interviewers to assist in these tasks if they demonstrate interest, reliability, and common sense. Such opportunities give interviewers a chance to expand their skill set and thereby enhance their value to their employer.

Workplace Policies

Workplace policies cover a variety of employee behavior and activities. This section focuses on the use of a pseudonym, standards of conduct, attendance, and performance evaluations. You are responsible for learning how your employer's policies differ from the policies presented here.

Using a Pseudonym

When you introduce respondents to a survey, you will almost always give your name. Most survey organizations allow interviewers to decide whether to use their first name only or both their first name and surname. The policy issue concerns whether and under what circumstances your employer will allow you to use a pseudonym instead of your real name.

> Interviewers with an unusual name should obtain their employer's approval to use a pseudonym instead of their real name when conducting interviews.

It is difficult to imagine routine situations in which telephone interviewers would have concerns about using their given names. Unlike face-to-face interviewing, which always contains an element of risk for interviewers, telephone interviewing gives you a certain anonymity because interviewers and respondents cannot see each other. In tens of thousands of telephone interviews conducted under my leadership, I cannot recall a single instance in which a respondent later called back or stopped by asking for an interviewer by name. Indeed, most respondents probably cannot remember the interviewer's name immediately after completing an interview. However, rare situations occur and some interviewers may want to protect themselves.

Most employers agree to pseudonyms for interviewers with an unusual name or a foreign name because they do not want your name to sidetrack a survey introduction. For example, an interviewer named Winter may find that he has greater success when introducing himself as Will. I know an interviewer named Noy who used the pseudonym Joy, because most Americans have never heard of her Thai nickname. Another interviewer, named Scott, was simply more comfortable calling himself John when conducting interviews.

If you wish to use a pseudonym or believe that you should use one, you must obtain your employer's approval in advance, preferably in writing. Then you must use that pseudonym consistently. You cannot use one name one day and another name another day. Nor can you change your name with every respondent. When supervisors call respondents back to conduct verifications, they will mention the interviewer's name; thus they must have the actual name that you used. For this reason interviewers must self-identify with the same name at all times.

Standards of Interviewer Conduct

When all telephone interviewers follow certain basic standards of conduct, they enhance the survey organization's ability to conduct its work efficiently, effectively, and harmoniously. Table 8.1 lists the basic standards of conduct in the survey workplace and gives examples of behaviors that violate those standards. These

TABLE 8.1. STANDARDS OF CONDUCT AND VIOLATIONS OF STANDARDS.

Standard of Conduct	Violations of Standards
Maintain high-quality work.	Unsatisfactory work. Careless mistakes. Failure to meet quality criteria.
Maintain the integrity of survey data.	Falsifying interview data, call disposition codes, or sample records.
Attend to one's work at all times.	Sleeping, loitering, or loafing during work hours. Soliciting during work hours or in work areas without authorization.
Arrive five minutes before the shift starts. Be ready to work when the shift starts. Work the entire shift.	Arriving late to work. Not being ready to work when the shift starts. Not working to the end of the shift, or leaving without prior authorization before the shift ends.
Complete all work-related documents fully and truthfully. Accurately record arrival and departure times. Take breaks of designated length. Honestly explain absences.	Willful dishonesty, misrepresentation, or lying on work records. Inaccurately recording arrival and departure times. Taking overlong breaks. Altering any employee's time card or attendance records, or asking someone else to do so. Lying about reasons for an absence.
Keep only sealed, spill-proof beverage containers in all work areas. Sip or drink between calls only.	Open beverage containers in work areas. Consuming fluids while dialing or speaking on the telephone.
Consume food and chew gum only on breaks and in designated areas.	Eating or chewing gum at the workstation or while using the telephone.
Turn off and put away cell phones while working.	Allowing one's cell phone to ring, or using it at one's workstation during work hours.
Make and take personal telephone calls only during breaks and on authorized telephones.	Using interview telephones for personal calls. Making or accepting personal calls at unauthorized times. Charging personal long-distance calls to a project's billing code.
Use computers only for work-related tasks, unless otherwise authorized in advance.	Using computers for personal tasks.
Treat coworkers with respect. Keep one's hands to one's self.	Gossiping. Conspiring to undermine coworkers. Using obscene or abusive language toward coworkers. Harassing others. Bullying or menacing coworkers on or off workplace premises. Inappropriately touching or attempting to do so.
Keep to one's own workspace, computer, and documents, unless otherwise authorized in advance.	Invading coworkers' workspaces, computers, or documents. Causing willful mischief in the computer system, network, or files. Stealing or removing the organization's or coworkers' property, equipment, or documents.
Follow workplace pledges, regulations, and safety rules.	Violating the pledge of confidentiality. Possessing, selling, or being under the influence of drugs or alcohol. Violating regulations or safety rules. Possessing firearms, explosives, or dangerous weapons.

(continued)

TABLE 8.1. *(CONTINUED)*

Standard of Conduct	Violations of Standards
Follow supervisors' work-related instructions.	Displaying insubordination, or refusing to obey instructions.
Treat property respectfully. Use equipment in the manner intended.	Willfully or through negligence damaging or destroying property, equipment, or documents.
Maintain appropriate behaviors in the workplace.	Engaging in or provoking violent acts (threats, fights, horseplay, and so on) or criminal conduct. Willfully or carelessly using words or engaging in deeds that endanger or harm an employee.
Keep workstations and communal spaces clean and neat.	Creating or contributing to unsanitary workplace conditions.

standards are presented with interviewers in mind, but they are equally applicable to all other employees in a survey organization.

Standards of interviewer conduct should be fully presented and discussed during general interviewer training. Violating these standards may result in a warning, formal disciplinary action, or immediate dismissal, depending on the seriousness of the offense. Again, the standards presented here address telephone interviewers' responsibilities. Most employers will also have a set of general standards for all employees, to which interviewers must also adhere.

Attendance

Unscheduled interviewer absences make survey planning extremely difficult. Such behavior also damages an interviewer's reputation with coworkers, because that person's *no show* denies another interviewer the opportunity to work. The rules for canceling scheduled work shifts, working partial shifts, and lateness vary across survey organizations. The following paragraphs represent reasonable rules and consequences, but interviewers should learn the extent to which their employer's rules differ from these.

> Do not work when sick or when recovering from an illness that affects your voice.

Illness Interviewers who get sick should call in immediately. Most survey organizations have a dedicated telephone number just for interviewers to communicate with schedulers and supervisory staff. Interviewers should give an employer as much time as possible to arrange for another interviewer to cover their shift.

Interviewers should never come to work sick. Call centers are often close environments in which viruses and germs spread easily, especially when interviewers share computer keyboards across shifts. Similarly, an interviewer should not come to work when recovering from an illness that affects their voice, such as laryngitis, a sinus infection, any type of cough, or cold. Stuffy noses, scratchy voices, coughs, sneezes, and mucous-filled lungs sound gross to respondents and distract them from their task.

Other Absences Interviewers who cannot work a scheduled shift for any reason other than illness should inform their employer twenty-four hours before they were scheduled to start their shift. Interviewers who inform their employer later than that (or their employer receives the e-mail or telephone message later than that) will receive a *late cancel* on their employment record.

Employees sometimes say that they have suddenly been taken ill when they have not. All too often the truth comes out when a coworker sees them jogging down the street, waiting for a bus, standing beside a soccer field, or shopping for groceries a few hours later. Lying about the reason for an absence is a violation of the basic standards of conduct in the workplace and could result in disciplinary action.

Tardiness Interviewers who learn that they will have to arrive late for a scheduled shift or leave early should inform their employer at least twenty-four hours in advance so that the organization can try to cover their shift with someone who can work it entirely. Failure to do this may also go on an interviewer's record. Most call centers do not tolerate partial shifts as it disrupts the workflow and distracts other interviewers. Some will try to be flexible with interviewers' class or bus schedules, but their patience has limits.

Interviewers who have not arrived and are not at their station ten minutes after their scheduled start time, and have not called in advance, will be recorded as a no-show. Those who arrive eventually cannot count on being allowed to work. A supervisor may not have time to repeat to latecomers the information they missed at the start of the shift. Similarly, interviewers should negotiate shift changes through regular channels and not as the work shift starts or during the shift, when supervisors are unlikely to be free to attend to these requests. These are all issues of respecting others' work.

Consequences of Poor Attendance Supervisors will record all interviewer absences, tardies, and other attendance problems in their personnel record. Interviewers who repeatedly cancel shifts or show up late, even with advance notice, will have to face the consequences. Each call center has its own tolerance limits.

One survey organization counts poor attendance in the following way. Two absences from scheduled shifts in a thirty-day period is regarded as excessive. Three late cancels or no-shows in a ninety-day period is considered a "consistent pattern of absence." Three late arrivals in a ninety-day period without advance notice is considered a "tardiness pattern." Early departures without advance notice are considered equivalent to late arrivals. Any of these patterns of poor attendance may result in the following consequences:

- Down scheduling, that is, giving problem interviewers fewer hours than they want to work, or not inviting them to the next project-specific training.
- Postponement or denial of the next scheduled pay raise.
- Disciplinary action (described in more detail below).
- Interpretation of the behavior as a voluntary resignation, which results in never again being invited to project-specific training sessions.

Performance Evaluations

Interviewer supervisors will continuously monitor interviewers' performance. This is necessary to maintain high-quality survey data. Interviewers will receive the greatest scrutiny and feedback in their first few weeks of interviewing, which employers often regard as a probationary period. After that interviewers should receive routine pointers and comments and formal periodic performance evaluations on the quality and quantity of their work.

Probationary Employment Period As discussed in Chapter Four, many survey research organizations require a probationary employment period for new interviewers of approximately twenty-five hours of interviewing or the first four to six work shifts, excluding training hours. During this period, employers will evaluate interviewers' suitability for continued work, and interviewers can decide if their employer and telephone interviewing suits them.

Supervisors will gauge interviewers' work habits, attitude, and attendance as well as the quality of their interviewing. They will take notes on how interviewers perform their work—including telephone etiquette, pace, tone of voice, sticking to the script, use of feedback and probes, tailoring, ability to discourage unrelated conversation, avoidance of leading comments, good judgment in on-the-spot decisions, and refusal conversion skills—and on how well interviewers respond to supervisor feedback. They will also consider interviewers' efficiency and productivity, such as dial attempts per hour and ratio of refusals to completed interviews. At the same time, new interviewers should be sizing up the workplace culture, the availability of work hours, and whether this is the kind of job you think you could enjoy doing well.

At the end of the probationary period, the supervisors will combine their notes into a formal evaluation. One or two will sit down with each interviewer to discuss your strengths and also the areas you need to improve. Interviewers should feel free to ask questions and present their observations at this meeting. The best interviewers show their sincere interest in doing the best possible job. Interviewers who are invited to join the interviewing team may receive a raise. Those who do not measure up to standards may be released or sent for remedial training.

Formal Performance Evaluations Interviewers' performance reviews should occur at predictable intervals. Following a probationary period, each interviewer should receive a formal performance evaluation after a certain period of time (hours, weeks, or months) or after completing a certain number of interviews, depending on the criteria your employer uses. Subsequently, interviewers should receive reviews in predictable periods. I prefer to conduct the first performance evaluation at the end of 400 hours of interviewing, which may take an interviewer three to six months to accrue, depending on the project availability and hours worked. Thereafter, I recommend reviews after every 1,000 hours of interviewing. No matter what sequence your employer uses, all interviewers should be able to request a review at any time.

Formal performance reviews are based on several sources of information: (1) supervisors' ongoing, documented observations about the quality and quantity of interviewers' work, including specific mentions of how they handled difficult situations; (2) statistical analysis of information collected automatically by the CATI system about interviewers' dial attempts, completions, and refusals across several surveys, in order to compare your productivity with that of other interviewers; (3) possibly, supervisors' evaluation of audiotapes of one or more interviews, perhaps taped without the interviewer's advance knowledge (such evaluations are the best way to determine the extent to which you consistently follow standardized interviewing protocols); and (4) information about interviewers' availability, attendance, ability to get along with others, contributions to teamwork, and adherence to standards of conduct. (The next major section, "What to Expect from Interviewer Supervisors," discusses the first two sources in more detail.)

Performance evaluations should give interviewers a balanced picture of their strengths and weaknesses as an interviewer, reinforce their good habits, and develop strategies to improve their weaker areas. Supervisors will let those interviewers who need to improve in certain areas know and suggest how to prevent mistakes in the future. They will also let interviewers who are doing a good job know. In this process, even very good interviewers can learn something about their interviewing of which they were unaware. This is also a good time for interviewers to discuss their interests, future goals, and whether their employer has additional opportunities.

A satisfactory or excellent formal performance review should result in a pay increase. However, some employers structure interviewers' pay increases to coincide with markers other than employee reviews.

Discipline

Interviewers who consistently abide by their employer's standards of conduct, have no attendance problems, and receive satisfactory performance evaluations should not find themselves the object of disciplinary action. Most supervisors prefer not to invoke the disciplinary process. Many avoid it by down scheduling a poorly performing interviewer. The problem with down scheduling is that these poor performers have no opportunity to learn about the underlying issues or correct them.

Interviewers who demonstrate a consistent performance or attendance problem should be taken aside by a supervisor for instruction or advising to develop a mutually effective solution. Failure to respond may result in disciplinary action. In addition, interviewers who violate one of the standards of conduct may find themselves in the grips of their employer's formal disciplinary procedure. Organizations handle employee discipline in various ways, but the formal procedures shown in Table 8.2 are standard; read them.

Although a three-step procedure like the one in Table 8.2 is typical for handling common issues such as attendance, some situations require more extreme intervention. Certain infringements of the standards of conduct, such as insubordination or treating coworkers disrespectfully, are often better handled by an external mediator, that is, someone skilled in dispute resolution. Other conduct violations are so serious, such as violating confidentiality or breaking safety rules, that an employer is justified in omitting one step of the formal discipline procedure or proceeding directly to dismissal. Certain less extreme situations, like chronic tardiness, may justify repeating a disciplinary step. For most employers, formal disciplinary procedures serve only as guidelines. Private employers in particular have a great deal of leeway in how they handle employee discipline problems.

TABLE 8.2. TYPICAL STEPS IN A FORMAL DISCIPLINARY PROCEDURE.

Step	What Happens
One	Oral reminder or warning. It remains in effect for six months and goes onto an employee's permanent employment record. For those showing no further performance or attendance problems in the six-month period, the disciplinary procedure is formally deactivated when six months is over.
Two	Written reminder or reprimand. If an employee's performance does not improve after Step One, the supervisor takes the person aside to discuss the issues and then generates a memo or reprimand, which they both sign. It remains in effect for six months and goes onto the employee's permanent employment record. At this point the employee may be placed on probation. If the employee shows no further performance or attendance problems in the six-month period, the disciplinary procedure is formally deactivated when six months is over.
Three	Decision on continued employment. If the problem recurs, the employee, the supervisor, and a senior person in the organization (such as a director, vice president, or president) discuss the problem. Unless the employee can demonstrate commitment to improve and abide by policies, he or she will be suspended without pay or terminated.

What to Expect from Interviewer Supervisors

Typically, a small cadre of interviewer supervisors oversees telephone interviewers' work. A call center with forty to sixty interviewers that operates about seventy hours per week needs at least five or six interviewer supervisors altogether. Because these supervisors affect telephone interviewers' work lives substantially, this section explains who they are, what they do, and what that means for interviewers' workplace experience.

Who Interviewer Supervisors Are and What They Do

Interviewer supervisors are usually former interviewers who rose through the ranks owing to their exemplary interviewing skills, work ethic, and interest in survey research. Because of their expert interviewing skills, supervisors should continue to conduct interviews at least part of the time, both to act as role models and to understand interviewers' experiences on particular surveys. Rarely do interviewer supervisors have prior supervisory skills or experience. For this reason most lack final authority in hiring, disciplining, or terminating interviewers, although they may exert influence in such decisions.

> Interviewer supervisors should continuously motivate interviewers, help them manage problems with respondents, further develop their interviewing skills, and transmit the value of high-quality survey data.

Interviewer supervisors' goals are to assist in maintaining the highest possible quality in survey data and to run the telephone interviewing part of the survey organization as efficiently as possible. The main tasks supervisors carry out to achieve these goals involve monitoring interviewers' daily work and tracking their performance. They may also schedule interviewer hours and maintain channels of communication with interviewers (via a Web site, e-mail, or telephone). To varying degrees, interviewer supervisors also participate in conducting interviewer training sessions, monitoring survey samples, and enforcing standards of conduct, but they do not usually bear full responsibility for these jobs.

This section of the *Handbook* focuses on interviewer supervisors' main tasks—interviewer monitoring and performance measurement—for these duties affect telephone interviewers the most.

Interviewer Monitoring

Interviewer supervisors continuously monitor and evaluate interviewers' job performance. The immediate goal of monitoring is to correct any data collection or data entry errors as soon as they occur. The long-term goal is to collect information for periodic performance evaluations. Most call center supervisors accomplish interviewer monitoring in two ways—from a centralized workstation and by wandering around.

Centralized Monitoring Many call centers monitor interviewers unobtrusively with a centralized system that allows supervisors to observe the computer screens of interviews in progress and to listen in on interviewers' conversations with respondents. With such a system, a supervisor can see each interviewer's computer screen exactly as they see it. Usually, a supervisor selects an interview in progress, without an interviewer's foreknowledge, and tracks all the key elements of a standardized interview. If needed the supervisor explains where you used a poor probe, failed to read a question completely, said something leading, or miskeyed an answer. This person should also congratulate you for doing a particularly good job under difficult circumstances.

Systematic monitoring is accomplished more formally. Supervisors use evaluation forms that prompt them to listen and watch for certain interviewer behaviors, note where these behaviors occurred during an interview, and then count the occurrences. Systematic monitoring often addresses such subtle features of interviewing as intonation, pace and timing, and use of feedback. Ideally, interviewers will have several systematic evaluations of their work during every survey. Systematic monitoring is an essential and effective supplement to interviewer training.

No interviewer should feel singled out for special or undue monitoring scrutiny, unless his or her work performance is clearly below par. However, you may request that a supervisor monitor your work if you are uncertain about your skills. For example, if you feel that you are getting too many initial or final refusals, ask a supervisor to listen in on several of your dial attempts and then offer suggestions on how you could improve.

The main problem with centralized monitoring systems from an interviewer's viewpoint is that supervisors sometimes overconcentrate on the computer screens and on eavesdropping. They can easily miss the frantic waving that signals that an interviewer needs immediate help with a particular respondent. For such reasons a centralized monitoring system alone is insufficient. It works best when combined with the supervisory style of *wandering around*.

Wandering Around For interviewer supervisors to do their job best, they must be available to interviewers when they need special help. They should be on hand when interviewers have impromptu questions about call disposition codes or need technical assistance with their hardware or software. If an interviewer requests help, a supervisor should be nearby to speak with a respondent, for example, to assure them of the call's legitimacy. Supervisors should be consistently available for spontaneous discussions with interviewers during work breaks. Interviewers will gain from supervisors' experience and their firsthand knowledge of your problems and concerns. Supervisors also should be ready to hear from interviewers when some aspect of a survey is not going according to plan, and they should be willing to carry that information to a project director or client if needed.

Toward these ends, interviewers should expect supervisors to spend a significant part of their work hours wandering among the interviewing stations.[4] Their job is to continuously motivate interviewers, help interviewers learn how to manage problems with respondents, further develop interviewers' standardized interviewing skills, and transmit the value of exceptional data quality. This also means, however, that interviewers must become accustomed to supervisors hovering over their shoulders, slipping them a note, and maybe pulling them aside between interviews—all with a goal of creating the best interviewers possible.

Ongoing Performance Measurement

In monitoring interviewers' work with technology and in wandering around, interviewer supervisors continually evaluate both the quality and quantity of interviewing work. Interviewers' daily interactions should give them a sense of how supervisors perceive your work. Supervisors should immediately congratulate an interviewer whom they observe doing something particularly well (such as converting a tough nut). They should immediately take aside an interviewer who errs. Most survey organizations have supervisors record specific examples of interviewer performance in a database, for future reference in formal performance reviews and to track changes in performance over time.

> Your employer should clearly communicate the expectations for interviewer productivity.

Supervisors typically evaluate interviewer performance and productivity in the six major domains outlined in Table 8.3: dial attempts, completions, refusals, verifications, attendance, interview quality, and a miscellaneous category that includes attitude, communication, and knowledge of your work. They gain the information for these evaluations by directly observing interviewers' work

TABLE 8.3. INDICATORS OF INTERVIEWER PERFORMANCE.

Domain	Examples
Dial attempts	Number of times an interviewer dials the telephone per hour
Completions	Number of completed interviews; completes per hour; average interview length
Refusals	Number of refusals; types of refusals; successful refusal conversions
Verifications	Interview confirmed; factual data items corroborated; professionalism conveyed
Attendance	Number of no shows, late cancels, and tardies
Interview quality	Consistent use of standardized interviewing techniques
Miscellaneous	Attitude, interest, knowledge, communication, standards of conduct, behaving as a team player

and by studying CATI records. Everything an interviewer does in the CATI system, such as making dial attempts, logging call disposition codes, and typing keystrokes while conducting interviews, is automatically recorded, with time and date stamps, each time an interviewer signs onto the CATI system with their interviewer identification number.

Dial Attempts Most survey organizations track the number of times interviewers dial the telephone. Each dial attempt requires interviewers to select an appropriate call disposition code and record it. Swiftness and skill in performing these tasks provide indicators of interviewer performance and productivity. The most common measures used are dial attempts per hour and dial attempts per completed interview. Interviewers usually log eight to fifteen dial attempts for every completed interview. Number of dial attempts per hour or per completed interview is often used as a measure of interviewer effort, or how hard an interviewer tries. Measures of dial attempts alone, however, are crude indicators of interviewer performance because they do not account for the quality or difficulty of completed interviews.

Completions Completed interviews are a fairly universal indicator of interviewer performance and productivity. Some survey organizations track interviews completed per hour or per shift, in order to compare interviewers to each other. Others use equations that compare one interviewer's completions, dial attempts, and refusals to those of other interviewers. As with measures of dial attempts, an interview completion rate should not serve as a sole performance indicator because it cannot account for obstacles, effort, or excellence.

Interviewers who excel in refusal conversion will naturally score lower in completion rates because answering reluctant respondents' concerns takes time and care. Interviewers with high completion rates per hour often have shorter interviews on average. But a pattern of overly short interviews can be a negative indicator, as it suggests that an interviewer does not fully probe "don't knows" and refusals or does not give respondents a chance to think adequately about their answers.

> The CATI system automatically tracks and records each interviewer's work, with time and date stamps. These data help measure interviewer productivity, but they cannot measure interview quality.

Supervisors understand, however, that interviewer productivity, measured by completions, varies by day of the week and time of day. Interviewers who work weekends tend to achieve more completions per hour than those who work weekdays, and those who work evenings achieve more than those who work daytimes. Yet not all interviewers can work the prime hours. In the predictable downtimes, dial attempts per hour may be a better measure of interviewer effort than completed interviews are.

Supervisors also know to take into consideration the life cycle of a telephone survey. For example, it takes interviewers longer and longer to complete an interview with each successive day of calling because respondents become harder and harder to locate. For the same reason, dial attempts per completed interview naturally increase slightly every day that a survey is in the field, as the easy-to-reach respondents are interviewed and you more often reach answering machines or make calls that no one answers. At the same time, the average number of refusals per hour should decrease slightly because interviewers speak with fewer people. Thus interviewers who tend to work at the beginning of surveys will naturally have productivity patterns that differ from interviewers who work more at the end of surveys.

For these reasons, most survey organizations do not (or should not) use overly mechanical or solely statistical means of comparing interviewers' productivity. Nonetheless, interviewers should expect to be evaluated in part on some combination of number of completed interviews and number of dial attempts.

Refusals Counts of interviewers' refusals also help to gauge their job performance. Supervisors may examine patterns of interviewers' refusals per hour worked, per one hundred dial attempts, or per one hundred completed interviews to determine who has the highest and lowest refusal rates.

Unusually high refusal rates could indicate that an interviewer is not trying hard enough to persuade reluctant respondents to participate or is passing off difficult persuasion work to other interviewers by accepting soft refusals too easily. It could also mean that that an interviewer does not understand how a refusal differs from a phone slam. In any case, an interviewer with markedly higher refusal rates compared with other interviewers will likely receive remedial training.

Interviewers who show a pattern of successful refusal conversions, on the other hand, will receive gold stars. A sustained pattern of refusal conversions could result in a bonus or merit raise.

Interview Verifications To verify interviewers' work, a supervisor recontacts a certain percentage of each interviewer's respondents within a day or two of the interview. (If supervisors wait longer, respondents might not recall the interview experience clearly, or at all.) The verification system varies across employers.

In its most basic form, the person conducting the verifications corroborates respondent's answers to several specific survey questions to make sure the interviewer recorded them correctly. The questions checked should always be factual (such as demographic or behavioral items) because respondents' attitudes, beliefs, and knowledge can change over a few days. (They may even change as a result of taking the survey if the questions have made respondents think about the subject matter more or in a new way.)

The verification process may also gather respondents' impressions of interviewers' professionalism and politeness and ask whether respondents have any lingering concerns. Almost always, recontacted respondents praise interviewers' skills when the interviews were conducted following standardized interviewing procedures. Of course, if a verification call shows that an interviewer fabricated an interview, he or she will be terminated from employment immediately.

Attendance Each time interviewers do not show up for a scheduled work shift, show up late, or cancel a shift late, a supervisor will note it in a personnel file or database. Such attendance problems will be part of interviewers' ongoing and formal performance evaluations.

Unreliable interviewers are a drag on the entire call center. They make it difficult to estimate how long a survey will be in the field. They deny potential work shifts to more reliable interviewers. Late arrivals disrupt the workplace. Unreliability is also an indicator of work quality in other domains, for rarely do unreliable interviewers have high completion rates or low refusal rates. Conversely, being a reliable interviewer will not compensate for a low interview completion rate or a high refusal rate, but your supervisors and coworkers will like you more.

Interview Quality Supervisors' routine monitoring should result in a sheaf of evaluation forms for each interviewer indicating how well that person sticks to standardized interviewing techniques. These forms will show how often interviewers adhered to the interview script; how well they used fill, optional language, and feedback; how consistently they probed; how well they used their voices; and related quality measures. Interviewers who use standardized interviewing techniques dependably produce high-quality interviews and gather survey data that researchers can trust. High interview quality can also compensate for a somewhat low completion rate and a slightly high refusal rate. Supervisors should have a method of tallying evaluations so that each interviewer can see how the quality of their completed interviews compares to that of the average interviewer.

Miscellaneous This performance domain includes the less tangible features of interviewers' work quality and workplace presence. It may include interviewers' approach to their work, their interest in survey research generally, how well they understand why they are supposed to use standardized interviewing techniques, how well they adhere to the standards of conduct, and how well they stay in touch with your employer. Also important is the interviewers' ability to accept constructive criticism from supervisors with grace and integrate it into the way they perform their work. This category also includes whether interviewers treat their coworkers in a professional manner and behave as a team player, for example by leaving good messages for the next interviewer. These miscellaneous features of interviewers' work are more difficult to quantify and measure than the other indicators, but they can make or break a performance evaluation.

Supervisors use the information in these six domains to compare and rank interviewers by their productivity and performance. The interviewers who regularly score highest are often asked to apply for higher positions, perhaps as lead interviewers or interviewer supervisors. Those who score lowest are usually sent to remedial training sessions, down scheduled, or let go.

Although each of these performance domains is important, the relative weight survey organizations place on them varies. Some value dial attempts and interview completions most highly. Others place more emphasis on interview quality. In day-to-day workplace interactions, the miscellaneous category often looms largest. Interviewers' employers should clearly communicate the organization's expectations for interviewer performance. Then interviewers should act accordingly to make their work lives as pleasurable and rewarding as possible.

Summing Up

This chapter described key parts of the survey workplace. It covered what you can expect in your interviewer workstation and workspace, interviewer equipment, daily workplace routines, typical work hours, pay and benefits, the policies that will affect your work, and what to expect from interviewer supervisors. This chapter can serve only as an introduction to the survey workplace, however, because settings and policies differ across survey organizations. Most organizations will have more detailed policies than the basic ones described here. Of course, you are responsible for learning about your employer's unique policies and routines.

CHAPTER NINE

CONCLUDING COMMENTS

When you call people on the telephone and invite them to participate in a survey, most do not know what to expect. Many are wary and uncertain, largely due to telemarketers' saturation calling in the late 1990s. After Do Not Call lists have been in effect for several years, potential respondents should become less suspicious of legitimate telephone survey research. Whether those who answer the telephone are suspicious or congenial, a professional interviewer must convey the survey's important elements—its purpose, how long it will take, the sponsor, the survey organization's name, the fact of confidentiality or anonymity, and the fact that participating is voluntary—and answer respondents' questions or concerns. This information enables respondents to make an informed decision to participate.

> Never forget that all research based on interviews is only as good as the interviewers who collect the data.

Once respondents agree to take part, remember that the interview itself is unlikely to resemble any of the respondents' prior conversations. Survey interviews are, by definition, artificial dialogues. But excellent interviewers can turn a highly structured interview into a naturally flowing conversation by judiciously modulating their voice and by carefully pacing the exchange. Active listening and the use of probes, fill, and optional language allow interviewers to tailor interviews to each respondent's needs and characteristics. Even though interviewers will utter the same words, sentences, and questions many times each day, it can seem almost like normal dialogue to the respondents.

Interviewing can be a great job if you genuinely enjoy human diversity. Most interviewers get to work on surveys of varying topics, sometimes at the same time. In any given month you might work on surveys about state transportation policy, elderly persons' experiences with their doctors, teachers' accreditation, violence in schools, and customers' satisfaction with a product or service. With each survey you learn about new and interesting things. Many interviewers feel gratified by the knowledge that their work is important to society and their role is crucial in survey research. Remember that all research based on interviews is only as good as the interviewers who collect the data.

In the long term, this volume should help to professionalize interviewers' work. It documents interviewers' specialized expertise, continuous training, unusual work hours, and important responsibilities in survey data collection. These facets of interviewing work deserve greater respect, better wages and benefits, and more influence in the survey process. Interviewers forming a professional association will bring themselves recognition and enhance survey researchers' appreciation of their work. Such an association will serve both to guide interviewers' work performance and to protect interviewers from exploitation. A code of ethics devised specifically for interviewing will enable interviewers to collectively self-regulate. Interviewers need the means to protect and reward members of their profession who perform well and to sanction and exclude those who do not. An interviewers' professional association operating side by side with the other survey professional associations will improve survey research and public opinion polling generally.

GLOSSARY

ACASI Audio computer-assisted self-interviewing. Respondents administer questionnaires to themselves with a laptop computer while viewing the instrument and listening to instructions on a DVD.

Active listening An interviewer's act of closely attending to what respondents say and how they say it, then combining that with their other knowledge and skills to determine what the person means.

Anonymity The respondent's identity is not known and cannot be determined.

Answer category An answer to a survey question with a numbered code category next to it, such as 1 YES. Also called a *response category*. See *ordered answer categories* and *unordered answer categories*.

Answer width The number of digits recorded in an answer to a question.

Answers to common questions A paper document posted in interviewer workstations containing sentences that interviewers should memorize to answer respondents' detailed questions about a survey. See Exhibit 4.2 for an example. Sometimes called a *fallback sheet*.

Back translation A process of translating a survey instrument from one language to another that ensures accuracy. For example, a bilingual interviewer might translate an interview script from English to Spanish. A second bilingual interviewer then translates the Spanish version back to English. Then the two translators compare the two English versions to determine if any differences arose and to resolve those discrepancies.

Bias Systematic error. Any influence that systematically distorts research results in a particular direction. Respondents' true answers not being recorded on the survey due to incorrect interviewing techniques, poorly worded questions, faulty skip logic, or incorrect interviewer instructions can all lead to bias. High refusal rates can also bias a survey's results.

Break-off A respondent who hangs up or refuses partway through a telephone interview.

CAI Computer-assisted interviewing. CAI includes all types of computer-assisted interviewing, including ACASI, CASI, CAPI, and CATI. When these methods are used, survey questions appear on a computer screen and answers are directly entered into a computer. When a survey instrument is properly programmed and thoroughly pretested before implementation, such methods speed data processing and reduce data entry and clerical errors.

Call center That part of a survey research organization where telephone interviewers accomplish their work.

Call disposition code In telephone surveys every dial attempt interviewers make must be assigned a code number indicating what happened on the other end of the line (busy signal, answering machine, nonresidential number, completed interview, refusal, and so forth). (These codes are discussed in Chapter Five.)

Call history The record of all calls made to each respondent, displaying the dates and times of days of all previous calls, the call disposition codes, and explanatory notes from previous interviewers about their experiences with the call attempts.

Call screen Usually the first CATI computer screen for a respondent, showing that respondent's telephone number and call history.

Call screening The use of telephone devices (such as caller ID) or persons (such as gatekeepers) to verify who placed a telephone call and to decide whether to answer the call.

Callback Another call to a telephone number that was called before. Callbacks can be scheduled automatically by CATI or deliberately by an interviewer.

Calling queue The group of telephone numbers waiting at an interviewing station to be called. It includes telephone numbers that can be viewed on the computer screen.

CAPI Computer-assisted personal interview. In a face-to-face interview, an interviewer uses a laptop computer to display the questionnaire and enter data directly, instead of using a paper-and-pencil instrument (see *PAPI*). Advantages include avoiding errors in skip patterns, receiving immediate edit checks, and expediting electronic data capture.

Case An individual respondent or a completed interview. See *unit of analysis*.

CASI Computer-assisted self-interviewing. A respondent self-administers a questionnaire, usually on a laptop computer.

CATI Computer-assisted telephone interviewing. Computer software that organizes and automates mundane data collection tasks for telephone interviewing.

Census A self-administered or interviewer-administered survey that results in a complete count of every unit in the population studied.

Client A person, an organization, or a person representing an organization that pays for a survey. See *principal investigator*.

Closed-ended question A survey question that allows only a specified selection of answer categories. Respondents must choose one answer from those provided. Also called a *fixed choice* question. *Partially closed-ended questions* include an "other → specify" option for respondents whose answers do not exactly fit the answer categories offered.

Code of ethics A document written, approved, and published by a professional association that formally defines acceptable and unacceptable behavior for its members in their field of expertise. Ethical codes serve as guidelines or standards for moral conduct in a profession. They include standards, norms, values, and best practices in the field of work. Each member must agree to abide by that code of ethics; failure to do so can result in censure, expulsion, and public humiliation.

Coder A person who codes data. See *coding*.

Coding A procedure for transforming raw data into a standardized format for data analysis purposes; assigning numbers to survey answers, which allows the survey data to be processed and analyzed by a computer. Coding open-ended answers involves identifying recurrent words, concepts, or themes and assigning numbers to them.

Combination questions Questions that combine open- and closed-ended formats. Combination questions have two forms: (1) questions that have closed-ended answer categories but allow an "other → specify" option for respondents who volunteer a different type of answer; (2) questions that sound open-ended to respondents because the question as read contains no answer categories, but the answer categories the interviewer uses are closed-ended. See *open-ended question* and *closed-ended question*.

Complete Shorthand for a completed interview. A happy interviewer might brag about "eighteen completes" in a three-hour work shift.

Confederate A person role-playing a respondent during the interviewer training process.

Confidentiality The researchers know or can learn the responses given by specific respondents, but respondents are guaranteed that their responses will be kept secret. Confidentiality is not the same as *anonymity*, where the respondent's identity cannot be determined by anyone, even the researchers.

Contingency question A question from which skip logic branches, such as, *Last week, did you work for pay, either full- or part-time?* Those answering yes go on to employment-related questions, and those answering no pass to another question group. See *skip logic*.

Convenience sample A nonrandom, nonscientific sample. Researchers use this kind of sample when they select the units of a survey based on their being readily available.

Conversational interviewing An "interviewing protocol that allows interviewers to interact freely with the respondent, to modify and adapt questions to the respondent's situation, and to assist respondents in formulating a response."[1] The goal of conversational interviewing is to reduce error in respondents' answers, including that which is attributable to interviewers.

Cooperation rate A survey's cooperation rate is the total number of households interviewed divided by the number of eligible households contacted, multiplied by 100. The detailed equation may be found in the American Association for Public Opinion Research publication *Standard Definitions*.[2]

Coverage The ability of surveys to reach all units selected for the sample.

Cross-sectional survey A survey that collects data at, essentially, one point in time from a random sample of persons who are specially selected to represent the entire target population. This is the most common type of survey design. Think of a cross section as equivalent to a slice of bread that represents the entire load of bread. See *longitudinal survey*.

Data Many pieces of information. The plural of the word *datum*.

Data correction report form A form that may be provided at interviewing stations for interviewers to record corrections to mistakes that they could not correct before completing the interview. The interviewer fills out the slip completely and puts it in the place designated. These slips are not used to comment on a respondent, on a specific question, or the survey in general.

Data set Organized data. Survey data are typically arranged in a numeric computer file, with each respondent's answers in a row and the survey questions in the columns.

Datum One piece of information. The singular form of the word *data*.

Descriptive statistics Statistical methods used to describe or summarize data collected from a sample or a population, including the mean (average), median (halfway point), mode (most frequently answered category), range, standard deviation, and frequency distributions.

Dial attempt A call to a telephone number. For every completed interview, interviewers may average eight to fifteen dial attempts. Each dial attempt is assigned a *call disposition code*.

Directive probe A nonstandard probe that interviewers create by phrasing respondents' answers for them in the way interviewers think respondents intend. For example, *Do you mean that you think bus services between cities are very important?* or, *Are you saying you drove a personal vehicle about ten miles yesterday?* Interviewers should avoid directive probes because respondents, especially uncertain respondents, tend to answer yes more often than no, potentially causing bias. See *positivity bias*.

Double-barreled question A question containing two clauses with different meanings, essentially asking two questions at once: for example, *Do you believe that exercise is fun and safe?* If the respondent answers yes, we do not know if the person means that exercise is fun, safe, or both fun and safe. Double-barreled questions should be split into two separate questions.

Down scheduling The practice of giving less productive and less motivated interviewers fewer hours to work than they would like. Often used as an indirect method of discipline.

Empirical Observed, counted, measured. Empirical approaches give a central place to experience and what is seen (rather than intuition) in the acquisition and testing of knowledge.

Enumerator Another term for *interviewer*, most often used in government surveys and censuses.

Enunciate Pronounce words clearly and accurately. Articulate each syllable.

Ethics Guidelines or standards for moral conduct. See *code of ethics*.

Ethnicity A human group that shares a cultural heritage that may include language, religion, food preferences, migration patterns, customs, and intermarriage. The United States officially recognizes only Hispanics and Latinos as an ethnic group. Hispanics and Latinos can be of any race. See *race*.

Fallback sheet See *answers to common questions*.

Feedback Short words and phrases used to reward respondents for good behavior as respondents.

Fill Words and phrases that appear in brackets and parentheses in interviewers' survey scripts, containing discretionary or optional language.

Fill, in brackets When fill appears in square brackets, interviewers may use their best judgment to determine whether a respondent needs to hear one of the fill words and phrases. Bracketed fill represents optional language. For example, *How many miles do you usually commute one way to work [as a passenger or a driver] [altogether]?*

Fill, in parentheses When fill appears in parentheses, interviewers must choose one of the fill words and phrases, as best fits the respondent. Parenthetical fill is obligatory language, but interviewers use their discretion to choose among the words or phrases offered, as for example, in this question: *How many miles do you usually commute one way to (work/school/work and school).* Sometimes both types of fill appear in the same question: *How many miles do you usually commute one way to (work/school/work and school) [as a passenger or a driver] [altogether]?*

Fixed-choice question See *closed-ended question*.

Frugging Fundraising under the guise of research. A practice used by telemarketers, who once often posed as interviewers for scientific research. This and related practices began fading away with the 1991 Telephone Consumer Protection Act (TCPA) and the 1995 Telemarketing and Consumer Fraud and Abuse Prevention Act and subsequent updates to those laws. Professional survey organizations publicly condemn frugging.

Gatekeeper A household member who tries to prevent an interviewer from speaking with the intended respondent, usually claiming that respondent is "too busy." Gatekeepers often volunteer to complete the interview themselves. See *call screening*.

Generalize Use of sample results to represent a population. *Generalizability* refers to the extent to which a relatively small set of observations provides evidence of a population pattern. Social science guards against *overgeneralization* by paying attention to the representativeness of samples and by testing whether research results can be replicated.

Household roster A list of all persons in a household, usually including their sex and age (or birthdate), and sometimes a nickname or initials, for the interviewer's future reference in subsequent questions in the interview.

Human subject A person who participates in research and provides data.

Human subjects approval The process of obtaining permission from an institutional review board to conduct a survey under 45 C.F.R. 46(A) (Basic HHS Policy for Protection of Human Research Subjects). (See Chapter Three.)

Hypothesis A statement that predicts the relationship between variables (specifically the relationship between the independent and dependent variables). A hypothesis may be directional or nondirectional: (1) directional hypothesis (or one-tailed hypothesis): a hypothesis that makes a specific prediction about the nature and direction of the relationship between the independent and dependent variables; (2) nondirectional hypothesis (or two-tailed hypothesis): a hypothesis that does not specify the nature and direction of the relationship between the independent and dependent variables.

In the field Description of a survey in the data collection phase; interviewers are conducting interviews.

Informant A human subject who helps fulfill the research tasks by supplying information about himself or herself or others. In surveys, a person in a household to whom an interviewer speaks before a respondent is chosen.

Informed consent Voluntary participation of individuals in research based on a full understanding of the possible benefits and risks. The respondent understands the survey purpose, hears informed consent language, hears that the interviewer is not selling or fund-raising, and agrees to participate in the survey.

Informed dissent A person understands the survey purpose, hears informed consent language, hears that the interviewer is not selling or fund-raising, and still refuses to participate in the survey.

Initial refusal Potential respondents who indirectly refuse to participate in a survey but leave open the possibility that they might later agree to participate. See *refusal conversion*.

Institutional review board (IRB) An office or committee in an organization that ensures that research on or with humans is conducted consistently with 45 C.F.R. 46(A) (Basic HHS Policy for Protection of Human Research Subjects). (See Chapter Three.) In the United States, organizations that conduct any type of research on or with humans and that receive federal funding (for research or for something else) are obligated to establish an IRB.

Instrument A survey instrument is a questionnaire: the words and questions in a survey. A survey is a scientific instrument, just like a magnetic resonance imaging machine. Surveys are carefully designed, tested, and then administered in a standardized manner to respondents. Any differences found between respondents should be due to their distinctiveness, not to how an interviewer administers the survey instrument.

Interview A method of data collection in which an interviewer asks a standardized series of questions and records answers from another person (a respondent), either face to face or over the telephone. See *self-administered questionnaire*.

Interview verification See *verification*.

Interviewer A trained professional who administers surveys to respondents and records their answers.

Interviewer briefing See *project-specific training*.

Interviewer ID # A unique number assigned to each interviewer and recorded at the end of each completed interview. (Remember yours!)

Interviewer observations See *thumbnail sketch*.

Interviewer training The structured learning environment in which new interviewers review specific skills that are designed to meet explicit objectives that produce satisfactory data collection.

Item nonresponse "Don't know," "refuse," and blank (no answer) answers to a survey question. Sometimes "no opinion" is also counted as item nonresponse. See *unit nonresponse*.

List sample Potential respondents for a survey are supplied in a list, usually by the client. For example, a hospital needing a patient satisfaction survey gives a survey organization a list of all patients treated within a certain time period. The survey organization usually selects a certain number of potential respondents at random from the list of all patients, then loads those selected into the CATI system. Such lists generally include respondents' names and telephone numbers and also certain background characteristics, such as age, marital status, and insurance status. Linking list data to survey data saves money, because interviewers ask fewer questions. Other examples include lists of employees at a certain organization, patrons of the local library, students enrolled at a certain college, and subscribers to a certain magazine. Survey organizations guarantee the confidentiality of client-supplied lists.

List vendor A private, for-profit business that compiles lists of telephone numbers and addresses from numerous sources and then sells those lists to survey researchers and others. Some lists also include names and the named persons' characteristics (for example, known tobacco users). List vendors rarely claim that their lists are totally complete or representative of a population.

Longitudinal survey A survey that collects data on the same individuals at multiple points over a period of time. Also known as a panel survey.

In contrast, a cross-sectional time-series survey collects data on different individuals in the same population at multiple points over a period of time. See *cross-sectional survey*.

Market research Studies devoted to the creation, development, and sales of products. Market researchers use surveys as well as other data collection methods.

Most-recent birthday method A way of randomly sampling adults within households by asking for the one "who most recently had a birthday." Because births in large populations are evenly distributed across the calendar, this is a simple and effective technique for choosing one adult, avoiding a household roster.

n A lowercase *n* refers to a sample size. For example, $n = 400$.

N An uppercase N refers to a population size. For example, Census 2000 found that the population of the United States was $N = 281,421,906$.

Nonsampling error Error due to everything except sampling error: for example, error due to respondents, interviewers, refusals, and data entry. This broad term encompasses both random error and bias.

Omnibus survey A survey with multiple sponsors and containing a separate question module for each sponsor.

Open-ended coding See *coding*.

Open-ended question A survey question that allows respondents to answer in their own words. No answer categories are provided. Sometimes called a *free response* question.

Operationalize Translate specific research concepts into observable and measurable phenomena, such as a survey question.

Ordered answer categories Answer categories that have codes assigned in a way that has some inherent meaning: for example, 0 NEVER, 1 RARELY, 2 SOMETIMES, 3 OFTEN, and 4 ALWAYS. It is meaningful to assign a 0 to "never" and the highest number, 4, to "always." See *unordered answer categories*.

Outlier A respondent answer that is very different from most other respondent answers.

Panel study See *longitudinal study*.

PAPI A paper-and-pencil survey instrument. An interview script printed on paper and administered by an interviewer either in person or by telephone.

Partially closed-ended question A closed-ended question that includes an "other → specify" or "if volunteered" option for respondents who do not fit the categories offered. See *closed-ended question*.

Phone slam A potential respondent hangs up the telephone before hearing the entire introduction with all elements of informed consent. A phone slam is not the same as a refusal because the person has not given informed dissent.

Pilot study A complete run-through of a project such as survey on a small scale to make sure the full-scale effort goes according to plan.

Poll A survey with very few questions, often conducted quickly with telephone or in-person interviews. *Political polls* test how voters feel about certain candidates for elected office. *Exit polls* ask voters how they voted as they exit a polling place.

Population The total membership of a defined group in a particular geographical area at a certain point in time. The set of all possible data values that could be observed in a certain area in a certain period. For example, all registered midwives working full-time in California in 2007 can be considered a population. Populations can include countries, states, cities, organizations, classrooms, households, people, animals, ranches, social roles, events, or social artifacts. In statistics a population's size is commonly symbolized by an uppercase N. For example, Oregon's population in Census 2000 was N = 3,421,399. See *sample*.

Positivity bias Respondents who lack strong opinions tend to give positive answers ("agree," "yes") rather than negative ones, especially when interviewers push them.

Pretest Interviews conducted with a small subset of the target population to examine question wording, to check question ordering, or to evaluate interviewing procedures. Usually conducted with a nonrandom sample specially chosen to test all dimensions of an instrument: for example, a survey of alcohol consumption should be pretested with teetotalers, social drinkers, binge drinkers, steady low-volume drinkers, and steady high-volume drinkers.

Principal investigator (PI) The professional researcher who develops a survey's ideas and obtains funding to conduct the research. PIs usually have doctoral degrees and often work in teams crossing several areas. For example, sociologists, psychologists, political scientists, economists, and demographers often work together on survey projects.

Probability sample See *random sample*.

Probe A technique used by interviewers to clarify respondents' answers or to obtain more information when respondents give incomplete, irrelevant, imprecise, or evasive answers to questions. A probe stimulates additional responses that explain or complete respondents' previous answers.

Probing The process of using probes as an interview progresses.

Project-specific training The preparation interviewers receive to work on a particular survey or research project. Sometimes called *interviewer briefing*.

Protocol A specified methodology for performing a research-related task, for example, a pretest protocol.

Push polls A telemarketing technique in which callers, posing as interviewers for a legitimate election poll, ask questions designed to manipulate or *push* voters away from a candidate by planting false or misleading information, creating negative feelings, or starting rumors. Professional survey organizations publicly condemn push polling.

Q by Qs The question by question survey objectives, delivered orally or in writing. A statement about each question to help interviewers understand its goals, how it fits with the rest of the questions, and how to handle potential problems.

Qualitative data Information gathered in narrative (nonnumeric) form, for example, narrative answers to open-ended questions.

Quantitative data Information gathered in numeric form, such as 1 for yes and 2 for no.

Question (Q) A type of sentence that asks people about their attitudes, knowledge, or beliefs about something or about their behavior or environment. A sentence that interrogates.

Questionnaire (Q're) See *self-administered questionnaire*.

Quota sampling Selecting specific numbers or proportions of units with certain characteristics for a survey. For example, a survey might need 400 completed rural interviews and 400 completed urban interviews. In a more complex quota sampling design, a survey might need 200 interviews with rural women, 200 interviews with rural men, 200 interviews with urban women, and 200 interviews with urban men. Usually the selection is made with nonrandom (or nonprobability) methods.

Race A human group that shares biologically transmitted traits that society sees as socially significant, such as skin color, hair texture, facial features, and body type. The U.S. Census identifies the following racial groups: white, black/African American, Asian American, Native Hawaiian and other Pacific Islander, American Indian/Native American/Alaskan Native, and "some other race." See *ethnicity*.

Random-digit-dial (RDD) sample A computer-generated, random list of telephone numbers from working telephone exchanges in a certain geographical area for a telephone survey. RDD sampling procedures provide new and unlisted telephone numbers, which would be missed if using a telephone book as a sample source.

Random digit dialing Calling from a list of telephone numbers that a computer generated randomly.

Random error Error associated with respondents, interviewers, refusals, and data entry that is due to chance. It is not systematic or directional, and it is difficult to detect.

Random sample Units that have been selected for a survey by using scientific methods that give each unit an equal or known chance of being included. Also known as a *probability sample*, because units of a population are selected by probability methods. In a simple random sample each member of the population has an equal, known, and nonzero chance of selection. In more complex types of random samples (stratified, quota, cluster), each unit in a population has a known chance of selection. Only randomly selected individuals can accurately reflect the attitudes, opinions, knowledge, or behavior of the entire population under study. A random sample must be very carefully selected so that it faithfully represents the entire population.

Random sampling The processes of selecting a random or probability sample. Accurate random sampling requires both a sound scientific design and rigorous execution. Interviewers must never substitute respondents, because doing so destroys the sample's representativeness.

Rapport A casual, trusting relationship between an interviewer and a respondent that helps ensure fuller, more accurate answers to survey questions (although too much rapport can cause bias).

Rating A response to a statement, idea, or product on a scale defined by the survey question: for example, *On a scale from 1 to 5, where 1 is strongly dislike and 5 is strongly like, how much do you like popcorn?*

Record # A unique number assigned to each unit of sample.

Refusal A potential respondent who hears all the elements of informed consent explaining a survey but is unwilling to participate. See *informed dissent*.

Refusal conversion The process of convincing reluctant respondents or respondents who have previously refused to participate in a survey. Interviewers do this by addressing respondent's concerns, providing the information they need, appealing to their sense of altruism or civic duty, and using other motivators. (See Chapter Six.)

Reliability The consistency and dependability of a survey instrument. A reliable survey should produce similar results over time and across groups of people, no matter who administers it.

Representative sample Synonymous with *random sample*.

Representativeness What a sample has when it possesses the same distribution of characteristics as its target population.

Research Repeated use of objective and systematic procedures by which what we think about reality is tested against what we observe, and what we observe is examined in the light of what is known.

Research assistant A semiprofessional technician who performs routine research-related tasks assigned by a principal investigator.

Research design The overall plan for a survey, stating how the sample will be selected, how key concepts will be operationalized into survey questions, and whether data will be collected at one or multiple time points.

Research method A specific procedure used to gather and analyze research data.

Respondent A person who has been chosen to participate in a survey and who answers survey questions.

Respondent # A unique number assigned to each completed interview.

Response category See *answer category*.

Response rate An indicator of the percentage of those invited to participate in a research study who actually did so. A survey's basic response rate is the total number of completed interviews divided by the number of all possible interviews, multiplied by 100. A more detailed equation may be found in the American Association for Public Opinion Research publication *Standard Definitions*.[3]

Role-playing Taking turns with other interviewers, pretending that one is an interviewer and the other is a respondent.

Salience The condition of standing out distinctly. Survey questions about salient memories tend to generate more accurate answers than questions about distant or indistinct memories. Salience is determined by direct, personal experience; how long ago the experience occurred; and the meanings individuals have attached to it, such as its distinctness and emotional impact.

Sample A small number of people specially selected from a population in such a way as to represent the entire population, making it possible to avoid the expensive and time-consuming procedure of taking a census. Commonly symbolized by a lowercase *n*. For example, *n* = 400. Compare *population*.

Sample bias Systematic distortion that occurs when a sample is not representative of the population from which it was drawn.

Sample design A strategy or method for selecting respondents to participate in a survey. Some examples are simple random, RDD, systematic, cluster, convenience, quota, and snowball samples. Not all sample designs seek to represent the total population.

Sample survey A survey administered to a random sample of people.

Sampling The process of choosing part of the population about which a study wishes to make generalizations. The sampling process differs for each sample design.

Sampling error The difference between a sample estimate and a population parameter. The extent to which a sample distribution differs from the distribution in the population from which the sample is drawn. Also, the normal fluctuation in the values of a statistic (for example, educational attainment or age) found in numerous different samples drawn from the same population.

Screener A short interview designed to seek units with certain characteristics for a survey.

Screening questions A few, initial survey questions that determine the units eligible to participate in the survey.

Self-administered questionnaire A standardized set of questions in a format designed for respondents to take themselves; the medium may be mail, e-mail, the Internet, CASI, or ACASI. Interviewers are not involved, which makes a questionnaire distinct from a survey interview.

Skip logic Many surveys have questions that only apply to certain groups of persons in the sample, for example, questions about jobs and about children. A CATI system is programmed to allow respondents to skip past inapplicable groups of questions. Some surveys have extensive skip logic; others have little. Skip logic can make each interview an interviewer conducts unique. See *contingency question*.

Social desirability bias Respondents' tendency to inflate their social status (for example, education, income, occupation), hide their unpopular beliefs and opinions (for example, racism), or disguise unfavorable characteristics (for example, age, illness) in order to boost their self-esteem or to please or impress the interviewer, survey research organization, or principal investigator.

Soft refusal See *initial refusal*.

Standardized interviewing ". . . an interviewing protocol that requires interviewers to ask questions as worded, to probe, provide feedback, and interact with the respondent in a manner which is consistent across interviews."[4] Standardized interviewing aims to minimize any error in respondents' answers that is attributable to interviewers.

Statement A type of sentence that declares or asserts something. In surveys, the role of statements is similar to that of questions, except that the answer categories are implicit or already known by the respondent. See *question*.

Statistic A characteristic of a sample, such as a mean and standard deviation. An estimate of a parameter calculated from a set of data gathered from a sample.

Statistical analysis Most statistical analysis is based on the principle of gathering data from a sample of individuals and using those data to make inferences about the wider population from which the sample was drawn.

Statistical inference A procedure using the laws of probability to infer the attributes of a population based on information gathered from a sample.

Statistical significance A measure of the extent to which the results of an analysis of data drawn from a sample are unlikely to have been caused by chance at a specified level of probability (usually .05 or .01).

Statistical test A procedure that allows a researcher to determine the probability that the results obtained from a sample reflect true parameters of the underlying population.

Strata Subdivisions of a population. For example, in a stratified sample, equal numbers of households might be selected from two strata—urban and rural.

Stratified random sampling A method of random (or probability) sampling in which the population is divided into subcategories, called *strata*, and then random samples are independently selected from each subcategory. Sample stratification can improve the effectiveness of a sampling effort or increase the understanding of population characteristics. For example, stratifying an election survey by sex allows researchers to understand voter behavior better by revealing differences in the way that males and females vote.

Study A synonym for a research project or a survey.

Sugging Selling under the guise of research. A practice used by telemarketers, who in the past often posed as interviewers for scientific research. This and related practices began fading away with the 1991 Telephone Consumer Protection Act (TCPA) and the 1995 Telemarketing and Consumer Fraud and Abuse Prevention Act and subsequent updates to those laws. Professional survey organizations publicly condemn sugging.

Survey A survey involves collecting data from a sample of people who have been specially selected to represent a population under study. Each person in the sample is asked the same series of questions. The answers obtained are put together in an organized way so that conclusions can be drawn. This information is then used to solve a problem or add needed information about the problem. *Survey* is an umbrella term for both self-administered questionnaires and interviews. Surveys are sometimes referred to as studies.

Survey research A research approach designed to collect systematic information on existing phenomena in order to describe or explain something; data are obtained through direct questioning of a sample of respondents.

Tacit knowledge Implicit knowledge of the rules of social life, including the procedures for conducting telephone interviews with accuracy and precision. This knowledge cannot always be articulated or made explicit by those who know it.

Tailoring Interviewers' practice of individualizing probes and feedback to meet each respondent's unique characteristics and needs, learned through active listening.

Target population The group of people to whom researchers intend to generalize their study's results. A random sample is drawn from a target population.

Thumbnail sketch Some survey research organizations invite interviewers to record their survey-related observations of respondents after the interview is complete. Interviewers use the thumbnail sketch to explain any questions, answer categories, or other circumstances that caused problems for a respondent or to describe their experience of the interview. (This is not the place to record corrections; see *data correction form.*) Unless interviewers are otherwise instructed, this task should take no more than two to three minutes.

Total error Sampling error plus nonsampling error.

TTY Abbreviation for *teletypewriter*, an electromechanical device used to transmit or receive messages via telephone lines. Sometimes telephone interviewers use TTY services or devices to communicate with deaf or mute persons.

Unit nonresponse A unit of analysis (for example, a respondent or household) refusing to participate in the survey. See *item nonresponse.*

Unit, or unit of analysis The households, individuals, or organizations that the interviewer intends to interview. The entity about whom (or which) the research gathers data.

Unordered answer categories Answer categories that have codes assigned in a way that has no inherent meaning. The code numbers for answers could be reversed or randomized without consequence. For example, code 1 could indicate male and code 2 could indicate female, or vice versa. See *ordered answer categories.*

URL Acronym for uniform resource locator, the address of an Internet Web site. For example, www.census.gov is the U.S. Census Bureau's URL.

Validity The extent to which survey questions accurately measure their underlying concepts.

Verbatim Word for word. When interviewers record respondents' narrative answers to alpha open-ended questions, they must type in exactly what is said verbatim, including "uh," partial sentences, ungrammatical phrases, and even profanity, never paraphrasing or interpreting what they think the person meant.

Verification The practice of calling back a subset of respondents who completed interviews, re-asking certain questions, and comparing the answers to the answers recorded earlier by an interviewer. Verification is a way of ensuring that interview falsification has not occurred.

APPENDIX B

EXAMPLE FORMS

Schedule Request Form

The form in Exhibit B.1 is an example of the type of form a survey employer might use to create interviewer work schedules. Often forms like these are distributed at each project-specific training, so interviewers should be sure to bring their personal calendars and be prepared to fill out a form for each study's duration. Interviewers who do not make their schedule requests in a timely way tend to get the fewest and worst shifts.

Daily Interviewer Work Schedule

Exhibit B.2 is a facsimile of the posted daily interviewer work schedule. Typically, a week's worth or more of these sheets are posted at one time. Some survey research organizations also post interviewers' work schedules on their Web sites, in a password-protected area.

Interviewer Check-In Time Sheet

Exhibit B.3 is a facsimile of an interviewer check-in time sheet. Although some survey research organizations have automated the process of recording interviewers'

EXHIBIT B.1. SCHEDULE REQUEST FORM.

Interviewer name:_____Tel.:_____

How many hours per week do you prefer to work in this period?_____

Please mark clearly all of the shifts that you prefer to work.

Shifts	Sunday	Monday	Tuesday	Wednesday	Thursday	Friday	Saturday
	Nov 6	**Nov 7**	**Nov 8**	**Nov 9**	**Nov 10**	**Nov 11**	**Nov 12**
9 to noon	Closed						
Noon to 4	Closed						
4 to 9							
9 to midnight							
	Nov 13	Nov 14	Nov 15	Nov 16	Nov 17	Nov 18	Nov 19
9 to 12	Closed						
12 to 4	Closed						
4 to 9							
9 to midnight							
	Nov 20	Nov 21	Nov 22	Nov 23	Nov 24	Nov 25	Nov 26
9 to 12	Closed				Closed for	Closed	
12 to 4	Closed				Thanksgiving	Closed	
4 to 9				Closed			
9 to midnight							
	Nov 27	Nov 28	Nov 29	Nov 30	Dec 1	Dec 2	Dec 3
9 to 12	Closed						
12 to 4	Closed						
4 to 9							
9 to midnight							
	Dec 4	Dec 5	Dec 6	Dec 7	Dec 8	Dec 9	Dec 10
9 to 12	Closed						
12 to 4	Closed						
4 to 9							
9 to midnight							

Please note any special schedule requests or circumstances here:

_____

hours, many still use paper time sheets such as this one. When interviewers arrive at work each day, they find a sheet like this one posted, indicating the date and the studies in the field on that date. Interviewers should fill in their name, the survey on which they will work, and their time of arrival. At the end of the work shift, interviewers should record their departure time. Interviewers who work on more than one survey should sign out and sign back in listing the new study to which

EXHIBIT B.2. DAILY INTERVIEWER WORK SCHEDULE.

Daily Schedule

Day And Date: Surveys in the Field:

Shift	Station 1	Station 2	Station 3	Station 4	Station 5	Station 6	Station 7	Station 8
9:00– 10:00		Nina						
10:00– 11:00	Joe			Nina				
11:00– 12:00	Joe			Nina				
12:00– 1:00	Sue			Nina				
1:00– 2:00	Sue			Nina				
2:00– 3:00	Sue			Nina				
3:00– 4:00	Sue			Nina				
4:00– 5:00	Clyde	Scott	Lee		Emma	Fred	David	Amy
5:00– 6:00	Clyde	Scott	Lee		Emma	Fred	David	Amy
6:00– 7:00	Clyde	Scott	Lee		Emma	Fred	David	Amy
7:00– 8:00	Clyde	Scott	Lee		Emma	Fred	David	Amy
8:00– 9:00	Clyde	Scott	Lee		Emma	Fred	David	Amy

they have been switched. Interviewers' usual activity will be interviewing, but they may also need to record project-specific training or some other assignment.

Data Correction Report Form

Exhibit B.4 is an example of a form for interviewers to use to correct a mistake that they could not or did not correct when it was made, but that someone needs to correct before the data are analyzed. Although survey research organizations vary in how they handle such corrections, one way is to use a form like the one shown here. Typically, a pad of these forms is provided at each interviewing station.

Interviewers should use these forms only when information they have typed needs to be changed and for some reason they were unable to do it themselves. Interviewers should fill out the slip completely, and either give it to their supervisor or put it in the place designated.

EXHIBIT B.3. CHECK-IN TIME SHEET.

Date: _____

Survey(s) in the field: _____

Name	Survey	Time In	Time Out	Activity

EXHIBIT B.4. DATA CORRECTION REPORT.

Date and time: _____

Survey: _____

Record #: _____

Respondent #: _____

Phone #: _____

Question name/description: _____

Describe the problem and the correction needed:

Interviewer ID #: _____

Interviewers should not use this form to clarify a respondent's answer, make personal observations about a respondent, point out something about a particular question, or comment on the survey in general. Interviewers should not use this form to report that a respondent's telephone number has changed. In most cases they should give a supervisor that information directly.

NOTES

Chapter One

1. The RDD sampling process is actually much more complex than this. For a concise description, see F. Scheuren, 1995, "What is a survey?" available at http://www.whatisasurvey.info, published by the American Statistical Association, Survey Research Methods Section.

2. In 1950, just 62 percent of U.S. households had telephones. This grew to 78 percent in 1960 and to fully 92 percent by 1970. See *The American almanac for 1974: Statistical abstract of the United States, 1974* (New York: Grosset & Dunlap), Table 804, p. 495.

3. This *Handbook* uses the term *interviewer supervisor* in a generic manner. Supervisors' duties may include hiring, training, scheduling, and monitoring interviewers, answering interviewers' technical questions, tracking their performance, enforcing standards of conduct, monitoring survey samples, conducting interview verifications, and conducting interviews alongside the people they supervise. But these duties vary widely by the size of the survey research organization. In large organizations different employees with specialized titles may conduct subsets of these tasks. In small organizations supervisors' duties tend to be wider.

4. M. Argyle and R. Ingham, 1972, "Gaze, mutual gaze, and proximity," *Semiotica, 6,* 32–49.

5. In a large, random sample survey of Oregonians in 1994, interviewers recorded respondents' sex by their voices and how they answered questions. About 1,200 were reinterviewed six months later and asked their sex. Researchers found that approximately 12 percent of respondents had their sex incorrectly recorded by interviewers the first time. Thus do not assume you can identify a respondent's sex by his or her voice.

6. R. Worcester, 1991, *British public opinion* (London: Blackwell); adapted from Sir Arthur Conan Doyle.

Chapter Two

1. U.S. Census Bureau, 2000, *Census 2000,* Table DP-2: Profile of selected social characteristics, retrieved November 2006 from http://www.census.gov/population/cen2000/DP2-4.pdf.

Chapter Three

1. Of course surveys also should cause respondents no physical harm, but it is difficult to imagine the circumstances in which participation in a telephone survey could cause respondents physical harm.
2. S. R. Gawiser & G. E. Witt, n.d., *Twenty questions a journalist should ask about poll results* (3rd ed.). National Council on Public Polls. Retrieved August 14, 2006, from http://www.ncpp.org/qajsa.htm.
3. Basic HHS Policy for Protection of Human Research Subjects, 45 C.F.R. § 46(A); retrieved November 2006 from http://www.hhs.gov/ohrp/humansubjects/guidance/45cfr46.htm.
4. Paperwork Reduction Act of 1995, 44 U.S.C. § 35.
5. See Federal Communications Commission, Consumer and Governmental Affairs Bureau, 2006, *Consumer facts: Unwanted telephone marketing calls,* retrieved August 10, 2006, from http://www.fcc.gov/cgb/consumerfacts/tcpa.html.
6. Telemarketing and Consumer Fraud and Abuse Prevention Act of 1995, 15 U.S.C. § 6101 *et seq.;* Telemarketing Sales Rule, 16 C.F.R. § 310; also see Federal Trade Commission, 2003, *Telemarketing Sales Rule,* retrieved November 2006 from http://www.ftc.gov/bcp/rulemaking/tsr.
7. See Federal Trade Commission, n.d., *Telemarketing information,* retrieved July 27, 2006, from http://www.ftc.gov/bcp/menu-tmark.htm. If you have questions about the Telemarketing Sales Rule, call 202-382-4357. For questions about the Telephone Consumer Protection Act, call 202-418-0200.
8. D. Krane, 2003, *National Do Not Call Registry popular, but public perception of impact on calls unrealistic: Estimate 60 million U.S. households eventually will register,* retrieved August 14, 2006, from http://www.harrisinteractive.com/harris_poll/index.asp?PID=400.
9. See American Association for Public Opinion Research, 2005, "Survey practices that AAPOR condemns," retrieved November 2006 from http://www.aapor.org/best_practices_for_survey_and_public_opinion_research_condemn.asp.
10. American Association for Public Opinion Research, 2003, *Push polls,* retrieved August 16, 2006, from http://www.aapor.org/pdfs/2003/2003pushpollstatement.pdf.
11. National Council on Public Polls, retrieved January 2, 2007, from http://www.ncpp.org/push.htm.
12. Public Opinion Strategies, n.d., *Push-polling,* retrieved January 2, 2007, from http://www.pos.org/research/pushpoll.cfm.
13. See H. O'Neill, 1996, *CMOR refusal rates and industry image study* (New York: Roper-Starch Worldwide).
14. See A. Kohut, 1996, *1996 poll on polls* (Princeton, NJ: Gallup Organization).

15. See the Oregon Annual Social Indicators Survey (OASIS) 2000, 2001, and 2002, retrieved January 2, 2007, from http://hdl.handle.net/1794/1051, http://hdl.handle.net/1794/1052, and http://hdl.handle.net/1794/1080, respectively.

16. See Council for Marketing and Opinion Research, 2003, *2003 Respondent cooperation and industry image study*, retrieved August 10, 2006, from http://www.cmor.org/rc/studies.cfm.

Chapter Four

1. Special thanks to Dr. Barnie Jones of the Oregon Department of Transportation for allowing the Transportation Needs and Issues Survey to serve as a continuing example in this book.

Chapter Five

1. American Association for Public Opinion Research, 2006, *Standard definitions: Final dispositions of case codes and outcome rates for surveys*, retrieved November 2006 from http://www.aapor.org/pdfs/standarddefs_4.pdf.

Chapter Six

1. Out of literally tens of thousands of telephone respondents in my twelve years of experience, just one respondent actually called his local police department. An officer called me, the survey center's director, and politely said that a man was claiming telephone harassment. I explained that because this survey was RDD and anonymous, I would need his telephone number to counter his claim. The officer supplied it, and I located the call record. The CATI system showed that in eight telephone calls over two weeks, an interviewer spoke with the respondent just once and recorded the call disposition code for "too busy." I explained our survey protocols to the officer. He said he understood, then apologized and wished us luck on the survey. Approximately ten other times in those twelve years, a respondent called my employer—once the president's office, a few times the IRB office, and a few times the general operator, who put those calls through to me. Not one incident resulted in the center getting "in trouble." Many more times my employer received calls of appreciation.

Chapter Seven

1. R. Tourangeau, L. J. Rips, and K. Rasinski, 2000, *The psychology of survey response* (New York: Cambridge University Press).

2. When, for example, a respondent to a health survey goes off on a tangent about his or her own aches and pains, some organizations' interviewer training manuals suggest that

interviewers say, *I am sorry to hear about that. The next question is . . .* I recommend not using this approach. Saying anything related to yourself or your feelings (being "sorry") can too easily be interpreted as an invitation by respondents who want to talk indefinitely.

3. These racial and ethnic categories are designed to implement Office of Management and Budget, 1997, *Revised standards for the classification of federal data on race and ethnicity* (Statistical Policy Directive No. 15), retrieved August 22, 2006, from http://www.whitehouse.gov/omb/fedreg/1997standards.html.

4. Gallup Organization, 2004, *Civil Rights and Race Relations Survey* (conducted by the Gallup Organization for the American Association for Retired People and the Leadership Conference on Civil Rights), retrieved August 23, 2006, from http://assets.aarp.org/rgcenter/general/civil_rights.pdf.

5. Pew Hispanic Center and Henry J. Kaiser Family Foundation, 2002, *2002 National Survey of Latinos*, retrieved August 22, 2006, from http://pewhispanic.org/reports/report.php?ReportID=15.

Chapter Eight

1. Council for Marketing and Opinion Research, 2000, *Telephone Survey Practices Study, 2000*, retrieved August 21, 2006, from www.cmor.org/pdf/final1999sum2a.pdf and http://www.researchinfo.com/docs/library/telephone_survey_practices_study_2000.cfm.

2. I have heard of survey call centers that customarily allow interviewers *drop-in* work. However, such organizations tend not to be the type that would assign their interviewers this *Handbook*. Their interviewer training tends to be minimal, as is their survey quality.

3. D. O'Rourke, 1998, An inquiry into declining RDD response rates: Part II. Telephone center operations and interviewers. *Survey Research, 29*(3), 1–3.

4. The principles of "management by wandering around" (MBWA) were developed and promulgated by Tom Peters, Bob Waterman, and others in the 1980s as American businesses adopted Japanese ideas of quality management. One principle idea is that productivity problems occur when supervisors and managers are out of touch with their employees. MBWA kicks these superiors out of their offices and into the halls, break rooms, and workspaces to chat casually with employees at all levels. MBWA practices are widely regarded as responsible for creating more effective leadership in the best-run organizations.

Appendix A: Glossary

1. P. P. Biemer and L. E. Lyberg, 2003, *Introduction to survey quality* (New York: Wiley), p. 154.

2. American Association for Public Opinion Research, 2006, *Standard definitions: Final dispositions of case codes and outcome rates for surveys*, retrieved November 2006 from http://www.aapor.org/pdfs/standarddefs_4.pdf.

3. American Association for Public Opinion Research, 2006, *Standard definitions: Final dispositions of case codes and outcome rates for surveys*, retrieved November 2006 from http://www.aapor.org/pdfs/standarddefs_4.pdf.

4. Biemer and Lyberg, 2003, p. 152.

BIBLIOGRAPHY

Adams, J. S. (1958). *Interviewing procedures: A manual for survey interviewers.* Chapel Hill: University of North Carolina Press.

American Association for Public Opinion Research. (2000). *Standard definitions: Final dispositions of case codes and outcome rates for surveys.* Retrieved January 2, 2007, from http://www.aapor.org/pdfs/standarddefs_4.pdf.

American Association for Public Opinion Research. (2003). *Interviewer falsification in survey research: Current best methods for prevention, detection, and repair of its effects.* Retrieved August 16, 2006, from http://www.aapor.org/pdfs/falsification.pdf.

American Association for Public Opinion Research. (2003). *Push polls: Not to be confused with legitimate polling.* Retrieved August 16, 2006, from http://www.aapor.org/pdfs/2003/2003push pollstatement.pdf.

American Association for Public Opinion Research. (2005). *Best practices for survey and public opinion research.* Retrieved August 16, 2006, from http://www.aapor.org/default.asp?page=survey_methods/standards_and_best_practices/best_practices_for_survey_and_public_opinion_research.

American Association for Public Opinion Research. (2005). *Survey practices AAPOR condemns.* Retrieved August 16, 2006, from http://www.aapor.org/default.asp?page=survey_methods/standards_and_best_practices/best_practices_for_survey_and_public_opinion_research_condemn.

American Statistical Association, Committee on Privacy and Confidentiality. (1998). *Surveys and privacy.* Alexandria, VA: Author.

Anderson, B. A., Silver, B. D., & Abramson, P. R. (1988). The effects of race of interviewer on race-related attitudes in SRC/CPS national election studies. *Public Opinion Quarterly, 52,* 289–324.

Anderson, D. A., & Aitkin, M. (1985). Variance component models with binary response: Interviewer variability. *Journal of the Royal Statistical Society*, Series B (Methodological), *47*, 203–210.

Angoff, W. H. (1974). The development of statistical indices for detecting cheaters. *Journal of the American Statistical Association*, *69*, 44–49.

Argyle, M. (1969). *Social interaction*. London: Methuen.

Argyle, M. (1975). *Bodily communication*. London: Methuen.

Argyle, M., & Ingham, R. (1972). Gaze, mutual gaze, and proximity. *Semiotica*, *6*, 32–49.

Arksey, H., & Knight, P. (1999). *Interviewing for social scientists: An introductory resource with examples*. Thousand Oaks, CA: Sage.

Axelrod, M., & Cannell, C. F. (1959). A research note on an attempt to predict interviewer effectiveness. *Public Opinion Quarterly*, *23*, 571–576.

Axinn, W. G. (1989). Interviewers and data quality in a less developed setting. *Journal of Official Statistics*, *5*, 265–280.

Bailar, B., Bailey, L., & Stevens, J. (1977). Measures of interviewer bias and variance. *Journal of Marketing Research*, *14*, 337–343.

Barath, A., & Cannell, C. F. (1976). Effect of interviewer's voice intonation. *Public Opinion Quarterly*, *40*, 370–373.

Bassili, J. N. (1996). The how and why of response latency measurement in telephone surveys. In N. Schwarz & S. Sudman (Eds.), *Answering questions: Methodology for determining cognitive and communicative processes in survey research* (pp. 319–346). San Francisco: Jossey-Bass.

Bell, R. (1984). Item nonresponse in telephone surveys: An analysis of who fails to report income. *Social Science Quarterly*, *65*, 207–215.

Belson, W. A. (1981). *The design and understanding of survey questions*. Aldershot, England: Gower.

Bennett, A. S. (1948). Survey on problems of interviewer cheating. *International Journal of Opinion and Attitude Research*, *2*, 89–96.

Bennett, A. S. (1948). Toward a solution of the "cheater problem" among part-time research investigators. *Journal of Marketing*, *2*, 470–474.

Bergsten J. W., Weeks, M. F., & Bryan, F. A. (1984). Effects of an advance telephone call in a personal interview survey. *Public Opinion Quarterly*, *48*, 650–657.

Berk, M. L., & Bernstein, A. M. (1988). Interviewer characteristics and performance on a complex health survey. *Social Science Research*, *17*, 239–251.

Bernstein, V., Hakel, M. D., & Harlan, A. (1975). The college student as interviewer: A threat to generalizability? *Journal of Applied Psychology*, *60*, 266–268.

Berry, S. H., & O'Rourke, D. (1988). Administrative designs for centralized telephone survey centers: Implications of the transition to CATI. In R. M. Groves, P. P. Biemer, L. E. Lyberg, J. Massey, W. L. Nicholls II, & J. Waksberg (Eds.), *Telephone survey methodology* (pp. 457–474). New York: Wiley.

Biemer, P. P. (2001). Nonresponse bias and measurement bias in a comparison of face-to-face and telephone interviewing. *Journal of Official Statistics*, *17*, 295–320.

Biemer, P. P., & Lyberg, L. E. (2003). *Introduction to survey quality*. New York: Wiley.

Biemer, P. P., & Stokes. S. L. (1985). Optimal design of interviewer variance experiments in complex surveys. *Journal of the American Statistical Association*, *80*, 158–166.

Biemer, P. P., & Stokes. S. L. (1989). The optimal design of quality control samples to detect interviewer cheating. *Journal of Official Statistics*, *5*, 23–39.

Billiet, J., & Loosveldt, G. (1988). Improvement of the quality of responses to factual survey questions by interviewer training. *Public Opinion Quarterly*, *52*, 190–211.

Bishop, G. F., Hippler, H.-J., Schwarz, N., & Strack, F. (1988). A comparison of response effects in self-administered and telephone surveys. In R. M. Groves, P. P. Biemer, L. E. Lyberg, J. Massey, W. L. Nicholls II, & J. Waksberg (Eds.), *Telephone survey methodology* (pp. 321–340). New York: Wiley.

Blair, E. (1980). Using practice interviews to predict interviewer behaviors. *Public Opinion Quarterly*, *44*, 257–260.

Bowen, G. L. (1994). Estimating the reduction in nonresponse bias from using a mail survey as a backup for nonrespondents to a telephone interview survey. *Research on Social Work Practice*, *4*, 115–128.

Boyd, H. W., & Westfall, R. (1955). Interviewers as a source of error in surveys. *Journal of Marketing*, *19*, 311–324.

Brehm, J. (1993). *The phantom respondents*. Ann Arbor: University of Michigan Press.

Brick, J. M., Montaquila, J., & Scheuren, F. (2002). Estimating residency rates for undetermined telephone numbers. *Public Opinion Quarterly*, *66*, 18–39.

Brick, J. M., Waksberg, J., Kulp, D. W., & Starer, A. (1995). Bias in list-assisted telephone samples. *Public Opinion Quarterly*, *59*, 218–235.

Bulmer, M. (Ed.). (2004). *Questionnaires*. Thousand Oaks, CA: Sage.

Bushery, J. M., Reichert, J. W., Albright, K. A., & Rossiter, J. C. (1999). Using date and time stamps to detect interviewer falsification. In *Proceedings of the Survey Research Methods Section, American Statistical Association* (pp. 316–320). Retrieved August 17, 2006, from http://www.amstat.org/sections/srms/Proceedings/papers/1999_053.pdf.

Campanelli, P. C., Martin, E. A., & Rothgeb, J. M. (1991). The use of respondent and interviewer debriefing studies as a way to study response error in survey data. *Statistician*, *40*, 253–264.

Campanelli, P. C., & O'Muircheartaigh, C. (1999). Interviewers, interviewer continuity, and panel survey nonresponse. *Quality and Quantity*, *33*, 59–76.

Cannell, C. F., & Fowler, F. J. (1964). A note on interviewer effect in self-enumerative procedures. *American Sociological Review*, *29*, 276.

Cannell, C. F., Miller, P. V., & Oksenberg, L. F. (1981). Research on interviewing techniques. *Sociological Methodology*, *11*, 389–437.

Cannell, C. F., & Oksenberg, L. F. (1988). Observation of behavior in telephone interviews. In R. M. Groves, P. P. Biemer, L. E. Lyberg, J. Massey, W. L. Nicholls II, & J. Waksberg (Eds.), *Telephone survey methodology* (pp. 475–495). New York: Wiley.

Cantor, D., Allen, B., Schneider, S. J., Hagerty-Heller, T., & Yuan, A. (2004, May 20–23). *Testing an automated refusal avoidance training methodology*. Paper presented at the 59th annual meeting of the American Association for Public Opinion Research, Phoenix, AZ.

Carton, A. (2000). An interviewer network: Constructing a procedure to evaluate interviewers. *Bulletin de Méthodologie Sociologique*, *67*, 42–53.

Casady, R. J., & Lepkowski, J. M. (1993). Stratified telephone survey designs. *Survey Methodology*, *19*, 103–113.

Catania, J. A., Binson, D., Canchola, J., Pollack, L., Hauck, W., & Coates, T. (1996). Effects of interviewer gender, interviewer choice, and item wording on responses to questions concerning sexual behavior. *Public Opinion Quarterly*, *60*, 345–375.

Catlin, G., & Ingram, S. (1988). The effects of CATI on costs and data quality: A comparison of CATI and paper methods in centralized interviewing. In R. M. Groves, P. P. Biemer, L. E. Lyberg, J. Massey, W. L. Nicholls II, & J. Waksberg (Eds.), *Telephone survey methodology* (pp. 437–450). New York: Wiley.

Choi, I. C., & Comstock, G. W. (1975). Interviewer effect on responses to a questionnaire relating to mood. *American Journal of Epidemiology, 101,* 84–92.

Clark, H. H. (1979). Responding to indirect speech acts. *Cognitive Psychology, 11,* 430–477.

Clark, H. H., & Schober, M. F. (1988). Asking questions and influencing answers. In J. M. Tanur (Ed.), *Questions about questions: Inquiries into the cognitive bases of surveys* (pp. 15–48). New York: Russell Sage.

Collins, M. (1980). Interviewer variability: A review of the problem. *Journal of the Market Research Society, 22,* 77–95.

Conrad, F. G., & Schober, M. F. (2000). Clarifying question meaning in a household telephone survey. *Public Opinion Quarterly, 64,* 1–28.

Converse, J. M., & Schuman, H. (Eds.). (1974). *Conversations at random: Survey research as interviewers see it.* New York: Wiley.

Converse, J. M., & Presser, S. (1986). *Survey questions: Handcrafting the standardized questionnaire* (Vol. 63 of *Quantitative applications in the social sciences*). Thousand Oaks, CA: Sage.

Cotter, P. R., Cohen, J., & Coulter, P. B. (1982). Race-of-interviewer effects in telephone interviews. *Public Opinion Quarterly, 46,* 278–284.

Council for Marketing and Opinion Research. (2000). *Telephone survey practices study.* Retrieved August 21, 2006, from www.cmor.org/pdf/final1999sum2a.pdf.

Council for Marketing and Opinion Research. (2003). *Callback procedures: Good response rates or harassment?* Retrieved August 10, 2006, from http://www.cmor.org/rc/rcnews.cfm?aID=0503 (membership password required).

Council for Marketing and Opinion Research. (2003) *2003 Respondent cooperation and industry image study.* Retrieved August 10, 2006, from http://www.cmor.org/rc/studies.cfm.

Council for Marketing and Opinion Research. (2005). *Respondent cooperation: Tools of the trade: What your rights are if you are interviewed?* Retrieved January 2, 2007, from http://www.cmor.org/rc/tools.cfm?topic=4.

Couper, M. P. (1994). Survey introductions and data quality. *Public Opinion Quarterly, 61,* 317–338.

Couper, M. P., Baker, R. P., Bethlehem, J., Clark, C.Z.F., Martin, J., Nicholls, W. L., II, et al. (Eds). (1998). *Computer assisted survey information collection.* New York: Wiley.

Couper, M. P., & Burt, G. (1994). Interviewer attitudes toward computer-assisted personal interviewing (CAPI). *Social Science Computer Review, 12,* 38–54.

Couper, M. P., & Groves, R. M. (1992). Interviewer reactions to alternative hardware for computer assisted personal interviewing. *Journal of Official Statistics, 8,* 201–210.

Couper, M. P., & Groves, R. M. (1992). The role of the interviewer in survey participation. *Survey Methodology, 18,* 263–278.

Couper, M. P., & Groves, R. M. (2002). Introductory interactions in telephone surveys and nonresponse. In D. W. Maynard, H. Houtkoop-Steenstra, N. C. Schaeffer, & J. van der Zouwen (Eds.), *Standardization and tacit knowledge: Interaction and practice in the survey interview* (pp. 161–177). New York: Wiley.

Couper, M. P., Hansen, S. E., & Sadovsky, S. (1997). Evaluating interviewer use of CAPI technology. In L. E. Lyberg, P. P. Biemer, M. Collins, E. D. de Leeuw, C. Dippo, N. Schwarz, et al. (Eds.), *Survey measurement and process quality* (pp. 267–285). New York: Wiley.

Couper, M. P., Holland, L., & Groves, R. M. (1992). Developing systematic procedures for monitoring in a centralized telephone facility. *Journal of Official Statistics, 8,* 63–76.

Crespi, I. P. (1945). The cheater problem in polling. *Public Opinion Quarterly, 9,* 431–445.

Curtin, R., Presser, S., & Singer, E. (2005). Changes in telephone survey nonresponse over the past quarter century. *Public Opinion Quarterly, 69,* 87–98.

Czaja, R., Blair, J., & Sebestik, J. P. (1982). Respondent selection in a telephone survey: A comparison of three techniques. *Journal of Marketing Research, 19,* 381–385.

Davis, D. W. (1997). The direction of race of interviewer effects among African-Americans: Donning the black mask. *American Journal of Political Science, 41,* 309–322.

Davis, D. W. (1997). Nonrandom measurement error and race of interviewer effects among African Americans. *Public Opinion Quarterly, 61,* 183–207.

Davis, P., & Alastair, S. (1995). The effect of interviewer variance on domain comparisons. *Survey Methodology, 21,* 99–106.

Dawes, R. M. (1997). Comment on survey biases: When does the interviewer's race matter? *Chance, 10,* 1.

De Leeuw, E. D. (1999). How do successful and less successful interviewers differ in tactics for combating survey nonresponse? *Bulletin de Méthodologie Sociologique, 62,* 29–42.

De Leeuw, E. D., & Hox, J. J. (2004). I am not selling anything: 29 experiments in telephone introductions. *International Journal of Public Opinion Research, 16,* 464–473.

De Leeuw, E. D., Hox, J. J., & Snijkers, G. (1995). The effect of computer-assisted interviewing on data quality. *Journal of the Market Research Society, 37,* 325–344.

DeMaio, T. J. (1980). Refusals: Who, where, and why. *Public Opinion Quarterly, 44,* 223–233.

DeMaio, T. J., & Rothgeb, J. M. (1996). Cognitive interviewing techniques: In the lab and in the field. In N. Schwarz & S. Sudman (Eds.), *Answering questions* (pp. 177–196). San Francisco: Jossey-Bass.

Dijkstra, W. (1983). How interviewer variance can bias the results of research on interviewer effects. *Quality and Quantity, 17,* 179–187.

Dijkstra, W., & Smit, J. H. (2002). Persuading reluctant recipients in telephone surveys. In R. M. Groves, D. A. Dillman, J. L. Eltinge, & R.J.A. Little, (Eds.), *Survey nonresponse* (pp. 121–134). New York: Wiley.

Dillman, D. A. (2000). *Mail and Internet surveys: The tailored design method.* New York: Wiley.

Dillman, D. A., Sangster, R., Tarnai J., & Rockwood, T. (1996). Understanding differences in people's answers to mail and telephone surveys. In M. T. Braverman & J. K. Slater (Eds.), *Advances in survey research* (pp. 45–62). New Directions for Evaluation, No. 70. San Francisco, Jossey-Bass.

Dillman, D. A., Brown, T. L., Carlson, J. E., Carpenter, E. H., Lorenz, F. O., Mason, R., Saltiel, J., et al. (1995). Effects of category order on answers: Tests of the primacy vs. recency hypothesis in mail and telephone surveys. *Rural Sociology, 60,* 674–687.

Downey-Sargent, K., & O'Hare, B. C. (2004, May 20–23). *A pre- and post-test experiment investigating the effectiveness of voice training for telephone interviewers.* Paper presented at the 59th annual meeting of the American Association for Public Opinion Research, Phoenix, AZ.

Drew J. D., Choudhry, G. H., & Hunter, L. A. (1988). Nonresponse issues in government telephone surveys. In R. M. Groves, P. P. Biemer, L. E. Lyberg, J. Massey, W. L. Nicholls II, & J. Waksberg (Eds.), *Telephone survey methodology* (pp. 233–246). New York: Wiley.

Durand, C. (2005). How to measure interviewer performance in telephone surveys. *Quality and Quantity, 39,* 763–778.

Durand, C., Gagnon, M., Doucet, C., & Lacourse, E. (2006). An inquiry into the efficacy of a complementary training for telephone survey interviewers. *Bulletin de Methodologie Sociologique, 92,* 5–27.

Durbin, J., & Stuart, A. (1951). Differences in response rates of experienced and inexperienced interviewers. *Journal of the Royal Statistical Society* (Series A, General), *114*, 163–195.

Dykema, J., Lepkowski, J. M., & Blixt, S. (1997). The effect of interviewer and respondent behavior on data quality: Analysis of interaction coding in a validation study. In L. E. Lyberg, P. P. Biemer, M. Collins, E. D. de Leeuw, C. Dippo, N. Schwarz, et al. (Eds.), *Survey measurement and process quality* (pp. 287–310). New York: Wiley.

Edwards, S., Slattery, M. L., Mori, M., Berry, T. D., Caan, B. J., Palmer, P., et al. (1994). Objective system for interviewer performance evaluation for use in epidemiologic studies. *American Journal of Epidemiology*, *140*, 1020–1028.

Edwards, T. P., Suresh, R., & Weeks, M. F. (1998). Automated call scheduling: Current systems and practices. In M. P. Couper, R. P. Baker, J. Bethlehem, C.Z.F. Clark, J. Martin, W. L. Nicholls II, et al. (Eds.), *Computer assisted survey information collection* (pp. 286–306). New York: Wiley.

Elinson, J., & Cisin, I. H. (1948). Detection of interviewer cheating through scale technique. *Public Opinion Quarterly*, *12*, 325.

Esbensen, F., & Menard, S. (1991). Interviewer-related measurement error in attitudinal research: A nonexperimental study. *Quality and Quantity*, *25*, 151–165.

Evans, F. B. (1961). On interviewer cheating. *Public Opinion Quarterly*, *25*, 126–127.

Federal Communications Commission, Consumer and Governmental Affairs Bureau. (2006). *Consumer facts: Unwanted telephone marketing calls*. Retrieved August 10, 2006, from http://www.fcc.gov/cgb/consumerfacts/tcpa.html.

Federal Trade Commission. (2003). *Telemarketing Sales Rule*. Retrieved November 2006 from http://www.ftc.gov/bcp/rulemaking/tsr.

Federal Trade Commission. Telemarketing Sales Rule, 16 C.F.R. 310 (2003).

Federal Trade Commission. (2003). *You make the call: The FTC's new Telemarketing Sales Rule*. Retrieved August 14, 2006, from http://www.ftc.gov/bcp/conline/pubs/tmarkg/donot call.htm.

Federal Trade Commission. (n.d.) *Telemarketing information*. Retrieved July 27, 2006, from http://www.ftc.gov/bcp/menu-tmark.htm.

Feld, K. G. What are push polls, anyway? (2000). *Campaigns and Elections*, *21*, 62–63, 70. Retrieved August 14, 2006, from http://www.findarticles.com/p/articles/mi_m2519/is_4_21/ai_62410241.

Fellows, C., & Mawhinney, T. C. (1997). Improving telemarketers' performance in the short-run using operant concepts. *Journal of Business and Psychology*, *11*, 411–424.

Fink, A. (2003). *How to ask survey questions*. Thousand Oaks, CA: Sage.

Finkel, S. E., Guterbock, T., & Borg, M. (1991). Race-of-interviewer effects in a pre-election poll. *Public Opinion Quarterly*, *55*, 313–330.

Foddy, W. (1995). Probing: A dangerous practice in social surveys? *Quality and Quantity*, *29*, 73–86.

Forsman, G. (1993). Sampling individuals within households in telephone surveys. *Proceedings of the Survey Research Methods Section, American Statistical Association* (pp. 1113–1118). Retrieved January 2, 2007, from http://www.amstat.org/sections/srms/Proceedings/papers/1993_191.pdf.

Forsman, G., & Schreiner, I. (1991). The design and analysis of reinterview: An overview. In P. P. Biemer, R. M. Groves, L. E. Lyberg, N. A. Mathiowetz, & S. Sudman (Eds.), *Measurement errors in surveys* (pp. 279–301). New York: Wiley.

Fowler, F. (1992). How unclear terms affect survey data. *Public Opinion Quarterly*, *56*, 218–231.

Fowler, F. J. (1991). Reducing interviewer-related error through interviewer training, supervision, and other means. In P. P. Biemer, R. M. Groves, L. E. Lyberg, N. A. Mathiowetz, & S. Sudman (Eds.), *Measurement errors in surveys* (pp. 259–278). New York: Wiley.

Fowler, F. J., & Mangione, T. W. (1990). *Standardized survey interviewing.* Thousand Oaks, CA: Sage.

Frank, L. L., & Hackman, J. R. (1975). Effects of interviewer-interviewee similarity on interviewer objectivity in college admissions interviews. *Journal of Applied Psychology, 60,* 356–360.

Freedman, D., Thornton, A., Camburn, D., Alwin, D., & DeMarco, L. Y. (1988). The life history calendar: A technique for collecting retrospective data. *Sociological Methodology, 18,* 37–68.

Freeman, J., & Butler, E. W. (1976). Some sources of interviewer variance in surveys. *Public Opinion Quarterly, 40,* 79–91.

Frey, J. H. (1986). An experiment with a confidentiality reminder in a telephone survey. *Public Opinion Quarterly, 50,* 267–269.

Frey, J. H., & Oishi, S. M. (1995). *How to conduct interviews by telephone and in person.* Thousand Oaks, CA: Sage.

Fuchs, M. (2002). The impact of technology on interaction in computer-assisted interviews. In D. W. Maynard, H. Houtkoop-Steenstra, N. C. Schaeffer, & J. van der Zouwen (Eds.), *Standardization and tacit knowledge: Interaction and practice in the survey interview* (pp. 471–491). New York: Wiley.

Gallup Organization. (2004). *Civil Rights and Race Relations Survey* (Conducted for the American Association for Retired People and the Leadership Conference on Civil Rights). Retrieved August 23, 2006, from http://assets.aarp.org/rgcenter/general/civil_rights.pdf.

Gao, S. (2001). Estimation of interviewer effects on multivariate binary responses in a community based survey. *Journal of Official Statistics, 17,* 149–161.

Gawiser, S. R., & Witt, G. E. (n.d.). *Twenty questions a journalist should ask about poll results* (3d ed.). National Council on Public Polls. Retrieved August 14, 2006, from http://www.ncpp.org/qajsa.htm.

Gilberg, C., Cox, J. L., Kashima, H., & Eberle, K. (1996). Survey biases: When does the interviewer's race matter? *Chance, 9,* 23–25.

Gostkowski, Z. (1974). Toward empirical humanization of mass surveys. *Quality and Quantity, 8,* 11–26.

Grobel, L. (2004). *The art of the interview: Lessons from a master of the craft.* New York: Three Rivers Press.

Grossman, R., & Weiland, D. (1978). The use of telephone directories as a sample frame: Patterns of bias revisited. *Journal of Advertising, 7,* 31–35.

Groves, R. M. (1979). Actors and questions in telephone and personal interview surveys. *Public Opinion Quarterly, 43,* 190–205.

Groves, R. M. (1990). Theories and methods of telephone surveys. *Annual Review of Sociology, 16,* 221–240.

Groves, R. M., Cialdini, R. B., & Couper, M. P. (1992). Understanding the decision to participate in a survey. *Public Opinion Quarterly, 56,* 475–495.

Groves, R. M., & Fultz, N. H. (1985). Gender effects among telephone interviewers in a survey of economic attitudes. *Sociological Methods and Research, 14,* 31–52.

Groves R. M., & Kahn, R. L. (1979). *Surveys by telephone: A national comparison with personal interviews.* New York: Academic Press.

Groves, R. M., & Magilavy, L. J. (1981). Increasing response rates to telephone surveys: A door in the face for foot-in-the door? *Public Opinion Quarterly*, *45*, 346–358.

Groves, R. M., & Magilavy, L. J. (1986). Measuring and explaining interviewer effects in centralized telephone surveys. *Public Opinion Quarterly*, *50*, 251–266.

Groves, R. M., & Mathiowetz, N. A. (1984). Computer assisted telephone interviewing: Effects on interviewers and respondents. *Public Opinion Quarterly*, *48*, 356–369.

Groves, R. M., & McGonagle, K. (2001). A theory-guided interviewer training protocol regarding survey participation. *Journal of Official Statistics*, *17*, 249–266.

Groves, R. M., & Nicholls, W. L., II. (1986). The status of computer-assisted telephone interviewing: Part II. Data quality issues. *Journal of Official Statistics*, *2*, 117–134.

Groves, R. M., Singer, E., & Corning, A. (2000). Leverage-saliency theory of survey participation. *Public Opinion Quarterly*, *64*, 299–308.

Gubrium, J. F., & Holstein, J. A. (Eds.). (2002). *Handbook of interview research: Context and method*. Thousand Oaks, CA: Sage.

Guenzel, P. J., Berckmans, T. R., & Cannell, C. F. (1983). *General interviewing techniques: A self-instructional workbook for telephone and personal interviewer training*. Ann Arbor: University of Michigan Institute for Social Research, Survey Research Center.

Guest, L. (1954). A new training method for opinion interviewers. *Public Opinion Quarterly*, *18*, 287–299.

Hagenaars, J. A., & Heinen, T. G. (1982). Effects of role-independent interviewer characteristics on responses. In W. Dijkstra, & J. van der Zouwen (Eds.), *Response behavior in the survey interview* (pp. 91–130). London: Academic Press.

Hague, P., Hague, N., & Morgan, C. (2004). *Market research in practice: A guide to the basics*. London and Sterling, VA: Kogan Page.

Hanson, R. H., & Marks, E. S. (1958). Influence of the interviewer on the accuracy of survey results. *Journal of the American Statistical Association*, *53*, 635–655.

Harrison, G. G., Stormer, A., Herman, D. R., & Winham, D. M. (2003). Development of a Spanish-language version of the U.S. Household Food Security Survey Module. *Journal of Nutrition*, *133*(1), 192–197.

Havis, M. J., & Banks, M. J. (1991). Live and automated telephone surveys: A comparison of human interviewers and an automated technique. *Journal of the Market Research Society*, *33*, 91–102.

Heneman, H. G., Schwab, D. P., Huett, D. L., & Ford, J. J. (1975). Interviewer validity as a function of interview structure, biographical data and interviewee order. *Journal of Applied Psychology*, *60*, 748–753.

Herzog, A. R., Rodgers, W. L., & Kulka, R. A. (1983). Interviewing older adults: A comparison of telephone and face-to-face modalities. *Public Opinion Quarterly*, *47*, 405–418.

Hess, J., Moore, J., Pascale, J., Rothgeb, J. M., & Keeley, C. (2001). The effects of person-level versus household-level questionnaire design on survey estimates and data quality. *Public Opinion Quarterly*, *65*, 574–584.

Hill, D. H. (1991). Interviewer, respondent, and regional office effects on response variance: A statistical decomposition. In P. P. Biemer, R. M. Groves, L. E. Lyberg, N. A. Mathiowetz, & S. Sudman (Eds.), *Measurement errors in surveys* (pp. 463–483). New York: Wiley.

Holbrook, A. L., Green, M. C., & Krosnick, J. A. (2003). Telephone versus face-to-face interviewing of national probability samples with long questionnaires: Comparisons of respondent satisficing and social desirability response bias. *Public Opinion Quarterly, 67,* 79–125.

Holstein, J. A., & Gubrium, J. F. (Eds.). (2003). *Inside interviewing: New lenses, new concerns.* Thousand Oaks, CA: Sage.

Hood, C. C., & Bushery, J. M. (1997). Getting more bang from the reinterview buck: Identifying "at risk" interviewers. In *Proceedings of the Survey Research Methods Section, American Statistical Association* (pp. 820–824). Retrieved January 2, 2007, from http://www.amstat.org/sections/srms/Proceedings/papers/1997_141.pdf.

House, C. (1985). Questionnaire design with computer assisted telephone interviewing. *Journal of Official Statistics, 1,* 209–219.

Houtkoop-Steenstra, H. (1996). Probing behavior of interviewers in the standardized semi-open research interview. *Quality and Quantity, 30,* 205–230.

Houtkoop-Steenstra, H. (2000). *Interaction and the standardized survey interview: The living questionnaire.* New York: Cambridge University Press.

Houtkoop-Steenstra, H., & Van den Bergh, H. (2000). Effects of introductions in large-scale telephone survey interviews. *Sociological Methods and Research, 28,* 281–300.

Hox, J. J. (1994). Hierarchical regression models for interviewer and respondent effects. *Sociological Methods and Research, 22,* 300–318.

Hox, J. J., & de Leeuw, E. D. (1994). A comparison of nonresponse in mail, telephone, and face-to-face surveys. *Quality and Quantity, 28,* 329–344.

Hox, J. J., & de Leeuw, E. D. (2002). The influence of interviewers' attitude and behavior on household survey nonresponse: An international comparison. In R. M. Groves, D. A. Dillman, J. L. Eltinge, & R.J.A. Little, (Eds.), *Survey nonresponse* (pp. 103–120). New York: Wiley.

Hox, J. J., de Leeuw, E. D., & Kreft, I. G. (1991). The effect of interviewer and respondent characteristics on the quality of survey data: A multilevel model. In P. P. Biemer, R. M. Groves, L. E. Lyberg, N. A. Mathiowetz, & S. Sudman (Eds.), *Measurement errors in surveys* (pp. 439–461). New York: Wiley.

Hox. J., de Leeuw, E. D., & Vorst, H. (1995). Survey participation as reasoned action: A behavioral paradigm for survey nonresponse? *Bulletin de Méthodologie Sociologique, 48,* 52–67.

Hyman, H. H., with Cobb, W. J. (1954). *Interviewing in social research.* Chicago: University of Chicago Press.

Ilgen, D. R., & Schneider, J. (1991). Performance measurement: A multi-discipline view. *International Review of Industrial and Organizational Psychology, 6,* 71–108.

International Organization for Standardization. (2006). *Market, opinion, and social research: Vocabulary and service requirements* (ISO 20252:2006). Geneva: Author.

Johnson, T. P., Parker, V., & Clements, C. (2001). Detection and prevention of data falsification in survey research. *Survey Research, 32,* 1–2.

Kahn, R. L., & Cannell, C. F. (1957). *The dynamics of interviewing: Theory, technique, and cases.* New York: Wiley.

Kane, E., & Macaulay, L. (1993). Interviewer gender and gender attitudes. *Public Opinion Quarterly, 57,* 1–28.

Keeter, S. (1995). Estimating noncoverage bias from a phone survey. *Public Opinion Quarterly, 59,* 196–217.

Keeter, S., Miller, C., Kohut, A., Groves, R. M., & Presser, S. (2000). Consequences of reducing nonresponse in a national telephone survey. *Public Opinion Quarterly, 64,* 125–148.

Kemsley, W.F.F. (1965). Interviewer variability in expenditure surveys. *Journal of the Royal Statistical Society* (Series A, General), *128*, 118–139.

Kerin, R. A., & Peterson, R. A. (1983). Scheduling telephone interviews: Lessons from 250,000 dialings. *Journal of Advertising Research, 23*, 97–112.

Kirsch, I. S., Jungeblut, A., Jenkins, L., & Kolstad, A. (1993). *Executive summary of adult literacy in America: A first look at the findings of the National Adult Literacy Survey*. National Center for Education Statistics. Retrieved August 16, 2006, from http://nces.ed.gov/pubsearch/pubsinfo.asp?pubid=93275.

Kish, L. (1962). Studies of interviewer variance for attitudinal variables. *Journal of the American Statistical Association, 57*(297), 92–115.

Kohut, A. (1996). *1996 poll on polls*. Princeton, NJ: Gallup Organization.

Krane, D. (2003). *The Harris Poll #51: National Do Not Call Registry popular, but public perception of impact on calls unrealistic*. Harris Interactive. Retrieved August 14, 2006, from http://www.harrisinteractive.com/harris_poll/index.asp?PID=400.

Krosnick, J. A. (1999). Survey research. *Annual Review of Psychology, 50*, 537–567.

Krosnick, J. A., & Fabrigar, L. R. (1998). *Designing good questionnaires: Insights from psychology*. New York: Oxford University Press.

Landsheer, J. A., Van Der Heijden, P., & Van Gils, G. (1999). Trust and understanding, two psychological aspects of randomized response. *Quality and Quantity, 33*, 1–12.

Lavin, D., & Maynard, D. W. (2001). Standardization vs. rapport: Respondent laughter and interviewer reaction during telephone surveys. *American Sociological Review, 66*, 453–479.

Lavrakas, P. J. (1993). *Telephone survey methods: Sampling, selection, and supervision*. Thousand Oaks, CA: Sage.

Lee, S. M., & Carlson, M. J. (2005). *Report on assessment of Spanish-language Oregon Medicaid Health Risk and Health Status Survey*. Portland State University, Department of Sociology, Center for Health and Social Inequality Research. Retrieved August 14, 2006, from http://www.sociology.pdx.edu/omhrhss.pdf.

Leigh, J. H., & Martin, C. R., Jr. (1987). 'Don't know' item nonresponse in a telephone survey: Effects of question form and respondent characteristics. *Journal of Marketing Research, 24*, 418–424.

Lemay, M., & Durand, C. (2002). The effect of interviewer attitude on survey cooperation. *Bulletin de Méthodologie Sociologique, 76*, 27–44.

Link, M. W. (2006). Predicting the persistence and performance of newly recruited telephone interviewers. *Field Methods, 18*, 305–320.

Link, M. W., Armsby, P., Hubal, R., & Guinn, C. (2004). Accessibility and acceptance of responsive virtual human technology as a telephone interviewer training tool. *Computers in Human Behavior, 22*, 412–426.

Link, M. W., & Mokdad, A. (2005). Advance letters as a means of improving respondent cooperation in RDD Studies: A multi-state experiment. *Public Opinion Quarterly, 69*, 232–245.

Link, M. W., & Mokdad, A. (2005). Leaving answering machine messages: Do they increase response rates for RDD surveys? *International Journal of Public Opinion Research, 17*, 239–250.

Lynch, M. (2002). The living text: Written instructions and situated actions in telephone surveys. In D. W. Maynard, H. Houtkoop-Steenstra, N. C. Schaeffer, & J. van der Zouwen (Eds.), *Standardization and tacit knowledge: Interaction and practice in the survey interview* (pp. 125–491). New York: Wiley.

Mangione, T. W., Fowler, F. J., & Louis, T. A. (1992). Question characteristics and interviewer effects in centralized telephone facilities. *Journal of Official Statistics, 8*, 293–307.

Matschinger, H., Bernert, S., & Angermeyer, M. C. (2005). An analysis of interviewer effects on screening questions in a computer assisted personal mental health interview. *Journal of Official Statistics, 21*, 657–674.

Mayer, T. S., & O'Brien, E. (2001). Interviewer refusal aversion training to increase survey participation. In *Proceedings of the Survey Research Methods Section, American Statistical Association*. Retrieved August 16, 2006, from http://www.fcsm.gov/committees/ihsng/ASA2001.pdf.

Maynard, D. W., & Schaeffer, N. C. (1997). Keeping the gate: Declinations of the request to participate in a telephone survey interview. *Sociological Methods and Research, 26*, 34–79.

Maynard, D. W., & Schaeffer, N. C. (2002). Standardization and its discontents. In D. W. Maynard, H. Houtkoop-Steenstra, N. C. Schaeffer, & J. van der Zouwen (Eds.), *Standardization and tacit knowledge: Interaction and practice in the survey interview* (pp. 3–45). New York: Wiley.

McCarty, C. (2003). Differences in response rates using most recent versus final dispositions in telephone surveys. *Public Opinion Quarterly, 67*, 396–406.

McConaghy, M., & Carey, S. (2004, May 20–23). *Training to help interviewers avoid refusals: Results of stage 1 of a pilot using Avoiding Refusal Training (ART) with interviewers at the Office of National Statistics, UK*. Paper presented at the 59th annual meeting of the American Association for Public Opinion Research, Phoenix, AZ.

McCracken, G. D. (1988). *The long interview*. Thousand Oaks, CA: Sage.

McKenzie, J. R. (1977). An investigation into interviewer effects in market research. *Journal of Marketing Research, 14*, 330–336.

Mensch, B. S., & Kandel, D. B. (1988). Underreporting of substance use in a national longitudinal youth cohort: Individual and interviewer effects. *Public Opinion Quarterly, 52*, 100–124.

Molenaar, N. J., & Smit, J. H. (1996). Asking and answering yes/no-questions in survey interviews: A conversational approach. *Quality and Quantity, 30*, 115–136.

Morton-Williams, J. (1993). *Interviewer approaches*. Aldershot, UK: Dartmouth.

National Center for Education Statistics. (2005). *A first look at the literacy of America's adults in the 21st century* (NCES 2006–470). Retrieved August 22, 2006, from http://nces.ed.gov/pubsearch/pubsinfo.asp?pubid=2006470.

National Council on Public Polls. (1995). *A press warning from the National Council on Public Polls, May 22, 1995*. Retrieved August 16, 2006, from http://www.ncpp.org/push.htm.

National Opinion Research Center. (1945). *Interviewing for NORC*. Denver: Author.

Newburger, E. C. (2001). *Home computer and Internet access in the United States: August 2000*. U.S. Census Bureau. Retrieved August 16, 2006, from http://www.census.gov/prod/2001pubs/p23-207.pdf.

Nicholls, W. L., II, & Groves, R. M. (1986). The status of computer assisted telephone interviewing: Part I. Introduction and impact on cost and timeliness of survey data. *Journal of Official Statistics, 2*, 93–115.

O'Brien, E., Mayer, T. S., Groves, R. M., & O'Neill, G. E. (2002). Interviewer training to increase survey participation. In *Proceedings of the Survey Research Methods Section, American Statistical Association*. Retrieved August 17, 2006, from http://www.fcsm.gov/committees/ihsng/asa02_interview.pdf.

O'Muircheartaigh, C. (1998). The relative impact of interviewer effects and sample design effects on survey precision. *Journal of the Royal Statistical Society* (Series A, General), *161*, 63–77.

O'Muircheartaigh, C., & Campanelli, P. C. (1999). A multilevel exploration of the role of interviewers in survey non-response. *Journal of the Royal Statistical Society* (Series A, General), *162*, 437–446.

O'Neill, H. (1996). *CMOR refusal rates and industry image study.* New York: Roper-Starch Worldwide.

O'Rourke, D. (1998). An inquiry into declining RDD response rates: Part II. Telephone center operations and interviewers. *Survey Research, 29*(3), 1–3.

O'Rourke, D., & Blair, J. (1983). Improving random respondent selection in telephone surveys. *Journal of Marketing Research, 20*, 428–432.

Office of Management and Budget. (1997). *Revised standards for the classification of federal data on race and ethnicity* (Statistical Policy Directive No. 15). Retrieved August 22, 2006, from http://www.whitehouse.gov/omb/fedreg/1997standards.html.

Oksenberg, L. F., & Cannell, C. F. (1988). Effects of interviewer vocal characteristics on nonresponse. In R. M. Groves, P. P. Biemer, L. E. Lyberg, J. Massey, W. L. Nicholls II, & J. Waksberg (Eds.), *Telephone survey methodology* (pp. 257–272). New York: Wiley.

Oksenberg, L. F., Coleman, L., & Cannell, C. F. (1986). Interviewers' voices and refusal rates in telephone surveys. *Public Opinion Quarterly, 50*, 97–111.

Oldendick, R. W., Bishop, G. F., Sorenson, B., & Tuchfarber, A. J. (1988). A comparison of the Kish and last birthday methods of respondent selection in telephone surveys. *Journal of Official Statistics, 4*, 307–318.

Oldendick, R. W., & Link, M. W. (1994). The answering machine generation. *Public Opinion Quarterly. 58*, 264–273.

Orton, B. (1982). Phony polls: The pollster's nemesis. *Public Opinion, 5*, 56–60.

Packard, D. (1995). *The HP way: How Bill Hewlett and I built our company.* New York: HarperCollins.

Pannekoek, J. (1988). Interviewer variance in a telephone survey. *Journal of Official Statistics, 4*, 375–384.

Parsons, J. A., Johnson, T. P., Warnecke, R. B., & Kaluzny, A. (1993). The effect of interviewer characteristics on gatekeeper resistance in surveys of elite populations. *Evaluation Review, 17*, 131–143.

Payne, S. L. (1951/1980). *The art of asking questions.* Princeton, NJ: Princeton University Press.

Peterson, R. A. (1984). Asking the age question: A research note. *Public Opinion Quarterly, 48*, 379–383.

Pew Hispanic Center & Henry J. Kaiser Family Foundation. (2002). *2002 National Survey of Latinos.* Retrieved August 22, 2006, from http://pewhispanic.org/reports/report.php?ReportID=15.

Phillips, D. L., & Clancy, K. J. (1971–1972). Some effects of "social desirability" in survey studies. *American Journal of Sociology, 77*, 921–939.

Piazza, T. (1993). Meeting the challenges of answering machines. *Public Opinion Quarterly, 57*, 219–231.

Pickery, J., & Loosveldt, G. (1998). The impact of respondent and interviewer characteristics on the number of "no opinion" answers. *Quality and Quantity, 32*, 31–45.

Pickery, J., & Loosveldt, G. (2000). Modeling interviewer effects in panel surveys: An application. *Survey Methodology 26*, 189–198.

Pickery, J., & Loosveldt, G. (2002). A multilevel multinomial analysis of interviewer effects on various components of unit nonresponse. *Quality and Quantity, 36*, 427–437.

Pickery, J., Loosveldt, G., & Carton, A. (2001). The effects of interviewer and respondent characteristics on response behavior in panel surveys: A multilevel approach. *Sociological Methods and Research, 29*, 509–523.

Podell, L. (1955). The structured interview as a social relationship. *Social Forces, 34*, 150–155.

Pothoff, R. F. (1987). Generalizations of the Mitofsky-Waksberg technique for random digit dialing. *Journal of the American Statistical Association, 82*(398), 409–418.

Presser, S., & Stinson, L. (1998). Data collection mode and social desirability bias in self-reported religious attendance. *American Sociological Review, 63*, 137–145.

Presser, S., & Zhao, S. (1992). Attributes of questions and interviewers as correlates of interviewing performance. *Public Opinion Quarterly, 56*, 236–240.

Public Opinion Strategies. (n.d.) *Public Opinion Strategies does NOT engage in push polling, voter ID, or GOTV programs.* Retrieved January 2, 2007, from http://www.pos.org/pushpoll.

Purdon, S., Campanelli, P. C., & Sturgis, P. (1999). Interviewers' calling strategies on face-to-face interview surveys. *Journal of Official Statistics, 15*, 199–216.

Reed, S. J., & Reed, J. H. (1997). The use of statistical quality control charts in monitoring interviewers. In *Proceedings of the Survey Research Methods Section, American Statistical Association* (pp. 893–898). Retrieved January 2, 2007, from http://www.amstat.org/sections/srms/Proceedings/papers/1997_154.pdf.

Reese, S. D., Danielson, W. A., Shoemaker, P. J., Chang, T., & Hsu, H. (1986). Ethnicity-of-interviewer effects among Mexican Americans and Anglos. *Public Opinion Quarterly, 50*, 563–572.

Reinecke, J., & Schmidt, P. (1993). Explaining interviewer effects and respondent behavior: Theoretical models and empirical analysis. *Quality and Quantity, 27*, 219–247.

Richardson, S. A., Dohrenwend, B. S., & Klein, D. (1965). *Interviewing: Its forms and functions.* New York: Basic Books.

Rizzo, L., Brick, J. M., & Park, I. (2004). A minimally intrusive method for sampling persons in random digit dial surveys. *Public Opinion Quarterly, 68*, 267–274.

Rogers, T. F. (1976). Interviews by telephone and in person. *Public Opinion Quarterly, 40*, 51–65.

Roslow, S., & Roslow, L. (1972). Unlisted phone subscribers are different. *Journal of Advertising Research, 12*, 35–38.

Ross, C., & Mirowsky, J. (1984). Socially desirable response and acquiescence in a cross-cultural survey of mental health. *Journal of Social Behavior, 25*, 189–197.

Rubin, H. J., & Rubin, I. S. (2005). *Qualitative interviewing: The art of hearing data.* Thousand Oaks, CA: Sage.

Schaeffer, N. C. (1980). Evaluating race-of-interviewer effects in a national survey. *Sociological Methods and Research, 8*, 400–419.

Schaeffer N. C., & Maynard, D. W. (2002). Occasions for intervention: Interactional resources for comprehension in standardized survey interviews. In D. W. Maynard, H. Houtkoop-Steenstra, N. C. Schaeffer, & J. van der Zouwen (Eds.), *Standardization and tacit knowledge: Interaction and practice in the survey interview* (pp. 261–280). New York: Wiley.

Schaeffer, N. C., & Presser, S. (2003). The science of asking questions. *Annual Review of Sociology, 29*, 65–88.

Schegloff, E. (2002). Survey interviews as talk-in-interaction. In D. W. Maynard, H. Houtkoop-Steenstra, N. C. Schaeffer, & J. van der Zouwen (Eds.), *Standardization and tacit knowledge: Interaction and practice in the survey interview* (pp. 151–157). New York: Wiley.

Scheuren, F. (1995). *What is a survey?* American Statistical Association, Section on Survey Research Methods. Retrieved August 14, 2006, from http://www.whatisasurvey.info.

Schober, M. F., & Conrad, F. G. (1997). Does conversational interviewing reduce survey measurement error? *Public Opinion Quarterly, 61,* 576–602.

Schober, M. F., & Conrad, F. G. (2002). A collaborative view of standardized survey interviews. In D. W. Maynard, H. Houtkoop-Steenstra, N. C. Schaeffer, & J. van der Zouwen (Eds.), *Standardization and tacit knowledge: Interaction and practice in the survey interview* (pp. 69–94). New York: Wiley.

Schober, M. F., Conrad, F. G., & Fricker, S. S. (2004). Misunderstanding standardized language in research interviews. *Applied Cognitive Psychology, 18,* 169–188.

Schuman, H., & Converse, J. M. (1971). The effect of black and white interviewers on black responses in 1968. *Public Opinion Quarterly, 35,* 44–68.

Shapiro, G. M. (1987). Interviewer-respondent bias resulting from adding supplemental questions. *Journal of Official Statistics, 3,* 155–168.

Sheatsley, P. B. (1951). An analysis of interviewer characteristics and their relationship to performance, Part II. *International Journal of Opinion and Attitude Research 5,* 79–94.

Shuttles, C. D., Skyrme, P. Y., Camayd-Freixas, E., Haskins, C. E., Wilkinson, D. L., Vallar, K. D., et al. (2006, January 11–15). *Hiring the right stuff: Development of a skills and personality assessment system for hiring effective telephone research interviewers.* Paper presented at the Telephone Survey Methods II conference, Miami, FL.

Singer, E., & Frankel, M. R. (1982). Informed consent procedures in telephone interviews. *American Sociological Review, 47,* 416–426.

Singer, E., Frankel, M. R., & Glassman, M. B. (1983). The effect of interviewer characteristics and expectations on response. *Public Opinion Quarterly, 47,* 68–83.

Singer, E., & Kohnke-Aguirre, L. (1979). Interviewer expectation effects: A replication and extension. *Public Opinion Quarterly, 43,* 245–260.

Singer, E., Van Hoewyk, J., Gebler, N., Raghunathan, T., & McGonagle, K. (1999). The effect of incentives on response rates in interviewer-mediated surveys. *Journal of Official Statistics, 15,* 217–230.

Singer, E., Van Hoewyk, J., & Maher, M. P. (2000). Experiments with incentives in telephone surveys. *Public Opinion Quarterly, 64,* 171–188.

Smit, J. H., Dijkstra, W., & van der Zouwen, J. (1997). Suggestive interviewer behavior in surveys: An experimental study. *Journal of Official Statistics, 13,* 19–28.

Snijkers, G., Hox, J. J., & de Leeuw, E. D. (1999). Interviewers' tactics for fighting survey nonresponse. *Journal of Official Statistics, 15,* 185–198.

Solano-Flores, W., & Hurtado, M. (2005). *CAHPS guidelines for assessing and selecting translators and reviewers* (Final draft). Agency for Healthcare Research and Quality. Retrieved August 14, 2006, from https://www.cahps-sun.org/Products/Healthplan/CAHPS%20Translator%20selection%20guidelines%201-06-051.pdf.

Stanton, H. K., Back, W., & Litwak, E. (1956). Role playing in survey research. *Journal of the American Statistical Association, 62,* 172–176.

Steeh, C., Kirgis, N., Cannon, B., & DeWitt, J. (2001). Are they really as bad as they seem? Nonresponse rates at the end of the twentieth century. *Journal of Official Statistics, 17,* 227–247.

Steinkamp, S. W. (1964). The identification of effective interviewers. *Journal of the American Statistical Association, 59* (308), 1165–1174.

Stocké, V. (2006). Attitudes toward surveys, attitude accessibility, and the effect on respondents' susceptibility to nonresponse. *Quality and Quantity, 40*, 259–288.

Stokes, L. (1988). Estimation of interviewer effects for categorical items in a random digit dial telephone survey. *Journal of the American Statistical Association, 83*(403), 623–630.

Stokes, L., & Yeh, M. (1988). Searching for causes of interviewer effects in telephone surveys. In R. M. Groves, P. P. Biemer, L. E. Lyberg, J. Massey, W. L. Nicholls II, & J. Waksberg (Eds.), *Telephone survey methodology* (pp. 357–376). New York: Wiley.

Suchman, L., & Jordan, B. (1990). Interactional troubles in face-to-face survey interviews. *Journal of the American Statistical Association, 85*, 232–253.

Sudman, S. (1973). The uses of telephone directories for survey sampling. *Journal of Marketing Research, 10*, 204–207.

Sudman, S., & Bradburn, N. M. (1974). *Response effects in surveys: A review and analysis.* Chicago: Aldine.

Sudman, S. N., Bradburn, N. M., Blair, E., & Stocking, C. (1977). Modest expectations: The effects of interviewers' prior expectations on responses. *Sociological Methods and Research, 6*, 177–182.

Survey Research Center, University of Michigan. (1969/1976). *Interviewer's manual.* Ann Arbor: University of Michigan Institute for Social Research, Survey Research Center.

Taylor, H. (2000). Does Internet research "work"? Comparing on-line survey results with telephone surveys. *International Journal of Market Research, 421*, 51–63.

Telemarketing and Consumer Fraud and Abuse Prevention Act of 2005 (15 U.S.C. 6101 *et seq.*).

Thornberry, O. T., Jr., & Massey, J. T. (1988). Trends in U.S. telephone coverage across time and subgroups. In R. M. Groves, P. P. Biemer, L. E. Lyberg, J. Massey, W. L. Nicholls II, & J. Waksberg (Eds.), *Telephone survey methodology* (pp. 25–49). New York: Wiley.

Thurkow, N. M., Bailey, S., & Stamper, M. R. (2000). The effects of group and individual monetary incentives on productivity of telephone interviewers. *Journal of Organizational Behavior Management, 20*, 3–25.

Tourangeau, R., Couper, M. P., & Conrad, F. G. (2004). Spacing, position, and order: Interpretive heuristics for visual features of survey questions. *Public Opinion Quarterly, 68*, 368–393.

Tourangeau, R., Rips, L. J., & Rasinski, K. (2000). *The psychology of survey response.* New York: Cambridge University Press.

Tourangeau, R., & Smith, T. W. (1996). A comparison of three modes of data collection. *Public Opinion Quarterly, 60*, 275–304.

Traugott, M. W., & Lavrakas, P. J. (1999). *The voter's guide to election polls* (2nd ed.). New York: Chatham Houses/Seven Bridges Press.

Tuckel, P. S., & Feinberg, B. M. (1991). The answering machine poses many questions for telephone survey researchers. *Public Opinion Quarterly, 55*, 200–217.

Tuckel, P. S., & O' Neill, H. W. (1996). Screened out. *Marketing Research, 8*, 34–43.

Tuckel, P. S., & O' Neill, H. (2001). The vanishing respondent in telephone surveys. In *Proceedings of the Survey Research Methods Section, American Statistical Association.* Retrieved August 14, 2006, from http://www.amstat.org/sections/srms/Proceedings/y2001/Proceed/00630.pdf.

Tucker, C. (1983). Interviewer effects in telephone surveys. *Public Opinion Quarterly, 47*, 84–95.

Tucker, C., Lepkowski, J. M., Casady, R. J., & Groves, R. M. (1992). Commercial residential telephone lists: Their characteristics and uses in survey design. *Social Science Computer Review, 10*, 158–172.

U.S. Bureau of the Census. (2004). *Current population survey interviewing manual*. Washington, DC: Author.

U.S. Department of Labor, Occupational Safety & Health Administration. (n.d.). *Good working positions*. Retrieved July 22, 2006, from http://www.osha.gov/SLTC/etools/computer workstations/positions.html.

Van den Berg, H., Wetherell, M., & Houtkoop-Steenstra, H. (2003). *Analyzing race talk: Multidisciplinary perspectives on the research interview*. New York: Cambridge University Press.

Van der Zouwen, J., Dijkstra, W., & Smit, J. H. (1991). Studying respondent-interviewer interaction: The relationship between interviewing style, interviewer behavior, and response behavior. In P. P. Biemer, R. M. Groves, L. E. Lyberg, N. A. Mathiowetz, & S. Sudman (Eds.), *Measurement errors in surveys* (pp. 419–437). New York: Wiley.

Van der Zouwen, J., & Smit, J. H. (2006). Effective repair in survey interviews. *Quality and Quantity, 40*, 245–258.

Vigerhous, G. (1981). Scheduling telephone interviews: A study of seasonal patterns. *Public Opinion Quarterly, 45*, 250–259.

Waksberg, J. (1978). Sampling methods for random digit dialing. *Journal of the American Statistical Association, 73*, 40–46.

Weeks, M. F., Kulka, R. A., Lessler, J. T., & Whitmore, R. W. (1983). Personal versus telephone surveys for collecting household health data at the local level. *American Journal of Public Health, 73*, 1389–1394.

Weeks, M. F., & Pierson, S. A. (1987). Optimal call scheduling for a telephone survey. *Public Opinion Quarterly, 51*, 540–549.

Xu, M., Bates, B. J., & Schweitzer, J. C. (1993). The impact of messages on survey participation in answering machine households. *Public Opinion Quarterly, 57*, 232–237.

INDEX